THE *Seven Tools* OF HEALING

Unlock Your Inner Wisdom and Live the Life Your Soul Desires

Steven M. Hall, M.D.

BALBOA.
PRESS
A DIVISION OF HAY HOUSE

Balboa Press books may be ordered through booksellers or by contacting:

Balboa Press
A Division of Hay House
1663 Liberty Drive
Bloomington, IN 47403
www.balboapress.com
1 (877) 407-4847

Because of the dynamic nature of the Internet, any web addresses or links contained in this book may have changed since publication and may no longer be valid. The views expressed in this work are solely those of the author and do not necessarily reflect the views of the publisher, and the publisher hereby disclaims any responsibility for them.

The author of this book does not dispense medical advice or prescribe the use of any technique as a form of treatment for physical, emotional, or medical problems without the advice of a physician, either directly or indirectly. The intent of the author is only to offer information of a general nature to help you in your quest for emotional and spiritual well-being. In the event you use any of the information in this book for yourself, which is your constitutional right, the author and the publisher assume no responsibility for your actions.

Any people depicted in stock imagery provided by Thinkstock are models, and such images are being used for illustrative purposes only. Certain stock imagery © Thinkstock.

Print information available on the last page.

ISBN: 978-1-5043-9762-9 (sc)
ISBN: 978-1-5043-9760-5 (hc)
ISBN: 978-1-5043-9761-2 (e)

Library of Congress Control Number: 2018901644

Balboa Press rev. date: 03/07/2018

Endorsements

"In *The Seven Tools of Healing,* physician Steven M. Hall presents us with an expanded concept of health and wellness — not as normal physical function, but a domain in which consciousness enters in vital ways. Hall is concerned with how love, compassion, hopes, and dreams — life's spiritual values — are essential aspects of a healthy life and which resonate in our physical wellbeing. If you want a glimpse of the medicine of the future, in which the spiritual, psychological, and physical are seamlessly combined, *The Seven Tools of Healing* is your book!"

- Larry Dossey, MD
Author: *One Mind: How Our Individual Mind Is Part of a Greater Consciousness and Why It Matters*

"*The Seven Tools of Healing* by Doctor Hall contains the wisdom of the ages. Its wisdom is universal and timeless and has been the message of the great sages of the past. Mind and body are not separate but are integrated units, and both must be considered when looking for the cause and cure of disease.

We are all exceptional and have the potential to achieve healing. It is built into us by our Creator. So read on, show up for practice, and the coach will guide you to becoming a star. This is not about avoiding dying, that is inevitable, but it is about true healing and the benefits it provides us with. And once your body knows you love it, your life it will do all it can to keep you alive. Read Steven Hall's book and learn the tools for healing. Please do not fear failure and, therefore, not undertake the attempt. Love yourself and participate in the healing. This book can be your life coach."

~Bernie Siegel, MD
Author of *Love, Medicine & Miracles* and *The Art of Healing*.

"Everyone is searching for health and contentment, yet it eludes so many of us. It is an act of supreme generosity to aim to assist others in achieving these primary goals. *The Seven Tools of Healing: Unlock Your Inner Wisdom and Live the Life Your Soul Desires* accomplishes precisely that aim. It is an outstanding book project.

To begin with, the overall structure is eminently clear, making the reader feel comfortable about what's ahead and able to digest each important insight as it arrives.

Secondly, the book successfully adopts a conversational tone, even incorporating humor, while addressing very challenging and personal topics. This, too, makes it an accessible, pleasurable read. In working through each chapter, one feels as if a good friend is gently and reassuringly guiding one to a more fulfilling life. Nowhere does the narrative voice become pedantic, condescending, or esoteric. This is a major achievement.

Most significantly of course, *The Seven Tools of Healing* offers a transformative experience to its readers, in a series of clear, readily adaptable steps. It thus strikes an impressive balance between supreme wisdom and straightforward practicality. I enjoyed it immensely and found it very useful personally."

~Edith Frampton, Ph.D.
Full-time Lecturer in the Department of English and Comparative Literature at S.D.S.U., the invited Guest Editor of *Contemporary Women's Writing: New Texts, Approaches, and Technologies*, and she has served as the Book Reviews Editor for *Contemporary Women's Writing*.

I would like to dedicate this book first and foremost to my beautiful wife, Patti, whose love, support, and wise-woman ways have helped me stay grounded and open-hearted in my constant searching for better medicine.

I would also like to dedicate this book to my early mentors: brave pioneers who also saw that something was missing from conventional medicine and were practicing integrative medicine before there was even a name for it: Jeff Fuson, MD and Stephen Bien, MD, my call partners in rural Maine, who were very open and accepting. To Ron Singler, MD, who greatly broadened my horizons regarding what kinds of alternative treatments are available and helped us land on our feet when we moved to Seattle. To Robert Anderson, MD, the founding president of the American Holistic Medical Association, who was very supportive of my early explorations and a wealth of information and wisdom. To Ralph Golan, MD, a veritable walking encyclopedia of alternative medicine and resources and a good friend over the years. And, most importantly, to Fernando Vega, MD, founder of Seattle Healing Arts. He created an office environment where I was not only supported, but encouraged, to practice all that I had been learning. He taught me much of what I know about herbs, nutraceuticals, and how to integrate alternatives into a busy family practice. But I am most thankful for his understanding, kindness, and support when it came time for me to fly under my own power.

And, lastly, I would like to dedicate this book to all of my patients, whose courage and persistence in the search for their own healing made all of this learning possible.

Contents

foreword

By Bernie Siegel, MD
Author of *Love, Medicine & Miracles* and *The Art of Healing*

The Seven Tools of Healing by Doctor Hall contains the wisdom of the ages. Its wisdom is universal and timeless and has been the message of the great sages of the past. Modern medicine still does not understand the truth about the human mind and body. Doctors are trained to treat disease. And so human beings are treated like mechanical objects as doctors treat the result and not the cause. Mind and body are not separate but are integrated units, and both must be considered when looking for the cause and cure of disease. Years ago, I wrote an article about my experience with patients' dreams, drawings, emotions, self-healing and mind body medicine at a time when I thought I was discovering things that were unknown to medicine. The medical journal I sent it to returned it with the comment "Interesting but inappropriate for our journal." So I sent it to a psychiatry journal which returned it also with the comment, "Appropriate for our journal but not interesting. We know all this." That is where medicine has lost its integrity and holistic qualities. Doctors in training do not really receive an education about caring for people. They just receive information about disease and ask people what is their complaint and not about what is going on in their lives that might make them vulnerable to illness at that time.

Fiction writers who observe life write about what I learned. W. H. Auden, in his poem Miss Gee wrote about cancer: "Childless women get it and men when they retire. It's as if there had to be an outlet for their foiled creative fire." Doctors have said to me, "Just because it rhymes doesn't make it true." But it is true. In his novel *Cancer Ward,* Solzhenitsyn sums it all up. When patients recover from a so called incurable cancer, doctors call it a spontaneous remission. Why? Because they don't ask the patient to tell them their story about why they got well and what changes they made in their lives that could have created the change and cure. In his novel, Solzhenitsyn speaks of "self-induced healing" and symbolizes it as a "rainbow colored butterfly" fluttering out of the book one of the men is reading to the others on the ward. Why that symbol and what does it tell us? The butterfly is the symbol of transformation and the rainbow represents the harmony and order of one's life that has been created by the transformation, and the cure is self-induced and not spontaneous. I learned that every patient who exceeded expectations had a story to tell when I asked them why they didn't die when they were expected to.

I was amazed, decades ago, by how few patients wanted to participate in my program for cancer patients entitled ECaP or Exceptional Cancer Patients, because they didn't feel exceptional. We are all exceptional and have the potential to achieve healing. It is built into us by our Creator. So read on, show up for practice, and the coach will guide you to becoming a star. This is not about avoiding dying, that is inevitable, but it is about true healing and the benefits it provides us with. And once your body knows you love it and your life, it will do all it can to keep you alive. The opposite effect is what we see on Monday mornings when there are more suicides and illnesses than any day of the week. Read Steven Hall's book and learn the tools for healing. Please do not fear failure and, therefore, not undertake the attempt. Love yourself and participate in the healing. This book can be your life coach.

~Bernie Siegel, MD author of *Love, Medicine & Miracles* and *The Art of Healing.*

Preface

I have had three major epiphanies in my medical career that have led me to write this book. The first two happened early and led me to spend my career studying deeper aspects of healing; the last came more recently as I started to realize that there are some concepts of major importance missing from the way most of us pursue our healing.

The first epiphany happened in my second year of medical school. I grew up in Salt Lake City, a bastion of conventionality and conformity. Since I was fairly healthy, how I understood the medical profession was based on idealized fantasy rather than personal experience. Chiropractic was the only alternative medical modality I was aware of and most of what I heard was derogatory. By the Seventies, acupuncture was barely making the news, and it was seen as *really* weird. So I started medical school assuming that there was only one real medicine worthy of consideration, and it either already had the answers to human disease and suffering, or was hot on the trail of the answers with medical research.

I met my wife, Patti, my senior year of college. When she came to join me in Salt Lake, she was interested in eating as naturally and organically as possible. As a teenager, my mom described me as having a hollow leg, so I pretty much ate anything in front of me that didn't get up and move out of the way. To think about what I ate ahead of time was a novel idea.

But we ran into a problem: there were no good health food stores in Salt Lake at that time (the late '70's). I don't know how she did it, but Patti found a woman who had organized a buying co-op where we bought organic food in bulk from distributors. We joined. Since it was a co-op and since I'd had math as an undergraduate, my job at the co-op was to do the bookkeeping. One evening, I was at the building we used as a drop-off site doing the books and the woman who organized the co-op was there doing inventory. While we worked, she told me about how she had cured her husband's Crohn's disease by putting him on an organic, whole foods diet. I thought that was great and I was very happy for him. But, of course, I didn't know anything about Crohn's disease at that time.

A few months later, we did study Crohn's disease in GI organ systems. It was described as this horrible inflammatory bowel disease that went from bad to worse and the treatments were worse than the disease (there are better treatments now (however, I rarely use them, as most of my patients with Crohn's get better by changing their diets)). No one talked about curing it and no one talked about changing diets as a possible treatment. Something inside me said, "Don't raise your hand and ask." So I just said, "Huh" to myself, and filed the experience away as an example of conventional medicine not having all the answers.

Over the next few years, as I got through the book work part of medical school and more into the seeing patients part, I became aware of the large number of conditions conventional medicine just managed but couldn't get to go away. I also saw patients with severe side effects from their medical treatments. Imagine my dismay when I started to realize how many people conventional medicine didn't really help. I also collected dozens of more cases of people getting better by using alternative treatments after conventional medicine did not help them.

To me, this was a problem. As an undergraduate, I not only studied scientific subjects but also how science worked. Without getting into a lot of boring details, the bottom line is that data is more important, more primary, than the theories used to try to explain the data. My first epiphany was that, since every experience you have exerts some sort of influence upon your health, the data that medicine needs to take into account is all of human experience. Since conventional medicine does not take all of human experience into account, it cannot be a complete system of healing. I needed to find a more complete model, one that includes all of conventional medicine but takes more of human experience into account.

This got me searching. Of course, I started from where I was. There is a saying in medicine: "you can't make a diagnosis if you don't think of it." So, we are trained to take a history, do a physical exam, look at any past medical records available, then come up with a list of as many possible diagnoses that might explain what the patient is going through as we can.

This list we call our "differential diagnoses." Then we decide what we need to do in order to make one diagnosis and rule out the others. So, while still a resident, I decided that perhaps we just needed to add more conditions to our differential diagnoses. From what I'd been hearing from my patients and reading on my own, I started considering conditions such as food reactions, adrenal fatigue, chemical sensitivities, overgrowth of yeast in the colon, other causes of increased intestinal permeability, trauma stored in the body, and the physical effects of limiting beliefs. By learning how to diagnose and effectively treat these kinds of conditions, I was able to help many patients that I couldn't have by using conventional medicine alone.

The second life-changing epiphany hit me in my sixth year of medical training. It was a busy time for me. Patti and I had two small children by then, I was in residency trying to learn Family Practice, which essentially encompasses all of conventional medicine, and follow my interest and patient leads into this broader approach to helping people. One afternoon, after finishing seeing my clinic patients for the day, I was walking back to the resident's room to dictate my chart notes. I was thinking about the people I had just seen and trying to sense into what motivated them to come in today. What were they seeking? Sure, they all has symptoms they wanted help with, but was there anything deeper? What if they were seeking healing? And I thought, "Well, what is that even? What is 'healing'?" And I stopped dead in my tracks in the middle of the hallway because I didn't know. I didn't know what healing was. In six years of medical training, we'd never discussed it. We all just went about our business of working with our patients as if we knew.

But medicine likes to be scientific, and science always defines its terms so that we have a precise language with which to communicate. Yet here was this vast, multi-billion dollar healthcare industry in which I had been participating for six years, and I didn't have a concise definition for health! This seemed ludicrous to me. So, on the spot, I resolved to rectify the situation and find a definition for "health".

Seven years later, after trying out and rejecting dozens of possible definitions, I started to appreciate why doctors might talk about an incision healing or a fracture healing but they rarely talk about a person's life healing. I was wanting a concise, non-circular, universally applicable, and clinically useful definition for healing. I did eventually find a pretty good one, which I talk about in this book, and though the search was not a trivial exercise, it was really worth it: it transformed my life ... and the way I practice medicine.

The third epiphany happened just a few years ago. By then, I'd been practicing Integral Medicine for a couple of decades. Integral Medicine is what I call the medicine that developed out of my first two epiphanies. I used Ken Wilber's integral world view[1] to combine all that I've been learning from conventional medicine, functional medicine, osteopathic medicine, naturopathic medicine, energy medicine, Chinese medicine, Ayurvedic medicine, homeopathy, Lakota shamanism, nutrition, psychology, clinical hypnosis, quantum physics, midwifery, philosophy, biodynamic farming, being married to Patti, raising four children, working on my own health issues, and just generally living life, into one seamless medicine that I think is better at treating a person as a whole human being than is conventional primary care.

One of the approaches I've learned helps people listen to and follow the advice from their own inner wisdom. Over the years, working with people with all kinds of health issues, from all kinds of backgrounds, holding all kinds of different world views, I've been able to discern a pattern to how people's inner wisdom helps them heal, grow, and change. My third epiphany came when I compared how people's own inner wisdom helps them heal, grow, and change with the advice on how to heal, grow, and change coming from the vast majority of the current self-help industry: they were not at all alike.

In other words, the advice you get from your own inner wisdom is not at all like the advice you get from most practitioners, self-help books, and programs. Our huge healthcare and self-help industries are omitting some concepts and practices that are critical for effective, long-lasting, deep personal growth and change. Once I saw that and considered how many millions of people are spending how many billions of dollars and decades of their lives trying to get themselves to heal, grow, and change, and most of them are not getting the results that my patients are getting, I just had to write this book.

My sincere hope is that this book will give you the answers you've been looking for, and that after you read it and master the use of the seven tools, all the time, life energy, and money you put into your healing will be much more productive.

Introduction

Are you ready to take your healing to the next level? Do you want to find and treat the real root causes of whatever problems you are facing? The current level in medicine, both conventional and natural, works to change what is already present in your life; in other words, what has already been created. The next level, then, works to change what brought that problem or issue into your life in the first place. The current level treats symptoms; the next level treats causes. When you do both, you have a complete system of healing that you can apply to any and all problems you are facing … and get good results. This book will show you how to add the next level to whatever you are doing now to help yourself.

The world we live in can be divided into two aspects: the tangible and the intangible. The tangible is everything that can be weighed and measured. I think of the tangible as those aspects of creation that are governed by the laws of nature: matter, energy, and information. The intangible are things like your hopes and dreams, your inspirations, meaning, fulfillment, love, symbolism, the spiritual. I think of the intangible as those aspects of creation that are governed by the laws of Consciousness. Science is devoted to discovering and exploring the laws of nature. Certain wisdom traditions are devoted to teaching and exploring the laws of Consciousness. In this book, we'll explore some of those laws as they relate to healing.

Consciousness is creative, so every aspect of creation, both the tangible and intangible, embodies or reflects some aspect of Consciousness. Even the laws of nature are created by Consciousness. So, if you want to work on the root causes of anything, including your health issues, or any other problem in your life, you have to work with Consciousness; specifically, with whatever determines the particular aspects of Consciousness that come forth and express themselves as your life. What are those determinants of

Conscious expression? Which ones do you have any say over? How do you find and change them? You will find the answers to these questions in this book.

We tend to think of them as either/or, but there are no reasons why you can't treat symptoms <u>and</u> find and treat root causes at the same time. I was recently talking to a friend, another functional medicine doctor, who has been going through a very difficult divorce. He took some supplements to support his adrenal glands and energy and felt much more able to stay active and productive in the face of the stress. But he didn't stop there. He was also learning a tremendous amount about himself. What was going on inside of him when he married her ... why he put up with the abuse and put-downs for so long ... the affects his upbringing had on his self-esteem and how to correct it ... it was a long list. He was emerging from this very difficult experience with a much deeper understanding of who he really is in his heart of hearts, beneath many of the limiting beliefs he'd been operating with his whole adulthood. He has extensive functional medicine knowledge, which he used to support his body/mind/energy, but he also recognized that this major life transition was a wake-up call to the need to make some deep and lasting inner changes. In this book, you will learn how to put the two approaches together like he is doing.

Like him, your life is giving you a constant flow of invitations to answer the question, "Who am I?" Every experience you have is another opportunity to know yourself better. Some people, once their symptoms are successfully treated, stop searching and questioning. If they did not simultaneously change the determinants of Consciousness that created those symptoms, they may, in the long view, be slowing their healing and prolonging their suffering. But once you've chased symptoms long enough to give yourself that long view, you are less likely to fall into that complacency trap. This book will give you the tools and techniques to really dig deep and get the full breadth and depth of what your life is offing you. Find the motivation to do so independent of your symptoms.

Who are you, in your heart of hearts? Get curious. Take a moment and imagine the life that you could create if you could really live the freedom that is your birthright. Imagine freeing yourself from limiting beliefs, from false or warped perceptions, and from that harsh, nagging inner critic. Imagine listening to your body and correcting imbalances so that your physiology works correctly. Imagine listening to your feelings and receiving all the information that your life feeds to you and then making good decisions in response. All these things I've witnessed in my patients as they've worked to heal their lives. This book gives you all the information you need to start healing your own life.

But even the best information, even the deepest truths, by themselves, are not enough: only you can put the information into practice for yourself; no one else can do that for you. But how do you know that what you are practicing will give you the skills you need? Toward that end, there are practical exercises, gleaned from years of clinical experience, sprinkled throughout the book to help you develop the skills you need to put this information to the best use for you. The good news: if you run into resistance, procrastination, or the trap of life getting too busy, you can use the tools in this book to overcome any blocks you may have to your growth. Nothing can stop you now.

This book contains new and revolutionary information. It is not one more book that tells you how to eat or how to exercise. It doesn't tell you how to visualize or say affirmations. It won't tell you where to tap. But it will show you how to work on the real roots of your issues. For example, many functional medicine doctors believe that when you change your lifestyle, you are changing the roots of your health issues. But how you eat and exercise are behaviors. There are always motivations behind behaviors. And there are deeper aspects of you that determine your motivations. If you keep following this line of searching back far enough, you will see that the real roots are Consciousness. By practicing the seven tools of healing, you will gain conscious control over how you manifest Consciousness.

This process of inner change has helped my patients more than anything I learned in medical school. And it is different from anything I've seen come out of our self-help industry. The process is fairly straight-forward, so let's walk through it. First, some basic concepts.

Consciousness is creative. An essentially infinite Consciousness is at the root of the entire universe. Everything in material creation, from the Milky Way, to the sun and earth, to all the plants and animals, to you and me, and even to all the blessings and challenges you face in your life, are all expressions of some aspect of that Consciousness. As a human being, you are creative. That means that you have volitional control over certain aspects of Consciousness. (You are not only creative in the artistic sense, you are creating your life, moment by moment, as it flows along. That is a given. I haven't found a way to get around that. So, since personal responsibility for your life is built in, you might as well learn how to use it to your best advantage. This book shows you how.) Now, how much of Consciousness you can control is an open question. Down through history, there have been people who have achieved phenomenal control, and could do all kinds of miraculous things. We all have that potential, including you.

But certain factors limit our ability to express aspects of Consciousness. Beliefs are the most important factor that you potentially have control over. Your beliefs have two main functions. First, they are like lenses that you peer through to see the world. In that way, they determine what reality looks like to you. Second, once formed, beliefs become the gatekeepers for your creative flow. You can't create something unless you first have a belief that allows it. Everything that you created has some kind of belief behind it that allows it to be there. That is the root of the saying, "if you want to know what someone believes, just look at their life." So, if you have a way to find and change your beliefs, you can have a big say over your creative flow.

At this point, we must then look at beliefs and how your mind works with them. You only have one mind, but we divide it into two parts to talk about how it works. You have your conscious mind (as opposed to being asleep, and though it is the same word, is not the same as Consciousness (this is defined in the book)) and you have the rest of your mind, the unconscious. By definition, you don't know what is contained in your unconscious mind, or what it does with that information. As soon as you are aware of something, it is in your conscious mind. What you may not realize, but is key to the success of this approach, is that any information in your unconscious mind can be accessed by your conscious mind, if you just know how (and you will, by the end of the book). The large majority of the Consciousness-regulating beliefs that are creating your life for you are in your unconscious mind.

So, putting it all together, for deep, lasting inner change, you need some sort of method for:

1. becoming aware of when something in your life is not working for you,
2. following that something back to the foundational belief that allowed it to be created in your life in the first place,
3. bringing that belief into the light of your conscious mind,
4. changing it into a belief that is more aligned with higher truth
5. then putting the corrected belief back into the unconscious mind where it starts letting different, more higher-truth-derived experiences into your life.

See? Straight-forward. How to do each and every step, along with exercises to help you get better at each new skill, is clearly and carefully explained in this book.

You might be wondering now, "If deep, lasting inner personal change is so easy, why does it seem so rare?" And you are right, real change is so rare that some researchers in the field of psychology have concluded that people basically never change[2]. I reject that pessimism. My experience in the office tells me that real change is so rare, not because it can't happen, but because we've been going about it the wrong way.

Most of the methods we've developed to help ourselves change commit two major errors. First, they fail to work effectively with how your unconscious mind works; and, second, they violate one or more laws of Consciousness. For example, saying affirmations is a great way to program your unconscious mind with new beliefs, so most of the big-name programs for change teach you how to use them. But, if you don't also remove the old, limiting beliefs (which saying affirmations doesn't do), they are still in there, and can raise their nasty, sabotaging head at the least opportune moments. In this book, you will learn how to get the old limiting beliefs out and replace them with beliefs more in alignment with your higher truth. Do not be intimidated by your unconscious mind: it is your great ally; and, once you see how to work with it, you'll be thrilled with how simple and straight-forward the process is.

As to the laws of Consciousness, these are rarely, if ever, talked about. But they are equally as important to healing your life as are the laws of nature. For example, one law of Consciousness states that your creativity flows to wherever you pay attention. Repression and denial are forms of attention. This explains that saying, "What you resist persists". But, if you think about this law carefully, you will see that whenever you start your efforts to change yourself from the position that there is something wrong (or inadequate, or not good enough, or _____ (fill in the blank)) with you that needs to change, you are already locking yourself into staying that way. This point is profoundly important. I don't know about you, but whenever I want to change some aspect of myself, it is because I don't like that aspect. But trying to force myself to change has never worked. How has it been working for you?

Whenever you focus on what's wrong with you, your creative flow goes there. Even focusing on the solution, and methods such as positive thinking[3], will keep you stuck if you also deny what is in any way. When you look at our current self-help industry with this one law of Consciousness in mind, you will be amazed at how often it is violated. Practicing the seven tools of healing allows you to change aspects of yourself without focusing your awareness on them or denying them in any way. And that is just one law; several others are also routinely violated by various self-help techniques. We will discuss each law as it comes up and you will see how the seven tools approach to personal growth works perfectly with each one.

As an example, have you ever noticed that when you try to make yourself be a certain way, there is always blow-back? I'm embarrassed to admit it, but I recently experienced this, even though I've read this book several times. (What can I say? Mastering this new way of inner change can occasionally fall prey to our old ways of being. But I caught on to what I was doing fairly quickly and was able to course correct, which helped.)

Here's what happened. I'm a bit fiery inside and can get really worked up about recent world events, even though I know in my head that I'm just contributing my energy to the problems. I don't want to do that, so when I notice that I'm filling with anger or falling into hopelessness and despondency, I remind myself of something Gandhi said: "be the change you want to see in the world." When I think of this, the change I want to see is much more open-heartedness ... toward ourselves, toward each other, and toward all of creation.

So, during a recent vacation, I told myself that I'm going to practice opening my heart. Several times a day, I focused my awareness into my heart center, breathed into it, relaxed into it, felt the peace and bliss there.

The result? I was much crabbier to Patti than I usually am. I would get easily frustrated and stuff would just blurt out of my mouth before I could stop it. She even asked me why I was being such an … well, I don't really want to write here what she said, but you get the picture.

Then I realized what I was doing. I really want to live with an open heart, but just telling myself to be that way and imagining how it felt was not working. Any time I try to make myself be a certain way, it backfires. This is a law of Consciousness often called "The Inverse Law of Human Effort," which we will get into. What does help with personal change is education: I can learn new ideas and information; and I can practice developing skills. When you practice a skill, what you are just naturally able to do changes.

I regrouped and started to practice the seven tools. Several times throughout the day, I took a moment to focus inwardly and see what was really going on. Whatever I saw, I admitted that was my personal truth in that moment, and then I chose to be kind to myself about it. So if I was angry, frustrated, or mind boggled that we're even in this situation, I could accept it and be kind to myself. And practicing kindness for myself for whatever the truth of my present moment happens to be turns out to be all the open-heartedness I need. When I respond to myself with compassion, I can respond to others with compassion, as well.

Let's talk about one more foundational concept that will help you see how much this book can help you. You have, deep within you, a wisdom that knows who you are, it knows what your soul prefers, and it knows how to help you create those preferences. That knowing is already in you. You don't have to create it; you just have to seek it. Once contacted, your own deep knowing can show you how to solve any problem or challenge you are facing. If you want to improve your life, improve your health, attain inner peace and happiness, find your gift and give it to the world, make more money, have more loving relationships, or achieve any other goal you have chosen, listen to your own knowing. For example, the deeper truth reveals you to be a divine, powerful, confident being worthy of love and all the good things life has to offer. Imagine knowing this truth beyond the shadow of any doubt. Imagine knowing this truth in every fiber of your being. Practice the seven tools of healing and you won't have to imagine, you will be living it.

Listen to what your heart knows at least as much, if not more, than to what your head knows. Trust your gut instincts. Have faith in your heart's knowing. Choose to trust yourself. It gets better with practice. This book will show you how.

I noticed this revolutionary new way to work deep, lasting, personal and spiritual change over years of helping my patients connect with and listen to their own deep knowing. Once contacted, it coached them on what to do to effectively respond to and resolve the very roots of their problems. Each patient had their own problems and their own place along their healing path, so it took time for me to see general patterns to the completely individualized, personalized advice the inner wisdom gives.

In the early years, I didn't talk much about this pattern that I started calling "The Seven Tools of Healing"; I wanted people to have a direct experience of them. But, there were many people for whom connecting with their inner wisdom was very challenging, sometimes taking months, sometimes not happening at all. When I shared the seven tools with them (and they practiced them) they then had a much easier time hearing and heeding their own inner knowing. I saw that listening to your inner wisdom and learning the seven tools have a chicken and egg sort of relationship. So I began teaching my patients the seven tools sooner rather than later and they started getting more out of their treatments, they healed more quickly (with less effort and expense on their part), and they got to know themselves on deeper and deeper levels. Once I realized that you, too, could similarly benefit from the seven tools, I just had to write this book.

As I mentioned, many of my patients often have difficulty hearing and heeding their inner knowing, as if it were buried deep in their psyche. So I want to give you the punch line to most of their stories: this deep knowing cannot be found anywhere in the mind: it is found in the heart. In this book, you will learn how to turn the steering wheel of your life over to your heart. Whatever changes you need to make in your life then rise up from your heart's knowing. After all, your ego mind is better designed to experience your life than to create it.

Practicing the seven tools of healing will give you more benefit out of whatever you are using to help yourself. And you will get better at choosing the practitioners, techniques, and modalities that will work for you the first time.

Your inner wisdom knows when you are blocked and it knows how to get around it. But, just in case, this book discusses most of the blocks to personal growth that people hit along the way and how to resolve them. The information in this book will help you advance your personal spiritual growth no matter where you are on the path now and no matter what blocks or challenges you are facing.

Now I want to teach the seven tools of healing to you so you can reap their benefits. Please read this book, take its teachings to heart, and practice the seven tools. Find your healing and your freedom.

Once again, who are you in your heart of hearts? Let's go find out!

Section One

Chapter One

What Are We Really Talking about Here?

Defining "Consciousness" and "Healing."

*You can search throughout the entire universe for someone who is
more deserving of your love and affection than you are yourself, and
that person is not to be found anywhere. You yourself, as much as
anybody in the entire universe, deserves your love and affection.*
—Buddha

*No man is great enough or wise enough for any of us to
surrender our destiny to. The only way in which anyone can
lead us is to restore to us the belief in our own guidance.*
—Henry Miller

One evening years ago, near the end of a stress class I was teaching, one
of the attendees, an artist with both words and paint, sat back in her chair,
surveyed the room, and observed, "We all have our own stuff that we're
working on, and we all have our own ways of doing that work, but we're
all really doing the same thing: we're all just learning how to love better."
She really hit the nail on the head, and the class sat there for a moment
contemplating the truth of what she had just said.

What if she, Buddha, and Henry Miller are all correct? How can you
put it all together? How can you know beyond a shadow of a doubt that
you deserve your own love? How can you connect with your deep, inner
wisdom and let it help you navigate the winding passages of your life

and show you how to meet whatever comes in your path with courage, competence, and confidence? How do you learn to love better?

In other words, how do you learn to heal? These and similar questions have pervaded my entire professional life. And I've been incredibly blessed to have had thousands of wonderful and amazing teachers, in the guise of my patients, helping me explore them. I'd like to share with you what I've learned in order to provide some possible answers.

How do I heal? This is a specific case of a more general question: how do I change? You need a way to make changes in yourself that works. The only changes you can make in yourself that last are those that allow you to become more of who you already are: your true, authentic self. Any other changes require ongoing effort to sustain them, which puts you at risk of fatigue or getting distracted and falling off the wagon. Practicing the seven tools of healing gives you a dependable, workable way to bring your true, authentic self to the surface without having to force anything. In other words, practicing the seven tools shows you how to effect genuine, lasting change in your life. There is no wagon to fall off of.

If you are experiencing any challenges anywhere in your life—with your health, in your relationships, in your career, with addictions—the information in this book will help you.

You have answers and possibilities within you that, could you access them, would astound you. Practicing the seven tools of healing will give you the skills you need to access those answers. It will give you the skills you need to bring forth and live as your true, authentic self to improve your physical health, your emotional health, and your relationships. It will help you find your right livelihood, to do with your life what you really came here to do: to live a life that pleases your soul. It will deepen and strengthen your connection to spirit, whatever that means to you personally. Practicing the seven tools of healing will give you the skills you need to be able to see the truth of what you are experiencing in your life, access your own inner guidance, trust it, and know how to act on it. All of this is healing. All of this I have witnessed in my patients.

What are we really talking about when we talk about health and healing? I made the mistake early in my career of just assuming I knew what healing was. Once I realized my mistake and started searching for a universal, concise, practical, actionable definition, I was amazed by the difficulty of the challenge. But the search was worth it because it transformed my thinking about health and healing, how I practice medicine, and how I live my life. Striving for clarity is worth it. In that spirit, I would like to define two words before we get started with the seven tools: "healing," because that's what this book is about and "Consciousness" because there is great confusion about this concept yet healing makes no sense without it.

We can look at the world in several different ways. Some promote healing; others promote suffering. I recommend that you try adopting a worldview that promotes healing. One such worldview that allows for real, lasting, deep healing sees Consciousness as primary. That means that Consciousness comes before matter and energy.

I regard consciousness as fundamental. I regard matter as derivative from consciousness. We cannot get behind consciousness. Everything that we talk about, everything that we regard as existing, postulates consciousness.
—Max Planck

Unfortunately, in English we use the word *consciousness* to refer to two very different concepts. One meaning, which I will denote with a small "c", refers to that usual state of awareness of ourselves and the surroundings in which most of us spend most of our waking hours. This is in contrast to being asleep or in a coma (although it has been recently discovered through PET and functional MRI scans that some people who appear to be in a coma are, in fact, conscious). The other meaning for *consciousness*, which I will denote from now on with a capital "C," refers to the Consciousness out of which all of the universe was created, the Consciousness that the Hindus refer to as *Brahman* or *Purusha*[4], that the Judeo-Christian traditions refer to as *God*, that the Lakota refer to as *Wakan Tanka*, and that Max Planck saw as fundamental to understanding quantum mechanics. These are just a few examples. Similar concepts of a singular Consciousness as the creator of, or contained within, all of creation can be found in different traditions all over the world and down through time.

When we work with healing, we work in depth with Consciousness. Consciousness follows basic laws similarly to the way nature follows basic laws. We need to put the laws of Consciousness next to the laws of nature if we want to get a more complete understanding of how healing works. The laws of Consciousness, as I've been able to discern them so far, will be presented throughout the book.

As a human, you are not only self-conscious; but you can also access universal Consciousness. You are simultaneously a unique individual and a seamless part of a greater Whole. I like to think that we are more accurately viewed as eternal, divine beings having occasional earthly experiences rather than as earthly beings having occasional spiritual experiences. You have free will and are potentially infinitely creative. Stop for a moment and take that in. You have free will: you get to choose; nobody, not even God, chooses for you. (Now, don't get too testy here. I'm not talking about all the things in life you have no control over. You don't choose your cancer or your sleep problem or your child's illness or the Holocaust or the weather—at least you as your conscious ego-self doesn't. But you do have control over certain things in your life, like how you respond to what you can't control, and for those things, you choose. We'll go into that more later.)

And you have the same Consciousness available to you that created the whole universe. Maybe not right now, as your ego-self, but with practice, there are no limits to your creativity.

Precisely because you have free will and can access Consciousness, the source of all creativity, you can heal: you can recover from diseases and injuries; you can live a meaningful and fulfilling life; you can be happy and loving. By using these two properties of your being, you can overcome adversity, free yourself from limitations, and follow your heart. You can take the hand life has dealt you and play it further than you or anyone else thought was possible. All it takes is the right practice.

Who are you? What is this world in which you live? What is truth, and how do you know it when you see it? What do you want to experience during your life? Are you interested in answering these questions for yourself?

If so, your challenge is to consciously use Consciousness to create a life that pleases your soul. That is the path of healing. Your health issues function as steppingstones and guideposts on that path. So the question is, how best to walk it? Do you want to dig deep and change the flow of Consciousness that is creating the problems that you want to change?

Or do you want to work more superficially: trying to change what has already been created, treating symptoms, or trying to make yourself be the way your ego mind thinks it wants you to be? Only you can answer these questions for yourself. You might want to work elements of both approaches, but definitely don't just work superficially. You can work and work to change the results of what you are creating. But unless you also make fundamental changes to whatever determines those aspects of Consciousness that you are allowing to flow through you—the aspects of Consciousness that are creating your life for you right now—your symptoms or patterns will reassert themselves.

You may or may not have seen this principle play itself out in your own life, but I bet you've seen it in your family and friends, in the way they keep treating themselves, in the kinds of relationships they keep getting into over and over, in their issues with their weight, with their addictions. If your efforts to alleviate your own suffering are working too superficially, your suffering will continue. You may have moments of respite, but eventually the same or similar forms of suffering will return. You need to work at the level of Consciousness to make real, lasting changes. I use these ideas in my practice every day. I know they work. I've seen them help thousands of people, many of whom had exhausted all of conventional medicine's options. I know in my bones that they will help you, too. I hope the medicine of the future will partner Consciousness equally with molecules, genes, and biochemistry; but you can create that advantage for yourself right now by practicing the seven tools of healing.

The second word I would like to define is "healing."

The purpose of this book is to explore healing. As I mentioned in the Preface, when I first asked myself the question, "what is healing?" I was a resident in my sixth year of medical training. The answer hit me like a giant lightning bolt: I didn't know. Asking myself that simple three-word question and being curious about an answer has changed my entire life.

The deepest essence of healing is a mystery and we will probably never have it all within our conscious control, but many practical benefits can be gained by learning how to work with the mystery.

Over time, as I worked down through the layers of my search for a definition of healing, I realized that healing has very little to do with how your body is working (or not) or how you are feeling, either physically or emotionally. As a physician, this came as a big surprise. It has little to do with changes in jobs, in relationships, or in living situations. It has little to do with diet or exercise. Any improvements in these areas are either the effects of treatments that will go away when the treatment stops or the results of the healing. Generally, relief of symptoms or improvement in your life circumstances are the outward results of healing, they are not the healing itself. This is a common confusion in our society.

To explain, let's assume for a moment that symptoms are clues that healing needs to happen. Then let's say that you received some treatment and the symptoms went away. Let's further assume that the treatment did not just suppress the symptoms (as do so many conventional and alternative treatments—for example, blood pressure medicines lower your blood pressure but do not cure you of your hypertension, insulin can lower your blood sugar but does not cure you of your diabetes, using your inhaler helps you breath but does not cure you of your asthma, and so forth) but actually resolved the imbalance behind the symptoms. So, if the symptom is truly resolved and does not need ongoing suppression to stay gone, since the presence of the symptom is a clue that healing needs to happen, the resolution of the symptom is a clue that the healing has happened. It is not the healing itself. I hope that distinction makes the confusion a little clearer.

As a simple example, suppose that you got diagnosed with high blood pressure. Let's also suppose that, instead of taking a medication for it, you went on a diet, lost fifteen pounds, and your blood pressure normalized. Have you healed your hypertension? My medical training would say "yes". But, from what I know now, I would say, "that depends." That depends upon what you did inside of yourself to lose the weight. What if, in six months, you put the weight back on, and your blood pressure went back up? In that case, you haven't healed your hypertension because maintaining your lower weight had not become who you are. Keeping the weight off was requiring your on-going effort, and when you fatigued or got distracted, the weight came right back on. If the changes you made inside of yourself that enabled you to lose the weight fully integrated and became a part of who you are, and your blood pressure stayed normal for years, then I would say that you healed your blood pressure.

I hope you get the point. So, if the resolution of the symptom is not the healing, then what is?

By the time I got around to asking myself that question, I'd noticed that, even though I couldn't state a succinct definition for healing, I could recognize it when it happened. True healing has its own distinct feeling or sense to it. I started observing my patients who had experienced healing with the following question in mind: What else has changed about them besides their symptoms going away?

And I saw that they had also learned something. And generally, what they had learned had to do with their own understanding of themselves, their relationship with themselves, and their place in their world. People who healed had deepened their understanding of themselves, they had improved the quality of relationship they were having with themselves (kinder, less judgmental, etc.) and they had found and freed themselves from some kind of limiting belief. They had changed some aspect of their world view to be more in alignment with a higher, spiritual truth.

I asked myself, "What if this learning, this aligning of their world view, is the healing? What if symptoms are really attention-getting devices calling our attention away from our busy externally-focused lives long enough to attend to some imbalance in our system?" So I came up with this definition of healing: Healing is the process of finding out who you really are and then living true to yourself.

Before having this insight, I had tried several other definitions of healing, eventually finding them to be too limiting, not true, or not practical. I have been working with this definition now for over twenty years and haven't outgrown it yet, so I'm starting to think that there may be something of use in it. But I also hold some suspicion that real healing is still a mystery beyond my ken, like the unveiling of your soul or something, and even this deep learning that my patients are experiencing is but a result of the healing as well.

As I mentioned earlier, I've been on a quest to find better and better ways to help my patients live happier, healthier lives. When I started medical school, I thought that conventional medicine had all the answers or was hot on the trail of the answers with active research. I had no experience or knowledge of alternative medicine. My conventional medical training is in family practice, so I have a broad understanding of conventional medicine and what it has to offer. Within the first ten years of completing residency training, I'd been the only doctor in a small town in rural Maine, a staff physician at a large, urban, multispecialty clinic in downtown Seattle, in private practice in a Seattle suburb, and the medical director of a free clinic for homeless people. All of these different practice settings have given me a broad understanding of how medical care gets delivered to people throughout the spectrum of our society.

While still in medical school, an awareness started growing in me that something was missing from conventional medicine: I started seeing patients for whom conventional medicine held no good answers. So I widened my search. I started to look at many different healing traditions around the world, their philosophies, and their practices. When I first started exploring beyond the bounds of conventional medicine, I hoped that alternative medicine had some better answers about healing. I studied a broad range of alternative medical systems, and looked into other ways to support and treat the body, mind, energy, and connect with higher knowing.

Disappointingly, I found that most kinds of alternative medicine do not necessarily help people change the flow of their creative Consciousness but, like conventional medicine, just treat symptoms; they just have their own ways of doing it. There are also many different theories among the variety of alternative medicines as to what causes disease. Neither conventional medicine by itself nor most of the alternative medicines are complete systems of healing. But a pretty good complete system of healing can be constructed by combining the best from all of them under a unifying world view. Much of what both approaches have to offer has its appropriate time, place, and person. Similarly, some ideas in both camps are valid and some are way out in left field with no rational justification.

By comparing and contrasting conventional medicine with several kinds of alternative medicine, I started to see patterns. In order to resolve some of the conflicts I witnessed in the broader medical profession, I started to think about what we do in medicine and how we do it in terms of process and content. If your practitioner's goal is to get your symptoms to resolve, to get your headache to go away, to get you over your sore throat, to get your tumor to go away, as a few examples, that is what I call "allopathic process." You can practice allopathic process with conventional content, like drugs and surgery, or with alternative content, like herbs or acupuncture, or a mix, like integrative or functional medicine. Realizing this, some of my naturopath friends call what they do "green allopathy."

But if your goal is to heal, to listen to what your life is telling you, to learn as much as you can from your experiences, to find and be your true, authentic, loving self and to get to and treat the real imbalance behind your symptoms ... that is radically different than just demanding your body be a certain way. I could find no name for this process in the medical literature. But this process generally involves integrating all aspects of your life into your healing process—as all aspects of your life exert some sort of influence upon your health—and the root cause may be anywhere in your larger life, not just in your physical body. The same process will also get you in touch with your own loving, wise guidance, which activates the roots of your vitality, hardiness, and health. Because this process integrates not just all of the different organ systems in your body but also all the different dimensions of who you are, I borrowed a term from Ken Wilber's Integral World View[1,5], and call this approach the "integral process". One can also practice the integral process with conventional content, alternative content, or a mix (but with a consciousness much more in alignment with real healing).

By thinking in terms of process and content, I don't have to get caught up in the arguments about whether herbs are better than antibiotics or if meditation is better than chemotherapy. They all have their best right time, place, and person. What you are ultimately trying to accomplish is more important to me than the technique you are using. Do you just want the symptom to go away or do you also want to learn what the experience is offering you? Once we are clear about that, we are free to choose the safest, most effective way to proceed from the entire palate of conventional and alternative offerings.

The poet and philosopher John O'Donohue sums up these concepts nicely in this excerpt from "**for a friend, on the arrival of illness**"[6].

> *May you find the wisdom to listen to your illness:*
> *Ask it why it came? Why it chose your friendship?*
> *Where it wants to take you? What it wants you to know?*
> *What quality of space it wants to create in you?*

What you need to learn to become more fully yourself
That your presence may shine in the world?
May you keep faith with your body,
Learning to see it as a holy sanctuary ...

Seeing illness as a friend, as an opportunity to learn and come more into your real self, may seem shocking or upsetting or too much of a stretch when we live in a culture that "fights cancer", "beats illness", and tells us to "just do it". We are raised to believe that illness is the enemy to be defeated and driven out. Drugs and surgery are our weapons. Unfortunately, this leaves your body as the battlefield. The war metaphor combined with the mechanical view of our bodies and of illness discourages us from asking deep and meaningful questions.

Yet, we are creatures of meaning. We seek meaning in everything, even in the movement of the stars through the night sky. Perhaps few things are more meaningful to us than our illnesses, disabilities, stressors, and other life challenges. To ignore the meaning of these experiences and only work to force them to your ego's will is to miss an incredible opportunity to find yourself, to come into your power, to find inner strengths and resources you didn't know you had, and, ultimately, to live your life in a way that is pleasing to your soul, to your heart. Practice the seven tools of healing, apply them to your illness, and you will reap the blessings buried within your suffering.

This is what I sense when I work on my patients. The center of your being is a solid white core of light about two and a half inches in diameter and running the length of your torso. The light is blindingly intense. Around that core is a transparent tube, much like the glass of a hurricane lamp. It sits right next to the core of light but lets the light through. Then around that layer of glass is a sheet of black plastic. It completely blocks the light. Peppered around the core are little pin-holes in the black plastic, letting some rays of light through to the outside world.

In this metaphor, the core of white light is pure Consciousness, the source of all of your creativity, your true, unchanging self. The pin holes in the black plastic are your beliefs. They are the curators, the gatekeepers, the determinants of what you are able to create in your life. The only creativity that can "leak out" into your life, so to speak, is that creativity that fits through the portals of your beliefs. The potential creativity available to you, through pure Consciousness, is essentially infinite. But what you are able to create in your life is determined by what you believe. (Please see Appendix C for a more in-depth theory about how Consciousness gets manifested as you and your life.) You need to change your beliefs if you want to change something in your life, otherwise, whatever situation or pattern you are in right now will just get re-created again.

This is a critically important point, so I'll say it again: if you want to really change something in your life for good, you need to change your beliefs so that you can create something different. Taking a medication or supplement might help with symptom management, but it won't necessarily change your beliefs. Tapping your forehead or solar plexus may change your present feeling state but won't necessarily change your beliefs. Saying affirmations may help implant new beliefs but doesn't necessarily change or erase the old ones. You need a reliable methodology for finding out what you believe right now and then changing those that are holding you back or creating your suffering. Practicing the seven tools of healing is just such a methodology.

Any and everything in your life can be used to get to know yourself better. With practice, you can control your beliefs and gain volition over your creative powers. This is how you can manifest what you want (ideally, what your true, authentic self wants, not just what your ego-self wants). You need two things in order to be a good student of life. First, you need some way to reliably identify and appropriately respond to the imbalances your symptoms are bringing to your attention. And, second, you need a way to identify and then to change aspects of yourself that are too limiting and are holding you back. Practicing the seven tools fulfills both of these needs.

Where do the seven tools of healing come from? Part of the work that I do with people in my office puts them in communication with their wise, loving inner guidance. Once they are in touch with it, people are able to ask the questions that have them the most puzzled, such as: "What do I really want to be doing with my life?" or "What is this illness asking of me and how can I heal it and move forward?" I then watch as people's inner guidance takes over as their personal coach and walks them through their own process of change. And I have been privileged to witness how those changes then manifest in their lives. Everybody has their own issues and their own challenges to face, but I've noticed a remarkably similar pattern to how the inner knower guides a person through their own personal growth and/or healing process. This similar pattern is independent of the person's age, gender, religious beliefs, level of education, or cultural upbringing.

I was able to discern seven major components to this pattern. These tools are very simple. You won't find anything in them you haven't seen before, yet they are incredibly versatile: applicable to virtually any problem you face. The genius of the seven tools lies in how your inner guidance combines these familiar concepts into a gentle yet powerful practice that, when followed properly, consistently leads to lasting, authentic change. They are simultaneously the journey and the destination; simultaneously practical, down-to-earth skills, and a process of deep personal awakening. They have all the earmarks of a spiritual path, yet you can practice them whenever and wherever you are, each and every moment of an ordinary day. They are all-denominational and compatible with any religious practices I've seen so far in my patients.

So let's run through a brief introduction to the seven tools. I want you know what they are and have a view of the bigger picture when we go through each one in more detail. Finding and being your true self is really no different than any other activity you engage in: to get masterful results generally requires actual practice. You can read about hitting a golf ball or riding a surfboard or baking a cake, but to become adept at those activities, the reading does not take the place of getting out there and practicing. The same holds true for the seven tools. Reading this book is great—and I'm very happy that you are—and, in addition to that, I strongly encourage you to practice applying these tools to the stuff of your life, by yourself or in study or support groups, until they become second nature to you. Please keep in mind that the seven tools individually are parts of one process. I speak of them separately and linearly because that is how our language works, but, as we go through them and as you practice them, I think you will see how they start to come together into one seamless practice.

So now let us dive into the Seven Tools.

Chapter Two

The Seven Tools of Healing : A Brief Overview

Faith, Awareness, Acceptance, Compassion, Forgiveness, Gratitude, Right Action

Faith

The first tool is faith. Faith is the foundation upon which nearly everything in your life is built. Coming from a strong scientific background, I was surprised to see this. But in science, we often forget how science works. Even our best scientific theories and models are built upon a set of foundational assumptions which are unproven ideas that we take on faith until we see how a deepening of our understanding of nature plays out. So faith is actually underpinning all that we think we know scientifically.

Faith is a word that we often associate with religion, but, in reality, it has a much broader application. Rather than using it in a limited fashion, people's inner guidance uses faith more like Webster[7] did: 1. confidence or trust. 2. belief that is not based on proof. The wisdom of the inner guidance is often more inclusive than exclusive and I have observed that people's inner wisdom is also okay with faith having a religious or spiritual connotation, if that fits the person's life.

I see the inner wisdom using faith as a foundation. All else is built upon it. Everything you think you know as facts are, if followed back far enough, seated on a foundation of faith. Faith also allows you to believe that you can make changes in your life and create something that you've not ever created before.

Faith is particularly helpful with the process of change. You can have faith that your life can indeed improve. You can have faith that you, as your true essential self, is enough: you don't have to be more than that in order to be good enough or lovable or acceptable. The first step in changing long-held limiting beliefs often requires a leap of faith in order to adopt new beliefs. A belief will sift through all of your sensory data and select for special attention those data that support itself, even if the belief itself is false. In this way, you accumulate lots of proof in your own mind that a particular belief is true. A new belief hasn't had time to collect all of that proof so you often need to take it on faith long enough for it to prove itself to you.

A simultaneous advantage and disadvantage of faith is that it requires no facts or data to support it. While some people use this quality of faith to adopt some pretty outlandish or oppressive beliefs, you can use it to believe in whatever is in your highest good, whatever helps you the most in your search for truth and growth, even if you do not have any personal proof of it yet. The proof of a belief often comes after you adopt that belief.

Coming from a background of science and conventional medicine, where I was trained to require verifiable, empirical evidence for everything, I had to do several years of soul-searching before I could start to comprehend how the inner knower utilizes faith. Faith is an antidote to fear. Until you overcome an obstacle in your life, you don't have any proof that you can. (Although when most of my patients take an honest look at their lives, and not just at those experiences flagged for special attention, they often see that they have indeed solved similar challenges on several earlier occasions but they had just brushed those experiences aside.) You were not put on this planet to live in fear. You are often being asked to explore and, hopefully re-think, your fear-based beliefs and choices when you have painful, scary or limiting experiences.

Doubt is the test of faith. Everything you learn about yourself and how you fit in with your surroundings will be tested. If doubt wins, your faith in what you've learned is not strong enough, at least not strong enough to continue to build upon that learning. I can't fully explain it, but there seems to be something very powerful about knowledge that comes from faith, about having faith and sticking with it through thick and thin. Scientific knowing doesn't seem to hold that power unless, of course, you have a strong faith in science.

Please, don't take my word for any of this. Explore faith in your own life. How does it work? What does it do? What do you have faith in? What happens when your faith is challenged?

Used unskillfully, faith can lead you to hold onto beliefs that have no grounding in reality. Faith needs to be tempered with reason. Faith is more powerful than reason, but the two need to consult with each other. Untempered, unreasonable faith has caused, and continues to cause, incalculable suffering on this planet. Faith in higher truths is very healing. Faith in dogma and false "truths" is very destructive. Faith in your own false beliefs, in your own dogma, will block your healing. Observe yourself, think about what is going on in your life, listen to and follow your clues, and your inner knower will help you discern truth from dogma. If you honestly and open-heartedly seek the truth, you will find it. This is a law of Consciousness.

Healing seems to require that you have faith in your spiritual guidance, in your own deep, compassionate knowing. Have faith in your own inner love, in its ability to guide you and give you what you need in life.

Awareness

The second tool is awareness. Awareness is the process of moving things from the unconscious mind into the conscious mind, from the not known to the known. Awareness is also called mindfulness. You can practice awareness of:

- Physical feelings—what information is my body sending me now?
- Emotional feelings—how am I feeling, what belief is behind it, what is a healthy response to it?
- Thoughts and mental activity—where did that thought come from? Are my thoughts in alignment with what I want to achieve?
- The energetic—how is my energy flowing? What is blocking it?
- Beliefs—what are the beliefs that make up my world view and what would my heart say about them?

- Dreams—what is my unconscious mind trying to tell me? What feelings did the dream bring up?
- Actions—what prompted me to act that way? What is the highest response to this situation? What influence do I want to exert here? Are my actions likely to bring about my desired results?
- Relationships—the eye (I) cannot see itself, what sides of me are being revealed in this symbolic "mirror"? What patterns keep showing up in my relationships?
- Surroundings—how am I affected by the people around me, by the environment?

All of the above categories are aspects of your personal truth. Use awareness to become aware of your truth: what is going on inside of you, what is going on outside of you, and how the two dance together. Your awareness operates on two levels of perception. You can look at your life through human eyes and you can look at your life through spirit eyes. You want to practice both. When you become aware of a thought, feeling, belief, or an action, etc., ask yourself, "how does this look through spirit eyes?" Or "what would God say about this?" Or "what would my heart say about this?" Or whatever similar question is compatible with your experience of the Divine.

All of the tools are skills that improve with practice. The practice of awareness keeps you grounded in the present moment and insures that you're getting the information that your inner knower wants you to have. Awareness lets you know that your life is offering you a clue … and it helps you interpret that clue correctly.

So now you're aware of some aspect of yourself—for example, about how judgmental you are toward yourself, or how hurt you are by what someone said or did, or that a conclusion you drew when you were five no longer fits your life—what does the inner knower guide you to do with that information? Fully admit the truth of it.

Acceptance

That's the third tool: accept your truth. Release yourself into that truth. Let go. It is what it is. Fully admitting the truth of the past or of your present moment allows you to move into a place of acceptance, where real change can happen. Resisting the truth traps you into using your creative energy to rail against what is, which entrenches you where you are. Once you accept your situation, the stage is set for the next step in your process of change.

There is an old adage that states, "You shall know your truth and your truth shall set you free." (This saying is actually another law of Consciousness.) Truth is the surest path to freedom that I've ever witnessed. You must deal with your own truth if you want to be free of a particular malady that you have or experience that you went through or are going through. Most of us, at a very early age, learned many ways to avoid facing our truth. We repress and deny it, we put spins on it, we sugar-coat it. You cannot know the truth if you're constantly telling it what it can or cannot be. Unfortunately the old adage is not, "you shall know your fantasy and your fantasy shall set you free" because fantasies are much easier and often more fun. How often do you use fantasy to escape your present moment? When you learn to pay attention to your truth of what is really going on in and around you, including how your past experiences are influencing you right now, you are in a much better position to make better choices for yourself. But you must let it in, just as it is, unconditionally.

Awareness and acceptance reveals that there are two truths that you are dealing with. You have your own personal truth: all the conclusions that you have drawn from your own personal experiences, how the world looks to you because of the language you speak and the culture you grew up in and such. And then there is a higher Divine or Spiritual Truth. Aspects of your personal truth may not be true from the Divine perspective, but because you have been holding them as true, they have been influencing your view of the world and your ability to create your life. You have to acknowledge and accept the fact that you have been perpetuating those false beliefs if you are ever going to change them.

The power of acceptance comes from how Consciousness works. Consciousness empowers your creativity and your creativity flows wherever you focus your attention. Resistance, repression, and denial are forms of attention. If you are using any of them on your feelings, beliefs, or life situation, you are inadvertently creating more of what you are resisting, repressing, and denying.

Acceptance is an exercise in self-honesty, in clear vision, in allowing yourself to trust the Divine. You are practicing accepting both your personal truth and the Divine Truth. Acceptance reclaims any of your creativity that has been going into resistance, repression, and denial and allows you to redirect it toward what heals you.

Building on a foundation of faith, become aware of what is happening inside and around you and admit the truth of whatever it is to yourself. What does the inner knower recommend next? Over and over, it says things like, "just be kinder to yourself about that." Or, "give yourself a hug; hold yourself in your arms." Or, "let yourself know that you're all right, that you are not alone." This leads us to the fourth tool.

Compassion

My patients are constantly being guided by their inner knower to just have compassion for whatever is: compassion for their pain, for their bodies, for their minds, for everyone in their lives, for both truths and, especially, for themselves. I often call compassion the "The Alchemist" because it can literally take this lump of lead in your life that is your illness or health challenge and convert it into a lump of gold, the gift or blessing buried in the experience. Often, the practice of compassion is all that is needed to start the process of change and healing. It is as if once you open-heartedly accept a part of yourself, and stop railing against it, the love steps in and finishes up what else needs to happen.

You may have to start by practicing compassion for yourself for having control issues, for how difficult it is to get out of the driver's seat, to stop doing, and to trust that a loving, wise part will take over and steer you in the right direction. I know I had to. If you believe that God is an infinitely compassionate being or entity outside of yourself but who works through you, that is a good image. Imagine giving the steering wheel of your life over to God. "Let go and let God." Be open to receiving God's guidance. There is an old saying to the effect that praying is when we speak to God and intuition is when God speaks to us. Trust your intuition.

The more I work with compassion, the more in awe I stand before it. Currently I believe that compassion is one of the most dominant traits of your true authentic self and the practice of compassion is the bringing forth and expressing of your true authentic self (which, by definition, is also healing.) The practice of compassion naturally invokes your deepest wisdom to call forth and create for you the best possible solution to your problem. You do not need to use your cognitive mind to create this solution. The surest path to your inner peace, happiness, and fulfillment is having faith in the power of compassion and applying your will toward the practice of applying compassion to whatever is your truth. It is the surest path to your health. There are good explanations based upon the natural properties of Consciousness that show why this is so. We'll go over that more in the expanded section on compassion.

The first four tools are the workhorses for the process of lasting, authentic, supportive change. They are skills that improve with practice. Here is what we have developed so far: on a foundation of faith in your inner love and whatever helps you the most, practice awareness, acceptance, and compassion for what is, then become aware of the next thought, feeling, or issue, accept the truth of it and put it in your heart, and so the spiral goes … deeper and deeper into the understanding of who you are and how you work. The practice of the first four tools is an excellent way to generate the beliefs, and hence the thoughts and feelings, that free you from bondage. (Again, you do not have to exert effort to come up with these thoughts.) The last three tools follow naturally from this practice.

Forgiveness

The fifth tool is forgiveness. It is truly a letting go. Forgiveness just naturally happens when you bring enough compassion to a situation. And after it does, that issue or experience is no longer a "button", there is no emotional rise or charge. Forgiveness is an extension of compassion: with enough compassion, forgiveness just makes sense. Forgiveness just makes sense once your beliefs around a particular issue in your life align with higher truth. Again, do not exert effort to repress, deny, or ignore painful, angry, or unsupportive thoughts and feelings. Simply note that they are there, open your heart to them and to yourself currently experiencing them, and follow them to their roots. That these thoughts and feelings naturally cease is a clue that real forgiveness has happened. Real forgiveness has the power to actually change your physiology. I feel these changes all the time while doing bodywork on people when they reach that moment of forgiveness.

There is much confusion in our society about forgiveness. Forgiveness does not mean that you condone what was done; it does not mean that you forget what was done. Forgiveness is for you, for your own healing and growth. Forgiveness allows you to navigate around the tar pits of anger and resentment. Many people practice forgiveness as part of their religion and that is because forgiveness is essential for moving forward, for the healing of life's inevitable hurts and injustices. But forced or intentionally practiced forgiveness does not have the same power to transform you as does forgiveness arrived at through the practice of compassion.

Forgiveness is a dawning realization that you can finally let go of any hope that the past will ever be any different. When I am working on someone and their head is telling them that they have to forgive someone, I feel no changes in their tissues. When they practice viewing themselves and their past from a place of compassion and spontaneously arrive at the realization of forgiveness, there is generally a big shift in their tissues. There is generally a relaxing of tensions and they report a growing sense of rightness inside.

Forgiveness is somewhat similar to acceptance but it has a deeper, more wise and loving resonance. Forgiveness is an act of your Divinity. It is a compassionate acceptance from the perspective of higher truth. Your Divinity has the power to release you from your regrets, from your need for revenge, from your self-flagellation, from your anger and frustration. But you need to allow it.

Being able to forgive others and yourself is essential for your healing but focusing on forgiving directly risks receiving shallow results. You may still be harboring un-dealt-with anger, for example. Practice arriving at forgiveness through the practice of compassionate accepting awareness of what is and see for yourself the difference it makes.

Gratitude

Once enough forgiveness happens, the sixth tool shows itself—a growing sense of gratitude. I've had hundreds of people come into the office and say things like, "I wouldn't choose to go through that again, but I'm glad I did for all that I've learned and gained by healing from this difficulty." People have said that about car accidents, cancer, being raped, or having any number of serious illnesses. This world really is an incredible place, the Divine works through amazing ways, and the human spirit is so beautiful and resilient. Gratitude is a recognition of all these things.

Besides letting it arise spontaneously from the practice of the first five tools, you can also practice gratitude directly. This can also be transformational as it keeps you aware of and in alignment with a deep spiritual truth: no matter what is happening to and around you, you are loved, cared about, and cared for.

Gratitude emanates from humility. Humility aligns you with spirit. Strengthening your connection to spirit is healing.

So you can practice gratitude directly or let it grow from a practice of compassion. The latter leads to gratitude that has deep knowing and conviction behind it, but the former seems to work pretty well, too.

Become aware of your truth, accept your truth, have compassion for your truth, and allow your Divinity to lead you to forgiveness of whatever aspects of your truth need forgiving. A sense of gratitude for your truth and the way that spirit works in your life then just grows. I often use this spontaneous and growing sense of gratitude as a yard stick, as an indication that the person has received the healing hidden in whatever experience they were working on. At this point, you are ready to choose your actions.

Right Action

Even though the Tao[8] says that the masters accomplish everything by doing nothing, I haven't quite embodied that one fully yet. I still need to take showers, fix my breakfast, and go to work. But, beyond the mundane, how do you know that your actions will bring about the results that you desire, or even better, that your soul desires? When they do, such actions are called Right Actions in many world traditions. Right Action is based upon right understanding. I've witnessed that the faithful and true practice of the first six tools leads to a right understanding and that you then just know how to act—what to do, what to say—in the moment.

Unless you are tightly controlling yourself, your doing comes from whatever your motivations happen to be in that moment, and studies show that most of those motivations are unconscious. Your actions—and the motivations behind them—are excellent windows into the inner workings of your being. As you uncover and bring forth more of your true essential self, more of your actions stem from there. Your actions just naturally become an expression of who you are and then serve to further attract to you the experiences you want to create.

You don't have to try to be yourself. You already are yourself. But most of us have a lot of learned "stuff" in the way that keeps us from expressing our full potential. The changes that you make that represent your real self coming forth in your life require no effort on your part to maintain. That is why we say that real change is effortless. You may have to work hard to recognize your limiting beliefs, but once those beliefs change and you come more into your own, your real self expresses itself that much more in your life and no one can take that away from you. The seven tools are the skills that allow you to effectively uncover and change limiting beliefs, attitudes, and perceptions; and, in the process, free your real self to come forth and just be.

Practical Application

We have just run through a brief description of each of the tools. How do you get started with all of this stuff? How do you find and change the deeply held beliefs that are behind all the thoughts and feelings you don't like, all the behaviors you don't like, all the patterns in your life you don't like, and even most of the physical symptoms your body is using to get your attention? How do you find and change these things?

Here is where you meet your first paradox, and I don't mean a couple of MDs walking down the hall. On one hand, you have within you all that you need in order to heal; yet, on the other hand, you will most likely access this information much more easily if you work with others. I would strongly suggest that you either find and join, or start, a seven tools practice group. Share this book with your family and friends and then set a time each week to meet and talk about what you have been doing and how it is working or not working for you. Ideally, you could find a good therapist familiar with the seven tools who is running or is willing to start a support group.

That said, how can you get started using the seven tools for yourself?

The seven tools are extremely versatile. You can apply them to help you heal your addictions, your mood swings or depression, your weight issues, or any residual effects of past traumas, as examples; you can apply them to help you manifest more wealth, improve your relationships, or find the right career. But as the example to illustrate their use right now, I would like to show you how to use the seven tools of healing to find and change limiting beliefs. Why did I choose this example? Because your beliefs are so foundational to the life that you are living right now and to the life that you hope to be living sometime in the near future. Because learning how to find and let go of old limiting beliefs and replace them with new, truer beliefs is one of the most important skills for healing and change. So let's lay a foundation by talking a little about beliefs and how your mind works with them.

You have no doubt heard the saying "mind over matter." It has good alliteration but is somewhat oversimplified. As we will discuss later, your mind is that aspect of you that makes conscious sense out of your sensory input. It literally bridges the physical world and Consciousness. Beliefs are considered contents of your mind. Appendix C aside, a simplified way to think about your mind and your body is to imagine that your mind runs your body. It monitors and manages all the information required to keep all your bodily systems in balance and harmony with your surroundings. Your mind uses your brain to translate the knowing in Consciousness into physical reality and relay it to your body. So, more precisely, the saying ought to be "Consciousness over matter" but that doesn't sound as cool. Semantics aside, the important point to remember here is that the mind matters. Master your mind and you master your life.

The job of your mind is to think thoughts. If there are not enough sensory stimuli coming in, the mind doesn't care, it just starts making up thoughts to fill in the gaps. Your mind is a thinking machine. Your mind can make its own reality and there is no law that says that reality has to have anything to do with anybody else's reality (especially your spouses'), natural law, or historical events. If you are hurting, if you are sick, not sleeping well, stressed and anxious, or are using drugs or supplements that alter your mind, chances are you are not thinking very clearly. So the first step is to stop believing everything you think. That is actually a good bumper sticker: "Don't believe everything you think." Also, because the conclusions that you drew at the time of any past experience were influenced by how you were thinking then, fostering the habit of questioning any conclusions that you've drawn is another good practice for studying your mind. Another good bumper sticker: "Question Conclusions."

Become a student of your mind. Be curious. How does my mind work? How does it take in and process information? What are thoughts? What are beliefs? You can do this by first choosing to have faith that you can deepen your understanding of the workings of your mind; then, use awareness to watch your thoughts.

You only have one mind but we divide it into two parts to describe how it works. There is the conscious mind, that part you are conscious of, those thoughts that you know you are having; and there is the unconscious mind, that part that you are not conscious of, that part that is running your body, monitoring all of your receptors, helping you make much of your day automatic so you don't tire yourself out thinking too hard. (Try staying fully conscious of every breath you take during a day, for example.) With mindfulness, meditation, and other practices of awareness, you can learn how to calmly watch your mind thinking thoughts even when it is freaking out. I would encourage you to search out some kind of mindfulness practice that works for you in your life and stick with it through thick and thin.

How you are feeling at any given moment is the result of your thoughts and experiences passing through the lens of your world view. Because most of the beliefs that make up your world view are in the unconscious part of your mind, your feelings are information about what is going on in your unconscious mind and in your body. Emotional and physical feelings are just two sides of the same coin, two ways of looking at the same subject. They are information for you to use. Practice becoming aware of how you are feeling, notice that every emotional feeling has a concomitant physical feeling associated with it and vice versa. Feelings are not facts. They are information, and your challenge is to learn how to receive the information, interpret it correctly, and take the proper actions that are in the highest good.

Your body is pretty much mindlessly obedient to your mind. This explains the whole mind-body connection. Try this exercise: imagine there is half a glass of water sitting before you. Look at that glass and choose to see it as half empty. Make note of how you feel inside. Now, clear your mind of that scenario, take another look at that glass and see it as half full. Again, make note of how you feel inside. Feel the difference? Most people feel a closing feeling, a sense of lack, or even despair when they see the glass as half empty. Most will also feel a sense of plenty, of reassurance when they see the glass as half full. These different feelings are actual physical, chemical changes in your body. Those physical, chemical changes happened purely in response to a conscious choice you made, a conscious choice about your perspective. When extrapolated to all the possibilities in your life, how you choose to look at the world can have incredible ramifications for you and your healing. And, what is perhaps most amazing, there wasn't even a glass of water there.

So get curious about how you work inside. What do you have control over in your life so that, with the proper practices, you can change it? And what is a given so you don't waste any of your time and energy trying to change it? Your challenge then becomes figuring out how you can work with whatever is going on in and around you in the healthiest way possible. You may recognize this as the crux of the Serenity Prayer[9].

Know that you get to choose both where you focus your attention and the perspective from which you view whatever it is you are focusing on…with practice. This is a most important point. This is how you claim the freedom that is your birthright. Pay attention, ask your inner wisdom to help you see things from the point of view that will create the greatest good. When it comes to making decisions and choices in your life, you generally get better results by following your inner guidance, your inner knowing—rather than going by what you are thinking and feeling. If you have good "gut instincts," that is most likely your inner knower guiding you.

Know your mind. Attend to your thoughts and feelings in a healthy way but don't give them more credence to direct you than they deserve. With that preparation, you are ready to start using the Seven Tools.

Faith is a choice. Think about what you could have faith in that would be most beneficial to you. If it is true that you get to choose your beliefs, why not choose to believe in whatever helps you the most? I remember I was working in a hospital owned clinic in downtown Seattle in the late 1980s when I first asked myself that question. One of the answers I came up with motivated me to move out of the existential agnosticism that I had been in since college, and into believing in a universal Consciousness that is pure love. That one belief has brought me much joy as well as, in my opinion, made me a better husband, father and physician. Take a moment right now to jot down a list of concepts that, if you had faith in them, would help you heal; then just hold that list in the back of your mind. You get to choose.

Your feelings are the key to uncovering your beliefs. When you watch your mind, you will notice that every thought that you think and every bit of sensory information that comes into your awareness creates a feeling. In other words, every experience you have, whether it is internally generated or coming in through your senses, gets translated into a feeling. Therefore, you can get the information buried in all of your experiences pertaining to who you are and how you work in the world by receiving the information encoded in your feelings. This is a grand, simplifying principle. Learning to be healthy with your feelings is a big step toward being able to heal your entire life.

Again, from watching your mind, you will see that a feeling is the net result of your experience—thought or sensory information—passing through your structure of interpretation—that is, whatever you believe. This relationship among your experiences, beliefs, and feelings is worth repeating because it leads to a most important observation: your feelings are never the problem … no matter how much you don't like them. They are just the result of some sort of input passing through your system of beliefs. So, either the input is the problem, or some part of your belief system is the problem. The feeling is just an innocent messenger. Running the mailman off does not relieve you from the responsibility of paying your bills. Controlling your feelings directly will never heal you.

To let the messenger deliver its message, first remember to put yourself into the perspective of the wise, kind observer of yourself, then become aware of the input, either what you are thinking or what you see, hear, smell, taste, or feel, then become aware of the feeling that comes up. Next, admit the raw, naked truth of how you are really feeling to yourself and then ask the feeling to take you to its roots. Generally, observing your experience and then observing the feeling that comes up allows you to also observe the belief that formed that feeling from the experience.

Notice what you just did. You started from the perspective of compassion, the fourth tool, used awareness, the second tool, to uncover the truth of your present moment; that is, what you were thinking and experiencing. Then you used acceptance, the third tool, to admit the truth of your present moment and asked that truth to take you to its roots.

Once you have uncovered the belief that spawned the feeling that you are exploring, just run it through tools two, three and four again. You have already done tool number two, awareness. You are now aware of the belief. Next, admit the raw, naked truth to yourself that you have been holding onto that belief as if it were true, whether or not it really is. Next, look the belief right in the eye and ask it if it is really true from a higher perspective. Generally, this is enough to get the belief to change and align itself with a higher truth. If not, then continue to hold yourself in kindness and compassion that this belief happens to be your truth, that you went through whatever experience led you to form that belief, and for all that that belief has been doing to you down through the years. That is, just be kind to yourself about it—tool number four. Over time, the kindness will change the belief.

You will just get locked into an arms race with the belief if you jump right in and try to change it. The energy you put into trying to make the belief change works to make the belief stronger. I bet you have already experienced this way of trying to work inner change. That this happens is just due to a law of Consciousness: your creativity flows wherever you pay attention. By using the seven tools approach to change the belief, you are fully aware of your truth (remember, denial and repression are forms of attention), but you are continuously focusing your attention on practicing compassion for yourself having your truth: never on trying to directly change your truth. The compassion then works any change needed in order to align your truth with higher truth. Focusing on having kindness for yourself holding onto a belief rather than focusing on changing the belief may seem like a subtle distinction, but it is critically important for working correctly with that law of Consciousness.

Compassion is love in action, so the practice of compassion is just practicing being your true self, letting your true self act in the world. This is healing, by definition.

Here are the steps summarized:

1. Choose an issue to focus upon that needs healing, for example, an injury, illness, relationship problem, problem at work, depression, anxiety or other health challenge, etc.
2. Become as aware of all of the feelings your chosen issue generates in you.
3. Admit the truth of your present experience to yourself. Be blunt and honest (but kind) with yourself.
4. Be kind to yourself that this is your present truth. Have compassion, open your heart to yourself and all that you've been going through.
5. From that perspective of unreserved loving kindness, ask your present truth to take you to its roots. When did you first feel these feelings? What was going on in your life at the time? What conclusions did you draw from that experience back then?
6. Once you uncover and are consciously aware of the root belief or conclusion, repeat steps 3 and 4: admit to yourself the fact that you have been harboring that belief or conclusion and be kind to yourself about that.
7. Next, ask yourself, "How do my root beliefs and conclusions look through Spirit eyes?" Another way to ask the question could be: "What would God think of my beliefs and conclusions?" or "How do my beliefs and conclusions compare with higher truth?" You get the point: ask in a way that works for you.

Most of the time, just uncovering your root beliefs, accepting them, being kind to yourself anyway and looking at them through spirit eyes is enough to get them to change to be more in alignment with higher truth. Occasionally, these steps need to be repeated a few times, or with closely related feelings, before the shift in belief happens. Just have faith in the process. Resist the temptation to get in there and try to force your root beliefs to change directly. You choose where to focus your attention. Focus on being kind to yourself no matter what you happen to be experiencing or feeling. This gets easier with practice.

Summary

We just went through a brief description of the tools and how to apply them in the real world. The bottom line: your truth will heal you. The more you can know your personal truth and get your truth to line up with a higher, spiritual truth, the healthier you become. You can look at your truth from four irreducible but interdependent perspectives. You can look at your truth as it is showing up in your body, in your energy, in your mind, and in your beliefs. Each of these four perspectives leads you back to those aspects of infinite Consciousness that you are manifesting in your life right now. You can then work to change what has already been created, if the symptoms or situations are that painful and intolerable; and, you can work to change what is getting created by changing the beliefs that are allowing those unwanted aspects of Consciousness into your life.

If all you do is work to change those things in your life that you don't like but do nothing to change how you work with Consciousness and creativity, you are likely to spend your life chasing your tail: continuing to create more of what you already have and not making much progress toward your real healing. But if you do both at the same time, you will make real progress towards finding out who you really are and making choices and creating opportunities that are right for you. Practice the seven tools; trust and act upon what you know deep inside and you will be able to both change those things in your life that are no longer working for you and start creating the body, thoughts, feelings, relationships, and circumstances that really do work for you.

I have noticed, both in myself and in my patients, that much practice is required before we just naturally, skillfully, and automatically apply the seven tools to the stuff of our lives, moment by moment. There are many detours and traps along the way, many subtle ways that we can use the tools incorrectly, all of which slow down or block our healing. I would love for you to benefit from our years of experience and help you do end runs around most of those mistakes. Again, a support group with similarly searching people would be one of your best resources. What I can do here to help you is explain these concepts in more detail and give you exercises to practice that will deepen your skill and improve the results you get from applying the tools. After that, we'll explore some of the common traps along the healing path and how to circumvent them.

Section Two

The Seven Tools of Healing

Chapter Three

Faith

The first tool is faith. But, interestingly, it was the last of the seven tools that I noticed. As an empiricist and a science nerd with strong family ties to Missouri (the "Show Me" state), it took me a long time to fully admit and clearly observe how my patients' inner guidance made use of faith. I put it first because of the way it functions in your life: it is the foundation upon which all knowing is built.

Faith is foundational for several reasons. First, all healing is spiritual healing and few relationships ask for more faith from you than does your relationship with spirit. Second, healing is heart-based more so than head-based, and so is faith. Third, real faith comes more from your guts than from your head; faith can be stronger than data and logic and reasoning; faith is a knowing in your bones. Faith that is deep enough to help you with your healing comes directly from your trust in your inner guidance. In fact, the word "faith" comes from the Latin *fidēs:* trust or *fidere:* to trust.

Coming to this understanding took me quite a bit of soul-searching. I knew by age twelve that I wanted to be a doctor. By age fourteen, I saw that I was good at and enjoyed science and math more than the humanities … and from that age on I've thought of myself as a man of science. In high school, *Star Trek's* Spock was my mentor and aspiration.

I probably would have devoted my life to hard scientific research if not for my love of the outdoors. In college, I worked summers as a river guide on the Green and Colorado rivers. Guiding people through wilderness adventures by day and engaging in scores of long conversations over campfires by night awakened in me a love, too, of philosophy and psychology, as well as a deep interest in the human condition. I really wanted to help people live better lives and my river experiences just affirmed and deepened my twelve year-old's conviction that a life of medicine was the way for me to contribute.

Still, the whole concept of faith, that faith was important or even necessary, seemed antithetical to the science-based medicine I was taught. But I also knew that one of the most unscientific things a scientist can do is discard data just because it can't be explained by the currently prevailing scientific model. And that is exactly where we are today: many human experiences, though affecting your health, cannot be explained by the medical model being used by conventional medicine. And if you try to talk with your doctor about one of those experiences, chances are it will be ignored, if not flat out ridiculed.

For example, have you ever had what could be called a paranormal experience? When surveyed, about eighty percent of elderly people admit to being visited by the spirit of a departed loved one[10]. Conventional medicine tries to explain this as a grieving hallucination. But even my older brother, a dyed-in-the-wool, card-carrying, conventional medicine nurse practitioner experienced my mother stopping by his bedroom late one night to say good-bye. She was in Salt Lake City and he was in Boise. He got a call the next morning that she had passed in the night. This couldn't have been a bereavement hallucination because it happened before he knew she had died. How does the current medical model explain that? I cannot discount his experience and write it off as an hallucination any more than I can for the majority of people in our society who've had similar "hallucinations."

There are many other human experiences that cannot be explained by the conventional medical model, from the common, such as the placebo effect, to the rare, such as near-death experiences. When I put all the out-lying data together, I concluded that the current medical model has very limited utility when it comes to informing our healing efforts. We can do better. Since all of your experiences affect your health, the science upon which medicine is based needs to take all of your experiences into account. The medical profession must keep improving the medical model until it does ... not keep forcing people's lives to fit the model or, even worse for the patient, ignore what doesn't.

But I need to be clear that by accepting that you had an experience does not mean that, as a physician, I need to accept at face value your explanation of your experience. I need to be able to draw my own conclusions based upon my training and clinical experience. Often the process of healing includes correcting or aligning your interpretations of your experiences with those arrived at from higher perspectives. But to discount your experience or ignore it altogether and give more credence to the dogma rather than to the data, is to practice medicinism, the religion of medicine, rather than to practice medicine.

Over the years, hundreds of my patients have come in with stories about how they've been discounted and disbelieved in other medical offices. I suspect the same is happening every day to millions of people all over the country. Science progresses much more slowly when data is ignored. Instead of blindly putting my faith in the current medical model, I've chosen to question the model and work to expand and refine it rather than discard so many of my patients' experiences. For so many of them, the faith-based experiences in their lives have been the most significant to them. By listening carefully to my patients' lives and staying true to empiricism and the scientific process, I came to the conclusion that faith is the foundation upon which all of our beliefs, our sense of safety, and all of our knowing—even scientific knowing—is built.

Some people react to the word "faith", but I'm choosing to use it because that is the word people's own inner guidance uses most often. Regardless of how you respond to the word, I trust you will see that faith is important to all of us, no matter our religious or spiritual beliefs. I have come to understand, after years of observing myself and my patients, that your inner wisdom, your inner love, your highest best self—whatever you choose to call this aspect of yourself—is pure Consciousness, spirit, or God working through you or attempting to communicate with your conscious mind. And it is continuously asking you to trust it and have faith in it.

What do you have faith in? How is faith operating in your life? Please take a moment and answer these questions for yourself.

You were conceived with the capacity to have faith, as you were conceived from spirit and you embody spirit within you, and hence are part of a universal spirit yourself. But that capacity blooms or withers in step with your early life experiences. Faith is first an experience in the body, then an intellectual concept. If your newborn and infant needs were just automatically met, if you were fed and changed and held and adored and not left to "cry it out" before you developed object permanence, or didn't experience some other form of abandonment, then you developed faith in your mother and father and in the world as a place where you can live and thrive.

If, on the other hand, your infant needs were not met, or you were abused or abandoned at a very early age, that bodily experience of faith didn't develop. Instead, you may have drawn the conclusion that the world is a harsh, threatening place and that you don't deserve to be safe and loved and cared for. Then your life will start creating lots of experiences to prove that those conclusions are correct. I've worked with people who were the result of unwanted pregnancies, with people whose mothers were drug addicts and constantly brought home pedophilic boyfriends. I even have one man in my practice whose stepfather was a military interrogator who thought it was funny to use his knowledge to keep the kids psychologically off balance. As a result, this man has chronic depression and anxiety and has never married. His brother is alcoholic and his sister is on drugs.

Whenever you look at a situation in which a baby is being abused, neglected, or abandoned by his or her parents, from our adult perspective it is easy to see that the baby is innocent and it's the parents who have the problem. But most fetuses, infants, and small children in abusive situations conclude that their parents are okay and how they are being treated is just how they deserve to be treated, that how they are being treated is all that they are worth. Very few people, in my experience, conclude that they are okay and that their parents are just messed up. To do so as an infant would feel intolerably unsafe. Also, by owning it, the child can hold onto the hope that if they could just be a better child, then their parents would be better parents. Such early conclusions about their self-worth go deep into their unconscious mind and act like immutable facts, continually creating experiences in their lives where they are under-respected and under-rewarded.

People who have been raised by narcissistic mothers, for example, have some of the deepest emotional and psychological wounds of anyone I've worked with. Narcissists need to be the center of the Universe, but then so do babies, at least for awhile. When the mother and the baby are competing for the same spot on stage, the mother generally overpowers the baby. For the baby, that deep need to be loved by the mother goes unmet. Without that direct experience of trusting and being loved by the mother, these babies are left with deep scars and disabilities. This can lead to depression, anxiety, problems with intimacy, borderline personality disorder, and the need to be hyper-vigilant all the time, which brings along with it all the diseases associated with chronic stress. These people often compensate by having faith in nothing or the complete opposite: blind unquestioning faith. That damage can be healed, but since faith is such an important and primary ingredient in the process of healing, healing damage to the very ability to form faith in the first place can be challenging.

If any of this sounds like you, take heart. You can heal. If you have difficulty having faith in yourself, in others, or in your ability to get better, find a therapist or other practitioner who has had years of experience and success working with abused people, even if you don't have any memories of such abuse. (Narcissistic mothers, for example, often do everything right on the surface and look like great mothers to the rest of the world. This can be crazy-making for the child experiencing the reality behind the façade.) Chances are this therapist will have a very deep understanding of what you have gone through, what you are going through now, and how to help you. Know that every instinct you have will scream against this, but challenge yourself to form a trusting bond with this person anyway. Consciously practice choosing to trust this person even in the face of what your mind is telling you. Remember, don't always trust what you think.

As will inevitably happen, when your trust of the therapist is challenged, look deeply within to see if you are reacting from old patterns or from your present experience. Since beliefs function like lenses that you view the world through, you will be viewing this therapist through untrusting lenses and you may not be able to tell if you are reacting from old patterns or if you just cannot trust this person. Challenge your belief systems that leave you feeling that trust is not possible. Trust enough, have the courage, to bring these feelings to your therapist for examination. Many of my most abused patients go through a phase where they get angry with me, even accusing me of abusing them. If they stick with the process, if they do not abandon themselves and quit therapy, they see that I will not abandon them and then they are able to let their guard down some and start a deeper therapeutic relationship. Find a therapist that you can get angry at and then work through it like two adults. This trusting therapeutic relationship can then form a foundation upon which you can build a trusting relationship with yourself, with your own knowing, and with other people.

Whether you need to start by healing your ability to form faith or if you already have faith automatically, notice that faith does not require any supportive facts or scientific proof. This is simultaneously a great strength and a great liability. Making good use of its strengths while minimizing its liabilities is your challenge with faith. This takes awareness (the second tool), practice, and skill. So next let us explore how you can get the most benefit out of your faith.

Because you have free will, you are just as free to think incorrect thoughts as correct thoughts. (Sometimes you are not even sure which are which until you have the advantage of 20/20 hindsight.) But whether correct or incorrect, you will experience the natural consequences of whatever you are thinking; that is a law of Consciousness. In this way, your life is constantly giving you feedback about what you are holding faith in and the strength of that faith. Therefore, becoming aware of what you have faith in right now is one window into your deeply-held beliefs. If you find that you have developed faith in destructive or limiting ideas, organizations or people, you can then use the seven tools to change the underlying beliefs and start to have faith in things that are more conducive to your health and happiness.

You will see that there are two origins to the objects of your faith. There are things you just unquestioningly have faith in because of the life that you've lived so far. This might include

- the conclusions that you drew from your experiences before your conscious memory developed,
- ideas and concepts that your family and/or culture just take for granted,
- the beliefs that you've formed that have become automatic and
- influences from the education that you've had.

Then there are also things that you have faith in because you've thought things through and chosen to have that faith. How do you wisely choose what to have faith in? You can use your faith to believe in ideas or concepts that have no basis in anything empirical, rational, or helpful; or, you can use your faith to believe in whatever helps you the most. You have to decide for yourself whether a belief is helpful or not. You might have to try some on for size and make a few mistakes along the way. The best use of faith is a skill that gets better with practice.

Our society is currently engaged in a huge struggle between faith and science. People who want to live their lives from a place of scientific rationalism think that they don't need faith. They base their beliefs upon what is known by science to be true and try to conduct themselves with reason and logic. But, as you know, you can make a rational choice but that does not control your emotional experience. If you try to live from pure reason and logic, you might find that your emotions keep popping up at inopportune times.

On the other hand, people who want to live a faith-based life develop very strong convictions in whatever their particular religion teaches and no amount of data, scientific proof, or opposing arguments can sway them (that is, after all, one of the defining characteristics of faith). Since faith is the root of all knowing, people with a strong faith in a particular teaching can feel like they have all the answers. And people who think they know it all really irritate those of us who do☺. Also, they risk being closed off to new, horizon-broadening experiences and the mystery of creation. As Brené Brown says, "Faith minus mystery and vulnerability equals extremism."[11]

But a few moments of contemplation will reveal that we need both faith and science. While every one of your experiences exerts some sort of influence upon your health, not every one of your experiences lends itself to exploration or explanation by our currently practiced scientific methods. So a complete system of healing needs something beyond science. And yet, a scientific understanding can, in certain circumstances, help you make better choices for yourself. William Egginton eloquently captures this need for science while, at the same time, stating the case for a need for humanness beyond science:

When science becomes the sole or even primary arbiter of such basic notions as personhood, it ceases to be mankind's most useful servant and threatens, instead, to become its dictator. Science does not and should not have the

power to absolve individuals and communities of the responsibility to choose. This emphatically does not mean that science should be left out of such personal and political debates. The more we know about the world the better positioned we are to make the best possible choices. But when science is used to replace thinking instead of complement it; when we claim to see in its results the reduction of all the complexity that constitutes the emergence of a human life or the choices and responsibilities of the person it may develop into; we relinquish something that Kant showed more than 200 years ago was essential to the very idea of a human being: our freedom.
—William Egginton[12]

Freedom is an important aspect of your true, essential self. You are a free being. You need a way to harness the strengths of both faith and science to help you with your healing. In his amazing book *The Marriage of Sense and Soul*[13], Ken Wilber lays one possible philosophical foundation for a way to resolve the differences between faith and science. He affirms that the scientific method, imperfect though it may be, is still the best process our species has yet devised for separating the valid from the bogus. If you doubt this statement, just look at how much the practical application of the scientific method has changed the human experience over the past two hundred and fifty years, and how it promises to continue to do so. Scientific breakthroughs and their subsequent technological developments are continuing to happen at ever increasing rates.

Wilber points out that we have three ways of knowing things—objectively, subjectively, and transcendentally. If I wanted to know you objectively, I could weigh and measure you, I could do blood tests and full body CT scans, EKGs, EEGs, and such. To do all of these measurements, I would not necessarily need to talk to you. So the objective way of knowing you is often called monological. I'm engaged in a monologue, as though I'm dictating all of my findings into a tape recorder as I'm examining you. I could learn a lot about you by examining you objectively, but there would still be much about you I can't find out that way, like what inspires you, what you are afraid of, what challenges you, and such.

I would need to talk with you to learn these things. In order to get your side of your life, your interpretation of your experiences, I would need to have a dialogue with you. So the subjective way of knowing is also called the dialogical way of knowing.

And have you ever noticed that if you just sit and stew about something, insights come? If you hold an object, thought, feeling, or experience you've had in your mind and really look at it, a deeper understanding comes to you. This is called contemplation. Contemplation, as a way of knowing, is frequently used by many of the world's great wisdom traditions. Also, many people just know things intuitively and can't logically explain how it is that they know them. This kind of learning and knowing transcends logic and reason so is often referred to as translogical knowing, the third way that we can know things.

Science almost exclusively limits itself to the objective, only relatively recently has started exploring the subjective, and seems to purposefully steer clear of the translogical. Wilber points out that there is really no logical reason why the scientific method couldn't be applied equally as effectively to all three ways of knowing. Doing so would lead to the development of what he calls a "broad science" that, in my opinion, would be better able to encompass a much greater range of human experience. A medicine based on broad science would be better positioned to help support you in your healing than our current medicine based on narrow science.

Interestingly, no matter what way of knowing the scientific method gets applied to, the method itself is still rooted in faith … or at least in assumptions. The scientific models that various branches of science use are all based on simplifying assumptions about nature. Until such time as those foundational assumptions need to change (see *The Structure of Scientific Revolution* by Thomas Kuhn[14]) they are "taken on faith," so to speak, and the rest of that discipline is built upon them. So, essentially, faith is at the root of everything we think we know as facts, even in science. Scientists have faith in the scientific method, they have faith in the knowledge that science has given them about nature, and they have faith that their foundational assumptions capture some aspect of truth about nature. If their faith in the current scientific model gets too strong, then they ignore outlying data and start practicing scientism, the religion of science.

Besides being at the root of scientific knowing, faith plays another role in knowing. We often live our daily lives as if we know things; yet, amazingly, the formal proof that a fact is indeed a fact has so far eluded us. My daughter asks, "How do you know <u>that</u> for a fact?" The answer is, "I don't." These question go back centuries. For example, Spinoza[15] set out "to find out whether there was anything which would be the true good ..." He was never able to prove the basis of knowing to his own satisfaction. I don't think he should feel too badly about that since, after three hundred years of working on the problem, philosophers of science have yet to agree on a methodology for arriving at the truth[16].

Despite all of the drawbacks and limitations of scientific proof, our society has adopted it as the gold standard for reliability; and that it is. We just have to keep this caveat in mind: even science is not certain. There is a good probability that currently held scientific truths will be replaced with newer scientific truths in the future. And they should, as our understanding of nature increases. But most of society—including many scientists—lose sight of the fact that faith is at the root of what we think we know as scientific fact—this pivotal role of faith is inescapable, as these foundational assumptions are inherent to the scientific process. As a result, some modern scientists have responded to philosophy's inability to arrive at a reliable way to know for certain what is true by saying, "Who needs philosophy, anyway? I know what I know." They don't see this view as an inherent contradiction: these hard-core rational scientists are taking science on faith.

Given all of this, we need to be open-minded about everything and continue to use our best powers of discernment, even with scientific facts. But to carry this argument to its extreme and lose faith in all facts is irrational, and even dangerous, leading to a post-fact world. As one of my students put it one day, in a humorous confusion between mind and brain, "I want to be open-minded but not so much so that my brain plops out on the floor."

So what if you don't know if what you think you know is in fact a fact? How important is all of this pontification if you are not a philosopher or scientist and are just trying to live your life? I'm reminded of an exercise my high school math teacher demonstrated one day in class. He had a boy stand at one end of the room and a girl at the other. He then asked them to halve the distance between them. Then halve it again ... and again. He pointed out that if they kept cutting the distance between them in half, mathematically they would never touch, but pretty soon they'd be close enough for all practical purposes. (And this was in Utah!)

The point is, in our day-to-day life, exactitude is not always necessary. Approximations and generalities are good enough, within reasonable bounds. Faith, especially in consultation with reason, is the foundation of our lives and it is good enough. I believe that philosophers have had such a difficult time arriving at a formal proof of knowing because mystery is the ground substance of existence. That is, mystery is the true nature of nature. I'm not a scientific nihilist, I think we ought to keep working to understand nature as much as we can. This knowing allows you to make better choices for yourself. Interestingly, in so many different scientific disciplines, as they hone in on that aspect of nature that they are exploring, the search keeps coming back to mystery. Because mystery is such a deep quality of nature, faith is the first tool.

The strength of your faith is basically a measure of how strongly you believe what you believe. Beliefs are just stable thought forms and the strength of your faith in them gives them their power to manifest in your life. Regular thoughts occur in your conscious mind. But once a thought stabilizes and solidifies into a belief, it can move into your unconscious mind. If thoughts are like the ripple of waves on the surface of a lake, beliefs are like the ripples of sand on the bottom of the lake. The former influences the latter but the latter are much more stable over time and represent aggregates of what the ripples on the surface have been doing. A belief, once formed, performs two simultaneous functions in your psyche. It becomes a lens through which you view the world, and it becomes a pin-hole in the sheet of black plastic that covers your infinite potential, only letting that potential through that is consistent with that belief. So beliefs not only make up your structure of interpretation, they also form your structure of creation. Beliefs function as the gate-keepers of your creativity. And they are very selective.

We have many sayings in our culture to this effect.

If you think you can, you can. If you think you can't, you're right.
—Henry Ford

Man is made by his belief. As he believes, so he is.
—Johann Wolfgang von Goethe

The world we see that seems so insane is the result of a belief
system that is not working. To perceive the world differently, we
must be willing to change our belief system, let the past slip away,
expand our sense of now, and dissolve the fear in our minds.
—William James

It's the repetition of affirmations that leads to belief. And once
that belief becomes a deep conviction, things begin to happen.
—Muhammad Ali

The idea that beliefs guide and direct your creativity, your power to manifest everything that is your life, is not new or surprising. But the observation that, with practice, you can shape and control your beliefs, thus freeing and redirecting your creative powers, is of ultimate importance for healing and personal growth. When I sit back and look at what I am actually doing with my patients through all of the different kinds of therapeutic ministrations I've learned over the years, I see that helping them identify and change limiting beliefs is the most important and conducive to long-lasting improvement in their lives. And helping you learn to work this process of change for yourself is the most important skill I, or any practitioner you work with, could teach you. Believe in yourself, trust what you know. Be willing to make mistakes, just take the time to learn from them so, as Robert Kiyosaki says, you can come back stronger and smarter[17].

What you believe, to a great extent, determines how your body responds to your life. Bruce Lipton wrote an entire book on the *Biology of Belief*[18]. Your beliefs determine your emotions and Candace Pert wrote an entire book on *The Molecules of Emotion*[19]. In their books, Lipton and Pert describe in very accessible detail, how the workings of your mind get translated into the workings of your body. Your beliefs determine the workings of your mind which in turn determines the workings of your body, including your brain. Of course there are exceptions in which genetic mutations, injury, or environmental toxicities and such take center stage in your health, but, even in these situations, there are opportunities to learn and deepen your understanding of yourself as you seek answers to your problems and healing for your wounds.

I do not take literally the New Age adage that you create your own reality. I see the process of creating as more complex than that. All that you have potential conscious control over is your present level of conscious understanding of yourself, and that potential is only achieved through years of intense discipline and practice. You, as your conscious sense of self, as your ego, don't create all that happens to you. Children don't ask to get sexually abused, the Jews didn't ask for the Holocaust. Remember, there is much more to you than you can hold in your consciousness. (You can't open all the files in your computer at once.) Your conscious mind can direct some of your creativity, but the rest is being run by all the rest of you—including those beliefs—that remains unconscious.

> *Until you make the unconscious conscious, it will direct*
> *your life and you will call it fate.* — C.G. Jung.

The only way the New Agers can be right is if you as spirit create your reality. In that case, your reality is then just one big invitation to know yourself as spirit, and that I can believe. If you are so inclined to believe that you create your own reality, and, by extension, everyone else is also creating their own reality, I would ask you to apply that belief with compassion and awareness or maybe just apply it to yourself in your own life. I recently had a patient who lost her young daughter to a chronic illness and a "friend" came up to her in church and asked her what she did to create her daughter's death. In unskilled hands, ideas that pass as spiritual truths can be uncompassionate and hurtful.

You are consciously aware of some of your beliefs, most you are not, but your inner wisdom is aware of them all. All of the beliefs that you formed while you were inside the womb, those you formed during your birth process, in your infancy and toddlerhood are, most likely, below the level of your conscious awareness. But they are there, nonetheless, functioning like lenses through which you view your world and directing the flow of your creative potential, your biology, your relationships, your wants and desires, and your fate.

Then, beyond the power of your own personal beliefs to direct your creativity, there seems to be a collective influence as well, as when a plane crashes, a war breaks out, or a landslide takes out an entire town. If that New Age adage is right, then how did one person create that reality and then impose their issues on everyone else? What about everyone else's right to create their reality? This point is illustrated by a comment one of my patients made one afternoon, "If I have a choice, when it is my time to go, I'd like to go like my grandpa did: peacefully in my sleep. Not screaming my fool head off like all the passengers in his car." "You create your own reality" is one side of the paradox and, as a bumper sticker recently put out by a lab that specializes in digestive function phrased it, "feces occurs." That is the other side of the paradox. Both are true. Paradoxes insure that mystery reigns supreme.

We tend to call the first seven years of life the formative years. During that time, your unconscious mind is operating much like a tape recorder with the record button on. Everything goes right in, without any filtering or discernment. For most of my patients, these early years function like the first act of a well-written play: all the major themes of their life are introduced. Then the rest of their life is like the rest of the play: the themes get worked through and, hopefully, resolved in some fashion.

Think about what happens during those first seven years and, remember, you are nine months old by the time you are born. You come into this world (from where?); you form a deep connection with your mother, whereby you feel what she is feeling; you go through a major transformation when you leave your mother's body and come into the world; you are totally dependent upon other people for every aspect of your existence; you learn how to move your body; you learn an entire language, sometimes two or more; you learn how to push people's buttons, to let your needs be known, to try to get them met; you start to become a social being, relating to people outside of your family; the list goes on. It is a busy time. You are like a learning sponge dropped into a bucket of water. You soak it all in. Oftentimes, a single experience of being abandoned, discounted, or abused during these years is all it takes to form influential and foundational beliefs about yourself.

One part of healing often involves doing an inventory of all the beliefs that got formed from going through all of those early-life experiences. You do this by learning to follow the tell-tale clues those beliefs are leaving in your life. Those clues lead you back to the beliefs, even if they formed long before you had language. You then use the seven tools to change any beliefs that need to be changed. You use awareness to make the previously unconsciously held belief conscious (tool two). You then admit the truth to yourself that you have been harboring that belief and, generally in that moment, you also see what that belief has been doing to you all these years (Acceptance, tool three). You then open your heart to yourself and have compassion for yourself for all that you've been going through: whatever experience that led to the formation of that belief in the first place, and then all the limitations you've endured because you've had that belief (Compassion, tool four). Then you compare that belief to a higher truth: you can ask, "how does that belief look through spirit eyes?" or "what would God say about that belief?" or "what would my heart say about that belief?" whatever phrasing works for you. Often that is all that is needed to get the limiting belief to release its hold on you and be replaced by a belief that supports the higher truth. With time and practice, the new belief that is based on an expanded understanding of what happened when the first belief formed and that is more in alignment with higher truth, sinks back down into your unconscious and becomes your new lens through which you view the world. It becomes a new guardian at the gate of your creative flow and then what you are able to create in your life just changes.

Abigail is now in her mid-twenties. As a child, she had learning difficulties and grew up thinking she was stupid. As a teen, she took very little responsibility for herself. Her parents were always "on me" because her room was a mess and she didn't help out around the house much. When she started having relationships, she was frequently physically and emotionally abused in them. By eighteen, she had a daughter out of wedlock. She developed chronic pain and anxiety and became addicted to prescription pain and anti-anxiety medications. She wanted to work in the schools as a teacher's assistant but could not get through any of the training programs. She started seeing me when she was twenty three. She had just quit another training program, was back living with her parents, and was very unhappy with how well she was parenting her daughter. And she was in yet another abusive relationship.

We tested her adrenal and bowel function for factors contributing to her chronic pain, treated what we found, then tried to wean her off of her medications … without success. Eventually circumstances came to a head in her life and her parents convinced her to go to an in-patient rehab program for three months. Shortly after getting out of rehab, she restarted her pain and anxiety medications. She didn't come see me for about a year and then, seemingly out of the blue, started coming in regularly for craniosacral therapy. By this time, she was clear that she needed to make some major changes in her life. Through the treatments, she was able to see many of the conclusions that she'd drawn early in her life, especially with respect to her self-worth and competence. She was able to see how those beliefs looked from an expanded perspective and release them.

Within weeks, she was off of her medications, using some of the skills she'd learned in rehab to help with the physical withdrawal symptoms. She ended her abusive relationship and got back in school. She stopped going out so much at night and started spending more time with her daughter. She said that these changes just "made sense" to her and she didn't miss going out in the evenings. She is now pain-free and not having anxiety. She is working part time in a classroom as part of her training and loving it. She is very clear and present now, and the children in her classroom really take to her.

We recently talked about how she got to where she is now. She credits the year of therapy followed by the inpatient rehab for planting some seeds of possibility in her mind and helping her to at least understand that change was possible. But it took repeating many of her mistakes to prove to herself that she needed to make some real changes inside. The second round of therapy worked better because she was "more open to it." Just like Abigail, you have your own timing to your healing path. Who knows when the seeds of change will take root and grow? Have faith in yourself. Don't give up on yourself, even if you've fallen off of the wagon several times. When you are ready, the seven tools will help you make authentic, lasting change.

However you are thinking, feeling, or acting can be used to reveal to your conscious mind any limiting or troublesome beliefs that are in the unconscious. Practicing the seven tools is one way to listen accurately to the information your life is presenting to you. You can then use that information and the tools to find the belief that is asking to be changed (by creating the problem in your life) and then actually change that belief into one that is more expanded, more freeing, more in alignment with spiritual truth. Because you are a child of God, a divine being, aligning your own personal deeply-held beliefs with spiritual truth is also becoming more of who you really are. That is healing. Faith is the foundation of it all.

That whole rack of lenses that you carry around inside your psyche has a name in psychology; we call it your "structure of interpretation." It includes not only how you see the world but also how you interpret those perceptions, how you see that they relate to you. I like that name because, even though the structure can be quite complex, made up of many different parts, it ultimately functions like a whole. Ideally, you want to be aware of your structure of interpretation and make changes to it when it does not mesh with reality. People who are closed off, people who are know-it-alls, people who hold onto their opinions despite evidence to the contrary, are not willing to modify their structure of interpretation and are blocked in their healing. This is one reason Tony Robbins[20] is fond of saying, "The four most dangerous words in the English language are "I already know that.""

Ironically, the opposite is also sometimes true. Sometimes what you know goes against all of the prevailing wisdom yet is still right for you. Our culture is full of stories of people who "stick to their guns" or persevere against all odds. Bernie Siegel[21] points out that medicine labels such people "difficult patients," because they often eschew expert opinion, but also that they are the patients who get better. What is the difference between the stubborn, stuck, pain-in-the-butt know-it-all refusing to admit reality and the rugged individualist marching to the beat of their own drum? I think the difference is the source of the knowing that they are living by. The former is often fearfully following some dogma; the latter has faith in deeper personal knowing and is courageously following that. Again, knowing which is which can be difficult until you learn to listen well to yourself.

All of your life experiences show up somewhere in your structure of interpretation. What language you speak as your native tongue[22], your cultural heritage, your religious upbringing, your education, your family issues, your level of sensitivity, your temperament, the list goes on. The chance of you coming out of your childhood with a structure of interpretation that allows you to view yourself and the world with kindness, compassion, wisdom, and understanding is fairly small. If you did, bully for you. Put this book down, go out and have lots of kids, and do the same for them. If you didn't, it is not too late. Healing is always possible. If you follow each of your life-shaping influences deeply enough into your psyche, you'll find that they eventually have a belief at their root. So having a methodology, a technology, so to speak, for identifying your beliefs and changing those that are too limiting or are not "true" in a higher sense, would be incredibly useful. The practice of the seven tools of healing is just such a methodology.

I'd like to take a moment and explain why I put "true" in quotes. As you know by now, one of my favorite laws of Consciousness is "You shall know your truth and your truth shall set you free." This means that if you want to be free of a particular malady in your life, you must work with your truth of it. Denial, repression, transference, and all those other Freudian coping mechanisms might change how you feel for a short time but don't help you find the deep, lasting change that you are looking for. Just as unhelpful are sugar-coating things, forcing yourself to think positively (when you don't truly feel that way,) putting spins on things, saying affirmations that are wishful thinking, and the like. In order to be free, you must work with your raw, naked, deep truth of whatever you are dealing with. This can be tricky because …

There are two truths. You have your own personal truth: the experiences that you've had and the conclusions that you've drawn from them; and you have a higher or spiritual truth. (I am not a post-modern relativist[23]. For example, I think kindness is inherently better than cruelty. I do believe in a gold standard for truth, a higher truth, a spiritual truth. I've noticed that the more my patients align their own structure of interpretation with this spiritual truth, the healthier they get. This does not seem relative to me.) For example, the truth is that you are holding a particular belief. That belief, in and of itself, may not be true from a higher perspective. When people see that they are holding a false belief, they almost always discount the belief and try to hold a better one. But until they admit the truth that they are holding the false belief, it generally does not change.

We live in a world where essentially nothing is as it appears to be. For example, you never truly know another person. All you know of them are your own impressions of them. And those impressions depends upon your own structure of interpretation. So, really, how you feel about someone else is saying more about you and your inner workings than about them. How you behave towards another person is saying more about you and your inner workings than about them. (The flip side is also true: when someone treats you badly, they are really just revealing to you their own inner workings. You may want to take their response to you under advisement, but you don't have to take it personally.) Another example, nature, despite all that we know scientifically about it so far, is still largely a mystery. Understanding the true nature of any aspect of nature generally requires very deep contemplation and training. So how do we ever know that we're working with the truth? That's the tricky question.

But, as much as I like to wax philosophical, in the office we need to keep things practical. I deal with the philosophical question, "how do you know when you're working with the truth of your health issues?" by trusting your own inner wisdom. You (the deep, inner you) know your own truth. Maybe your conscious mind doesn't know it yet, but, deep down, some aspect of you knows it. Learning how to access that deep knowing, to trust it, and act appropriately on its information are skills that you can develop with practice; they are skills that are very helpful to your healing. Faith in your deep knowing is the foundation upon which these skills are built.

Often your deep knowing will reveal the truth to your conscious sense of self in layers. I see this most often when people are working on healing the residual effects of traumas that they experienced when they were very young, before they formed their conscious memory. It is as if your inner love must lay some kind of foundation or clear some things out of the way before it reveals your truth to you. You have your own timing to your healing and that timing needs to be honored. To be pushed to heal faster than your inner timing is to just get abused more. Most likely, you have been abused enough by life. You don't need your therapies to abuse you more. In fact, it can be very healing to have your therapies model how to be kind, empathetic, accepting, and loving toward yourself, others, and the world.

Understanding these concepts is one thing. Experiencing them and putting them into action in your moment-to-moment life is another. It takes practice; be patient with yourself but keep practicing. I recently received the following e-mail from a woman who has been working on healing years of childhood abuse and how that abuse has been affecting the relationship she has with herself and how she's been able to live her life:

> "I had the thought that inherent in true healing is a trust and deepening of the relationship one has with oneself. A relationship that allows more kindness, understanding, acceptance, compassion, love, etc. (things you talk about in the *Seven Tools of Healing*). When I look at my own experience this idea makes sense ... When I look at the way you practice (treating within the context of the whole person's life and allowing or calling on that inner healer/knower as integral to the process) this seems clear."

It has taken her three years of work to get to this point. But as she is more and more able to develop a loving relationship with herself—as she is deepening her faith in her own knowing—she is spending less and less time in dark thoughts and despair ... without forcing herself or exerting effort directly on her feelings.

You may have to hear these concepts over and over. As your skills grow, what you are able to hear, understand, and actually put to use deepens, so you may have to revisit the same issue several times before you've plumbed it to its full depth. You have your own timing. Just hold the intention that you can get better and better at listening to your physical feelings, listening to your emotional feelings, watching your thoughts, watching how you respond to people and situations in your life, and using all of that information to see what you really believe.

Hold the intention that you can grow in your kindness toward yourself and your understanding will also grow. As your understanding grows, you will see new options for yourself, new therapies to try that may be effective where others were not, new ways of seeing yourself and your place in the world, new ways of acting. Have faith that this process works, allow it to germinate, take root, and grow. Once it grows, you will have plenty of personal proof that it works. People will sense your inner peace and kindness and respond to you according to their own structure of interpretation. If someone is living a very fear-based existence, they may well be threatened by your happiness and feel the need to attack you. Others may want to be with you to absorb by osmosis what you have.

By now, you can see how important beliefs are. They are the lenses through which you peer out at the world while, simultaneously, they are the windows through which pass the creativity that forms your life. There are a few more things beliefs do that are important to understand. Beliefs tend to be self-reinforcing. First, they are constantly scanning your experiences, thoughts, and feelings and bringing to your conscious awareness those that support or align with themselves. Maybe you've noticed that, when you buy a new car, suddenly you see a lot more of that brand of car on the road when you didn't notice them before. Or, if you or your spouse gets pregnant, suddenly you see a lot more pregnant women around.

Second, since beliefs also direct your creativity, they will continually create situations from which you conclude that the belief is correct. For example, if you believe that you are not worthy of respect, you constantly find yourself surrounded by people who don't respect you. Then every time someone disrespects you, you conclude once again that you are not worthy of respect.

Once you adopt a new belief as your own, it will start scanning your experiences and flag for special attention those that prove to you that it is correct. And, it will start creating experiences that lead to conclusions that support it. Pretty soon, you will have plenty of proof the new belief is true. But early in the process of changing your beliefs, since you have no proof yet, it takes a leap of faith to adopt that belief long enough for it to start collecting and creating its own supportive data. This is how any new belief will act, whether or not the new belief is any closer to a higher truth. That is why I like to let your wise, loving, inner guidance choose the new beliefs that supplant old, limiting beliefs: there is a better chance they will embody some deep wisdom.

I learned the hard way that, even when you've drawn conclusions directly from your own experiences, you may need to be open to reconsidering them. When we moved to rural Maine, we lived on a 250-acre farm that we rented from the doctor who had lived in that town before. The old farmhouse only had wood stoves as a source of heat and used fourteen cords of wood a year. The owner wanted the woods thinned around the edges of his pastures, so, being who I am, I figured I would put up our wood myself. I spent any spare time I had falling trees, piling slash, and cutting, splitting, and stacking wood. I was getting in pretty good shape.

The hayloft of the barn also served as a full basketball court and there was a trampoline up there as well. One Saturday morning, our neighbor came over to play some basketball. I was jumping on the trampoline, did a seat drop, and my legs got locked straight and my torso flexed forward as I landed. I felt a sensation in my lower back like pulling a glass rod through rubber tubing. That was the start of a long relationship between me and low back pain. I played a little basketball with my neighbor but had to stop because things just didn't feel right down there. The pain hit a few hours later and went down my left leg.

Of course, being who I was then, I didn't do anything to take care of it. Eventually, I did see the only local chiropractor, who was a stack 'em, rack 'em, and crack 'em kind of chiropractor. I'm not sure it actually helped much. I continued to work on wood and, every time I would spend a few hours splitting and stacking wood, my back would hurt. This went on for the two and a half years that we lived there.

When we moved to Seattle, all I had to do to heat our house was turn a knob on the wall, so I needed some other form of exercise. My back was doing a little better, so I took up jogging. We lived near a wonderful park that was a ravine carved by a small creek through the hill between Greenlake and Lake Washington. It had woods and hills and trails all through it. I started slowly and gradually built up my mileage. As soon as I got up to about three miles, two or three times per week, I started to get over-use injuries. One time I'd get an inflamed knee cap, another time a stress fracture in a foot bone, another time tendonitis in a hip. This went on for months and I was not able to increase my mileage. I saw the PT who worked in my office and followed her advice. I bought new shoes. Nothing worked.

This was back in the '80s and I was just learning to listen to my own body about what it was saying. One morning I was practicing listening to my creaky knees while I was running up one of the hills on the side of the ravine and suddenly I saw it: while I had been in Maine, I'd developed a belief, without realizing it but as a direct result of my own experience, that, for me, exercise was bad, that exercise would lead to pain. I was shocked. I reminded myself that I sit in my office all day long encouraging people to exercise. While still running, I asked, "Is that really what I want to believe for myself?" A big resounding "NO!!!" welled up from inside.

Once I realized that I had drawn that conclusion from my own experience and was able to let it go, I was able to up my mileage within weeks to around six to eight miles, five days per week, without injury. This experience boggled my mind at the time. I was getting real injuries: real patellar syndrome, real stress fractures, real inflamed tendons and joints. How could my mind fabricate those, just because I believed that I'd get hurt if I exercised? I still don't fully understand the precise mechanism by which thoughts and beliefs get translated into physical realities, (Appendix C offers some interesting theories based upon quantum mechanics) but I'm convinced that they do. The conclusion that I'd automatically drawn as a direct result of my own actions and experiences made perfect sense, yet it was still wrong in the sense that it was limiting. How, I don't know, but clearly an unconsciously held belief was determining how my body functioned and, by listening to how my body functioned, I was led to the belief. Just seeing the belief was enough to get it to change. Bodily changes followed almost immediately.

Something has to change if you want change. Embarking on a new path, seeing yourself and your life in new ways, dreaming new dreams—all often require leaps of faith. When a belief is limiting, problematic, or just plain false, faith in your knowing is essential to change it. As your beliefs change, your relationship with your body changes, your biochemistry changes, your energy changes, the possibilities you see for yourself in your life change, and your relationships with others change. All of these things are just correlates of each other, they are all interconnected and interdependent: when one changes, they all change.

Faith is the foundation upon which all of your knowing is built. Faith plays a very pivotal role when you need to change your beliefs, and changing your beliefs is essential if you are to grow and heal.

To summarize, faith is the foundation of what you know, faith allows you to connect with spirit, faith strengthens your beliefs, and beliefs both determine how the world looks to you and what you are able to create as your life. Faith also helps you change limiting beliefs into more supportive beliefs. Faith serves another very important function I'd like to discuss next: you use your faith to develop an inner sense of security.

In a world where you can never really know anything for sure, where all you can know of another person is your own impression of them, where you can never completely predict the outcomes of your actions, faith helps grout in the gaps, smooth out the rough edges, construct a stable sense of yourself and your place in the world, so that you are not consumed with doubts and insecurities. A sense of security, a sense of surety, is vital to your ability to function in your life (without chronic anxiety). In the hierarchy of human needs, Maslow places a sense of security second[24], just above food, water, and shelter. Maslow observed that people were much more successful in their lives if they met their needs in order, that is, if they met the needs lower in the hierarchy first, then they were able to more successfully meet the needs higher on the hierarchy, such as fulfilling work and satisfying intimate relationships. But later research suggests that that hierarchy is not so rigid. For example, people in poverty can still be in love and benefit from friends and self-esteem[25].

Anxiety, depression, and the whole host of stress-related physical problems are common. Problems in careers and in relationships are common. When people come to me with these problems and we look carefully at what is going on in their lives, we often find that their sense of security is either based on illusion or lacking altogether. They were having such problems in part because they had just skipped over that step when climbing up Maslow's hierarchy.

Nothing you can do on the material plane can absolutely guarantee your safety. This is a major problem we all face. For example, you could have all the money of Bill Gates and you could have a year's worth of food in your basement and Mount Rainier could still pop off. Or, if you don't happen to live in the Northwest, you could step out your door and get hit by a car or you could wake up with MS. All sorts of weird things can happen … and do.

As an example, so often it happens that when someone has just been in a car accident, they get anxious or nervous when they have to drive again. They may come in complaining about the anxiety. I tell them that they are the sane ones. Anyone who just blithely gets into their car and drives off heedless of the risk they are taking are deluding themselves. Most of us derive our sense of safety in life and in the world from a very similar process of delusion: we just don't think about it. But that is just a pseudo-solution for your need to feel safe and doesn't provide enough of a foundation upon which to build the rest of your life. Any sense of security you get from your worldly circumstances is an illusion. It can be plucked away in a heartbeat.

So, is it a sadistic cosmic sense of humor that, on one hand, we're hard-wired to need to feel safe and then, on the other hand, we get plopped down on this planet with no guarantees ... or is something deeper going on?

I believe the answer is the latter. The only true, unshakable sense of safety I've witnessed in my patients has come from their own deep personal relationship with spirit. (I use the word "spirit" purposefully to keep this discussion all-denominational. I've witnessed that faith holds the same benefits for people no matter the religious denomination in which it is rooted; indeed, it still works even if it is not rooted in any religion.) Your sense of safety needs to be the result of your own deep personal relationship with spirit if it is going to be any more than an illusion.

Your soul, your Atman, your immortal aspect, remains untarnished by anything that happens to you on this earthly plane. Your sense of safety is found on the level of your soul. Therefore, if you are to meet your needs sequentially, as Maslow suggests, you need a deep personal relationship, not just a lip service relationship, with spirit. Whoever made our need to feel safe so foundational is a genius. Once you genuinely forge your own indestructible relationship with spirit, you then have that incredible grounding and support to take with you as you work on your career, family, and other hierarchical needs. (Sort of ironic, don't you think, that connecting with spirit helps us ground?)

Spirit is beyond physical reality and so does not lend itself to examination by our currently practiced scientific tools (but Zen Buddhism[26] is a pretty good example of the application of the scientific method to spiritual exploration.) Therefore, we must base our relationship with spirit on faith (if you're not a Zen Buddhist).

What do I mean by spirit? For many years, I thought about things organized in levels. There was the physical level; so some problems occurred on the physical level and some therapies worked on the physical level. There was the mental level and the emotional level and the energetic level and the spiritual level. I thought of symptoms or problems occurring predominantly on one level or another, even if their influence could be detected on other levels. Therapies also worked predominantly on one level or another. Drugs worked on the physical, Reiki on the energetic, and so forth. But one day I asked myself what was the spiritual level? After some contemplation I realized that it was all the other levels at once—not separate, not isolated. Spiritual equals unity. No matter which terminology you use, there is only one God, only one Consciousness, only one Universe (other "universes" that physicists hypothesize could all be lumped together into one, total Universe and the Universe that we inhabit would be more like a galaxy in that mega-universe, so the argument of unity still stands). Spirit is not its own level, it is everything at once.

So the idea of different levels fell away and I started seeing physical, mental, emotional, and energetic as just different ways to look at what Spinoza[15] called "divine substance," the mysterious stuff we're really made out of. More simply, I thought of them as different arms on a mobile: if some influence causes one arm to start moving, the whole mobile starts moving. This view easily explained the mind-body-energy connection, as I thought of it then. I don't think of a mind-body-energy connection now because, in order to be connected, they first have to be separate; and they are not. This unity is why Native Americans see spirit wherever they look: in the clouds and trees, in the animals and streams, in each other and in themselves. Spirit, or Consciousness, is at the causal root of everything in existence and everything in existence contains spirit or Consciousness.

How then do you relate to spirit in such a way as to feel safe? The answer my patients have shown me over and over is that, when you identify yourself as that unity, when you are aware of it and feel a part of it (rather than apart from it), you just feel safe. Many believe that the root of all human suffering is our sense of separation from God. If this is true, then the answer to our suffering is to feel united with that totality that some call God, which is synonymous with Consciousness. If spirit is all of the Universe in all of its aspects, then you, too, are spirit: no separation, no duality. When you have an intense direct experience of this, when you know this in your heart of hearts, when you trust this and have faith in it, you feel safe.

If doubt, insecurity, and anxiety have been challenges in your life, then an in-depth examination of how faith works for you—its strength, where it's focused—would be fruitful for you. Ask yourself the question, "where is my sense of safety to be found?" Don't give up until you have a satisfactory answer. And perhaps you have some early traumas in your life to heal.

Faith is a skill; it gets better with practice. You can have faith that your life can indeed improve, that you can heal. You can have faith that you, as your true essential self, is enough. In order to change and grow, you need to free yourself from old limiting beliefs and adopt new beliefs. Since you often have no personal experiences to support the new beliefs, the first step in changing long-held beliefs is often a leap of faith. You can choose to practice faith in whatever is in your highest good, whatever helps you the most in your search for truth and growth, even if you do not have any personal proof or experience of whatever that is yet. Just know that when you work within yourself this way, your inner wisdom often brings up whatever needs to be healed. This may get expressed in your life as new symptoms, new problems in relationships, and such. This is a good time to practice the seven tools, especially compassion for yourself.

The stronger the faith, the better it works. You can practice faith in something until it has the strength of certainty. Many stories of human experience attest to the power of faith when it reaches the level of certainty.

Until one is committed, there is hesitancy, the chance to draw back. Concerning all acts of initiative (and creation), there is one elementary truth that ignorance of which kills countless ideas and splendid plans: that the moment one definitely commits oneself, then Providence moves too. All sorts of things occur to help one that would never otherwise have occurred. A whole stream of events issues from the decision, raising in one's favor all manner of unforeseen incidents and meetings and material assistance, which no man could have dreamed would have come his way. Whatever you can do, or dream you can do, begin it. Boldness has genius, power, and magic in it. Begin it now.
—W. H. Murray (Note: this quote is often mistakenly attributed to von Goethe.)

Doubt is a test of faith. If doubt wins, then your faith is not strong enough. Double check to make sure that you really want to have faith in what you are doubting. If you are sure, then remind yourself that whatever you have faith in is your choice. Faith can be practiced until it is stronger than all doubts. When I feel doubts coming on, I strengthen my faith by giving myself little pep talks. If I'm getting butterflies before public speaking, for example, I tell myself something like, "these people have come because they need the information I'm about to offer, and I'm the one to give it to them." I like to include spiritual truths in my pep talks. For example, if I start to doubt that my back pain will ever go away, I tell myself, "healing is always possible...even for me." And then I can settle down and listen more carefully to my back pain. When you feel doubts rising inside, try giving yourself little pep talks. Unpack the situation into smaller steps and have faith in yourself at each step. See what works for you.

Over-intellectualization can block the advantages of faith.

Analysis kills spontaneity. The grain once ground
into flour, springs and germinates no more.
—Henri Frederic Amiel

Have you heard the term "analysis paralysis"? We live in a culture that literally worships the intellect. As a result, we seem to love the question "why." Questions are powerful tools to engage your mind, focus your thoughts, and, hence, your creativity. But "why" type questions are analytical; they keep you in your intellect, generally stuck where you are.

For years "why" was my favorite kind of question: my intellectual curiosity really wants to know the why's of things. I love to think about how things work. So, if you ask, "why did I get in that car accident?" the answers will be all the reasons you got in that car accident. You didn't see the car coming, the other person ran a red light, or you took the corner too fast—whatever you see about your own situation. These answers might help you prevent another similar experience and they might satisfy your intellectual curiosity, but are they going to help you heal from the car accident?

Compare the "why" question to: "okay, I was just in this car accident. I wonder what I can learn from this experience?" If you were injured, there is a better question to ask. "I wonder how I can best heal this injury?" Can you feel the difference in your body as you imagine asking yourself these kinds of questions? As a rule of thumb, the answers to "what" or "how" type questions help you focus on moving forward. "What" or "how" questions open your heart and mind to new possibilities. "Why" questions often keep you in your intellectual, analytical mind which keeps you where you are.

The quality of your life is determined by the quality of the questions you ask. So watch yourself. See what kinds of questions you ask yourself. Imagine how you would use any possible answers. Keep reworking the questions in your mind until you find those whose possible answers move you closer to your goals. I bet you'll find that you make more progress and forward motion in your healing if you reframe "why" into "how" or "what" kinds of questions. At first, I had a very difficult time giving up my "why" questions. But I found that if I focused on the learning and how to best move forward, the whys made themselves known. By changing to what or how questions, my intellectual curiosity still gets assuaged and I have the added benefit of deepening my understanding and making useful, helpful changes at the same time.

You don't want to paralyze faith with doubts or over-intellectualizing, but you don't want blind faith either. You don't want your brain to plop out onto the floor. Walk that balance by giving yourself plenty of opportunities to practice faith…then learn the lessons you are supposed to from the results.

Kristine (not her real name) and her family recently moved to town, from the Mid-West. She has a strong Christian faith but shared with me the observation that she and her family have been hurt the worst by others who also profess to be Christian. It was starting to shake her faith. She told me about what happened to her just before she moved here. She and her family were going to a local church. She needed physical therapy for a problem she was having and wanted to support a physical therapist she'd met at her church. During her first visit with him, he took her history and examined her. Something about his manner gave her "the creeps." But she told me that she wanted to practice her faith and trust people, especially people in her church, so she made a second appointment with him. During that second appointment, he sexually assaulted her.

She did all the right things: she protected herself and got herself out of there as soon as she could and she filed a complaint with the State and the man lost his license. But she couldn't understand why that had happened to her when she was trying to be trusting. I pointed out that she was indeed being asked to trust. But to trust herself. The heebie-jeebies she got from him on their first visit were accurate. She was being asked to trust her own sense of knowing, not blindly trust another just because they profess a certain set of beliefs. All trust of others boils down to trusting yourself. If you listen well and know yourself well and trust what you know, you won't let others lead you astray (most of the time). The practice of the other tools will also help you know how to balance your faith between pure gullibility on one hand and cold hard scientific skepticism on the other.

You choose your beliefs, even those being held in your unconscious mind, with the right practice. Beliefs determine what you are able to make manifest in your life. So, what life do you want? Take a moment and write down three to five qualities or characteristics of the life of your dreams. Where do you see yourself living? What career do you have? What are your relationships like? What is your health like? Now imagine what you would have to believe in order to pull it off. Have faith in yourself. Practice, practice, practice.

Here are some beliefs that I suggest you practice having faith in:

- Your true authentic self is enough. You don't ever have to be more or different than you really are.
- The inner teacher in your life has your best interest at heart and is feeding you the exact right curriculum for what you need right now. (See Metaphors, Appendix B.)
- If you seek your truth, you will find it (and it will set you free).
- You are competent to deal with whatever life puts in your path.
- Healing is always possible, including for you.
- You can control your beliefs and adopt those that help you live a life that is pleasing to your soul.
- You can adapt your beliefs to serve you the best as you go through your life.

When you find certain beliefs that you want to hold, have faith in them. If you are holding any beliefs that are counter to the new beliefs that you are adopting, they will show themselves, and you can practice the rest of the seven tools to help you free yourself from them.

So faith functions as the foundation. Everything we know in our life sits on a foundation of faith. Faith helps us meet our primal need to feel safe and faith helps us in the early stages of adopting new beliefs and new ways to see and be in the world. Faith is a skill that can be practiced, strengthened, and honed to balance the mystery of life with reason and rationality. Faith is powerfully creative when it reaches the level of certainty.

Have faith in yourself. Have faith that you know what is right for you and that you can find and live that knowing. The best you can be is who you are, and that is healthy no matter how your body is or isn't working. Decide what beliefs will help you in your life and have faith in them. Practice strengthening your faith until it reaches the power of certainty.

Faith lays the foundation for your happy, healthy life. So now let's build on it.

Chapter four

Awareness

The second tool is Awareness. The true nature of healing may be a mystery, but as I watch my patients live their lives and make progress on their healing, it is as if they are being asked to grow their consciousness. You grow your consciousness when you expand your awareness, come into your personal power, and exercise your volition where you can.

Awareness moves information from the unconscious into the conscious; from the not-known to the known. Your personal growth and healing progress in relation to your power of observation. I have yet to observe one of my patients heal and remain oblivious at the same time. You may have noticed that you tend to have a much easier time working on an issue, belief, or feeling if you know it is there. Believe me, I know. Most of the big issues I'm dealing with today are a result of blind spots I have had about myself. I practice awareness followed by the other tools to work through these things.

Awareness is a big topic. Your life is feeding you clues from many sources—physical feelings, emotional feelings, your actions, your dreams and intuitions, how people respond to you, the stream of thoughts that come into your mind in between the thoughts you choose to think, and more—and you want to be able to get that information no matter how it comes. All of it is relevant to your health. Expanding your awareness is vital to your healing so we are going to take an in-depth look at each one of these major sources of information about your present moment. As we go along, I will give you some ways to practice your awareness, so that you can get the most out of each experience. There are so many aspects to awareness and how to apply it that I don't want to gloss over any of them; they are all important. Once again:

> *Until you make the unconscious conscious, it will*
> *direct your life. And you will call it 'fate.'*
> —*Carl Jung*

You need to be able to acquaint yourself with, and even be able to shape, the contents of your unconscious if you want to be the "master of my fate ... the captain of my soul[28]". You are not a victim of fate: you just have most of your creative power operating unconsciously. I cannot overstate the importance of awareness if you ever hope to gain conscious control over your creativity, including your ability to create health. John A. Bargh[29], a professor of psychology at Yale University, observes that "when psychologists try to understand the way our mind works, they frequently come to a conclusion that may seem startling: people often make decisions without having given them much thought—or, more precisely, before they have thought about them *consciously* ... The ability to regulate our own behavior—whether making friends, getting up to speed at a new job or overcoming a drinking problem—depends on more than genes, temperament and social support networks. It also hinges, in no small measure, on our capacity to identify and try to overcome the automatic impulses and emotions that influence every aspect of our waking life. **To make our way in the world, we need to learn to come to terms with our unconscious self.**" (The emphasis is mine.)

Your unconscious mind has its own awareness, its own problem-solving abilities, and draws its own conclusions. Your unconscious is quite powerful. The practice of awareness and the rest of the seven tools gives you precisely the ability you need to tap into that power and use it to help you in your life. You can make specific aspects of your unconscious conscious when you need them, you can see what your unconscious has concluded and how those conclusions are affecting you, you can gain some modicum of conscious control over your otherwise automatic responses (especially those that get you into trouble), and you can take conscious control of your creativity, and, hence, make your way in the world (with grace.)

By practicing awareness, you can increase the amount of information coming to you from your life and you can bring to light those deeply-held beliefs that are keeping you in your dysfunctional or ineffective patterns. Awareness makes known what is going on in and around you, and this puts you in a better position to make good choices for yourself. Awareness:

- makes the unknown known, the unconscious conscious
- connects you to your inner workings
- connects you to your surroundings
- determines what information you have access to in your conscious mind

People seem to differ widely in their natural levels of awareness (the absent-minded professor comes to mind). But awareness gets better with practice, no matter what level you are starting from. I used to think that being aware was difficult (now there's a limiting belief!) until I realized that to be aware is simply a normal property of the mind. As I was watching my mind, I noticed that wherever I focused my attention, it just naturally started taking in and processing the information it was receiving. Imagine that your mind has a spotlight and wherever the spotlight is aimed is where your awareness is focused.

Try this short exercise: take a moment and look around you. Notice that wherever your gaze lands, you start taking in details about whatever it is that you are looking at. For example, I am gazing out the window. I see the large oak tree in our lower pasture. I see how the sunlight illuminates its south side and its north side is in shadow. I see the bare branches gently waving in the breeze. I see the buds of next Spring's leaves forming on the twigs at the end of the branches. Move your eyes around wherever you are, notice what information comes into your mind from wherever your eyes land. Now imagine that you are curious about whatever you are looking at. Notice how much more detail you take in and retain.

In the Vedic model of a human being (see Appendix A), your mind functions as the bridge between the world as you perceive it through your senses (for example, your retinas are just perceiving colored patches and your ears are just hearing sound waves) and conscious meaning. The job of the mind is to take in and process data. By "process" I mean the mind tries to make conscious sense out of the data. It compares what you are seeing, hearing, smelling, etc. to what you already know. It just naturally does that wherever it is focused. For this reason, if you wish to increase your awareness of something, simply choose to focus your attention upon it. This was the breakthrough insight that helped me overcome my limiting belief about awareness. And where you put your focus is your choice.

To expand your awareness of something—for example, what feelings are in your body—choose to focus your attention upon your body. Your mind will then just start taking in and making sense of the sensory data from that source. You may start to notice feelings, properties, and qualities of your body that you were previously unaware of. Here is where your sensitivity comes in handy. With it, you can notice fine and subtle details. To heal, become aware of the important information pertaining to your present health challenge, interpret the information correctly, and take whatever actions seem most appropriate. We will go over each of these steps as we go along. Let's start by taking a deeper look at awareness and what you could become aware of.

These are the major avenues of information coming to your conscious mind that I'd like to explore with you:

- Physical feelings — what information is my body sending me right now?
- Emotional feelings — how am I feeling? What belief is behind it? What is a healthy response to it?
- Thoughts and mental activity — what am I thinking? What stimulated that thought? What belief(s) is/are influencing my conclusions? Are my thoughts in alignment with what I want to achieve? This thought is showing me how I'm currently directing the flow of my Consciousness and creativity. Is this how I want my Consciousness flowing right now?
- The energetic — how is my energy flowing? Are there any blocks? How is my vitality right now? What is influencing it? What is it asking of me?
- Beliefs – what are the beliefs underlying my thoughts and feelings? What are the beliefs that make up my world view? How do these beliefs look from a higher or spiritual perspective?

- Dreams — (Dreams can be viewed as an important means of communication between the conscious and unconscious aspects of the mind.) What feelings do the dreams evoke? What symbolic meaning does the dream have?
- Actions — how do (did) I respond to various situations? What thoughts, feelings and beliefs are influencing my actions? What are the results of my actions? Are they congruent with what I want for my life?
- Relationships — what sides of me are being revealed in this symbolic "mirror"? What feelings come up in me as a result of the interactions I have in this relationship? What are the cultural and social influences?
- Surroundings — how do shapes, colors, textures, and the arrangement of the physical environment influence how I feel? How am I influenced by the weather, traffic, world events, or other factors in the environment?

We'll look at each of these categories in more detail, but first a few simple ground rules for paying attention.

Awareness is much easier if you first clear out any distractions. I have a little visualization that I use to get centered and grounded that I would like to share with you. If you like it, please adapt it to your own needs. I use it any time I need to think or get focused and I do this every time I'm getting ready to do craniosacral therapy on someone: I put my attention into my body and scan up and down inside and just observe how I'm feeling. Then I ground my feet to the Earth. I often do this by visualizing copper rods that are about one inch in diameter and six feet long extending from the bottoms of my feet into the earth (this works even if I'm several stories up.) Next I "ground" my head to the heavens by imagining a hollow cord extending from the top of my head and disappearing into infinity above me. Energy, information, or whatever needs to can flow into me through that cord, course through me and into my patient or into the Earth through the copper rods. In this way, I've completed some kind of circuit and am in the flow. Some spiritual teachers believe that one purpose of the human being in creation is to function as a bridge between Heaven and Earth and this grounding exercise helps me participate in that.

Once I'm grounded in both directions, I set an intention about what I want to pay attention to. When I'm working on someone, I set the intention that that person will find their healing, whatever that means to them. Otherwise, I set an intention that is appropriate to whatever situation I'm dealing with. I often use the body meter (discussed soon) to help choose those intentions.

The third step is to create a desire to know about whatever I'm paying attention to. I'm generally pretty curious, so often the desire is just there. Most of us are literally dying to know who we are and that, in itself, ought to be motivation enough.

To summarize, get clear in your mind about what you want to become aware of; get centered, grounded, and curious; then turn the spotlight of your mind on whatever you choose … and see what happens.

So now let's look at each of the major categories of information through which your life is talking to you.

Physical Feelings

Your body is much more than a machine that occasionally breaks down and leaves you stranded by the side of the road. It is literally the physical expression of your own personal access to Consciousness. As such, it functions like the physical spokesperson for your soul, your inner love. I often think of the body as an attention-getting device. If your deep inner knowing knows something and it wants your conscious mind to know it too, it can put the information into your body.

There is also another way to think about it. A symptom is a clue that something in the system of who you are is out of balance. That imbalance will show up in all aspects of you. The Vedic model of a human being explains this observation very well (see Appendix A). This model says that you have six aspects; but, for practical purposes, let's focus on the outer four: your body, energy, mind, and belief structures. These four function not as independent aspects but as correlates of each other. They are interconnected and interdependent, just like different bars on a hanging mobile.

If you bump one part of a mobile, the whole mobile starts moving. In a very analogous fashion, if I pour a drug into you and change your body's biochemistry, there will be some kind of simultaneous change in your energy and mind. If I stick you appropriately with acupuncture needles or do Reiki or therapeutic touch on you to change your energy, there will be some sort of change in your biochemistry and thoughts and feelings. If we engage in EMDR[30] or cognitive behavioral therapy[31] or some other form of psychotherapy and change your thoughts and beliefs, there will be some sort of correlating change in your biochemistry and energy.

Your mind, body, and energy are inextricably linked to each other (see Appendix C). So a change anywhere in your system—your beliefs, the environment around you, your energy, etc.—will show up in your body somehow. Listening to the physical body is generally fairly easy for most people, unless you have a dissociative disorder, so the body is where we start with the practice of awareness. As you practice awareness of your body, remember, that is just the first step. You will also need to be able to correctly interpret whatever your body is telling you and then take the appropriate action. This is where practicing the other tools and listening to your inner wisdom comes in handy.

The interrelatedness of these four parts of yourself explains the mind-body connection—which really ought to be thought of as the mind/body/energy connection. This perspective or insight has very important consequences for your healing because it clearly points out that not every physical symptom has a physical cause. Conventional medicine often misses causes that may be found in other aspects of you because it focuses primarily on the body and how diseases are being expressed through it.

When I started running, back when my family and I first moved to Seattle, I was getting tendonitis and stress fractures not because I was running too much or had bad shoes, but because I held a set of beliefs that were out of balance with higher truths. Those overuse symptoms were my body's attempt to get my attention and motivate me to find and align my personal beliefs with higher truth.

If you are like most of my patients, listening to your body is easier than listening to your energy or mind or going straight to your belief systems. But, because your body, mind, and energy are correlates of each other, listening to any one of them will work equally well to help you find the primary imbalance behind your symptoms. I worked with a man a few years ago who found that, for him, listening to his energy was the easiest and clearest source of information about his inner workings. He was much more in tune with his energy than with his physical body, yet he was still able to follow his own clues back to his deeply held beliefs and make significant changes in his life patterns.

As an example, let's look at a hypothetical situation. Let's say for the moment that you don't know how to interpret the sensation of thirst in your body. When you start to feel thirsty, you could say to yourself, "oh, I'm having these symptoms, I better take a hand full of vitamins." Or you could go to the gym for a workout, or take a nap. If you had no idea what was going on in your body or how to help yourself, you could choose from thousands of possible therapies. Some may quell the symptoms for a time but none will ultimately work until you drink some water. So the question is, "how did you learn that those symptoms of thirst mean 'go drink some water'?"

You probably learned that too young to remember. When you were young, you could listen to your body and trust your instincts. I contend that this kind of listening and learning gets trained out of us at an early age. I bet when you started school, you were told to sit at a desk and be quiet. I further bet that what you really wanted to do was get up and run around and talk to the other kids. What happened to you if you followed your natural inclinations? Chances are you learned very quickly that what you naturally wanted to do was not going to be tolerated. So what did you have to do inside of yourself to make yourself sit there? You had to learn how to stop listening to the messages coming to you from your body. I have some patients who work at Microsoft and they often get so engaged in their work that they don't even know when their bladders are full. And if you become an athlete, your training to ignore the messages from your body and push it harder just intensifies. All of these kinds of experiences can interfere with your ability to get clear and usable information from your physical feelings. But you can overcome these learned blocks by practicing paying attention to whatever you are feeling in your body, along with the third tool—accepting the truth of whatever you are aware of.

Perhaps because we get isolated from our bodies and learn to objectify them, we blame our bodies when they don't work so well. Many people with chronic illness are at war with their bodies when I first start seeing them. They hate their bodies; they feel let down or betrayed by their bodies;

they feel trapped and helpless inside these bodies that aren't working right. They just want to annihilate their disease and get better. But by gently explaining about the body as messenger and pointing out that all of the attack and destroy techniques that they've tried so far haven't worked, most are willing to give listening to their body a chance. You can get a head-start by learning to listen to the messages coming to you from your body sooner in your process rather than later.

Your body can lead you to the primary imbalance by focusing your attention—especially your kind and open-hearted attention—on your body and trusting what you see, hear, and feel. Once you find that imbalance, you can once again focus your awareness on it and get a sense of the best way to respond to and resolve it. You may need to change your diet; you may need to take an herb or a medication; you may need surgery or to change careers; or you may need to change beliefs—whatever will put the imbalance to rights. This is where all of the different therapies and treatment modalities come into play: you use whatever approach will best alleviate the primary imbalance in your system.

Some people are living their lives somewhere in the near vicinity of their bodies. Their bodies feel totally unsafe. The thought of putting their awareness into their bodies and listening to the information there feels overwhelming, too painful, or too scary. They would much rather be off in their mind somewhere else. Psychologists call this dissociation. Most people call it being checked out. I would say that most of the people I've met who dissociate experienced fairly severe traumas at a young age. Leaving their bodies like that was a survival technique and they continue to use it. Often, when a young child is abused, they reason that the abuse happened to their bodies; so, if they just didn't have a body, then this abuse wouldn't have happened to them. Logically, they conclude that the abuse is their body's fault. From an adult perspective, this is obviously childish reasoning; but, nonetheless, this kind of conclusion drawn at a young age often determines the kind of relationship abused people have with their bodies.

June had one of the most severe childhoods of anyone I've ever met. She was the baby in her family. Her sister was so much older that June and her niece were almost the same age. Her older brother was very abusive, often dragging her around the house by her hair and sitting on her until she couldn't breathe. Her father left before she was born and her mother was impoverished and emotionally absent. June grew up white and blonde in inner city neighborhoods and experienced firsthand the destructive effects of discrimination. Her brother-in-law was a pedophile who abused her and her niece (his own daughter) during their entire childhoods. Her niece grew up to be a drug addict and prostitute but June took a different path.

As a young adult, she was a dancer and also had a corporate job. She was never successful in intimate relationships but kept her good heart and sense of humor. She developed juvenile onset rheumatoid arthritis and colitis as a teen. She also had severe asthma. In her mid-thirties, she left her corporate job to move back to Seattle to care for her elderly mother who was overweight and had diabetes. She was able to resolve her arthritis by the time I met her and had learned how to keep her colitis in check most of the time. But she still had problems with her asthma. She came to see me for her fibromyalgia, chemical sensitivities, and depression. She was still caring for her mother when we first started working together and had been for ten years by that time.

We did the usual functional medical evaluation for fibromyalgia, looking for environmental allergies, food reactions, adrenal fatigue, increased intestinal permeability, liver overload, hypoglycemia, hormone imbalance, and hidden causes of immune system activation. We also started craniosacral therapy (CST) to help heal the effects of her severe childhood abuse.

She was very surprised to find that when she tried to look inside, all she found was a black emptiness. She had no sense of information coming to her from her body. After several months of persistent practice, she was able to get into her body a little bit. But all she could feel was pain. Whenever we did CST, she felt as though someone was driving a spike into her belly, just above her pubic bone. She much preferred to hover around rather than be in her body. Eventually she was able to dialog with the pain and get the pain's side of the story, so to speak. It turned out that her body was angry with her for going off and having a "good time" while it was left alone to go through all the abuse. She'd learned to dissociate as an infant and had continued to do so ever since. It helped her survive.

Over time, she was able to work things out with her body and the pain eased. She was able to be more and more present with and for herself, so we were then able to go deeper. I experienced her as very intelligent, kind, and caring. She experienced herself as worthless. She had a very deep and enduring belief that life just went from bad to worse and then you die. In many ways, her life, up to that point, had been proof of that. Beliefs are funny that way. Because they determine what aspects of Consciousness we are able to bring forth into our lives, they create experiences that fit with them; then we use those experiences as proof that those beliefs are correct ... and off we go on the hamster wheel.

We worked together for years to help her with her healing, so there is much more to her story than I can get into here, but the important point is that she learned how to listen and just be with whatever was going on inside of herself. That one skill, along with her courage and determination, really started her on her path to healing.

She was living on Social Security Disability and her asthma medications alone took a third of her monthly income. She had no resources for supplements or other medications, so our therapeutic options were quite limited. But just with the craniosacral therapy, we were able to stabilize her asthma and get her colitis to go into remission. Her fibromyalgia improved enough that she didn't have to spend all day in bed but had a few hours of productive time per day. Her depression continued to improve, despite all the stress she was under. I think that if she'd had the money to do some of the treatments that were indicated, she would have improved enough to get a job and get off of disability, but such is the state of the social safety net in our country. Even without being able to take a lot of supplements, just listening to her physical feelings was a major turning point in her life.

If you dissociate, or if the idea of putting your awareness into your body causes you to have a panic attack, find a good therapist who works with such issues, as trying to practice body awareness on your own might be too threatening. But persevere, because your body is not the enemy, it is not the battleground; it is one of the best members of the team that is you. Your inner wisdom uses your body as a spokesperson to guide you on your healing journey.

You can get your body's side of the story by listening. Debra was a thirty-five-year-old woman who'd been experiencing stabbing pains between her shoulder blades for the past fifteen years. She'd seen chiropractors, orthopedists, and acupuncturists; she'd done years of physical therapy, had tried yoga, massage, everything she could think of. Her x-rays and CT scans were normal. She ate well, exercised regularly, and practiced yoga. She was in good health except for this pain that was a major detractor from her happiness. It was nagging and, as she said, "never leaves me alone." Anti-inflammatory medications didn't help much, nor did pain medications. She was getting pretty discouraged.

I spoke with her briefly about using craniosacral therapy to both treat the pain and listen to it as possibly one more option to try. She was skeptical, as nothing had helped but, out of desperation, was willing to give it a try. She lay back on the exam table and I started working at her feet. I asked her to allow her awareness to settle into her body as she took a few slow, deep breaths. I asked her if anything was catching her attention and she said, "The pain between my shoulder blades is." I asked her to describe the pain. She said it was sharp, like a knife. She was silent for a moment then added, "Like a sword in the stone." I thought to myself, "Now this is a bit freaky", because I was reading EB White's *Once and Future King*[32], a story about King Arthur and Merlin, to my children at that time. This visit happened early in my CST work and I wasn't yet used to how other people's inner wisdom could always tell what was going on inside of me, too.

So I asked her which part of her could step up and pull the sword out. I could see her eyes moving under her eyelids as she was looking around inside and then she said, "My thirteen year old can."

"What happened when you were thirteen?" I asked.

She was silent for a moment and a tear squeezed out of the corner of one eye and she said, "That was when my mother died." Memories of that time started coming to her and she described what happened and what she had been going through. She stopped short and said, "Oh, I remember one day I was so sad and grief-stricken about my mom's death that I made a vow to myself that, if I was ever happy, that would be betraying my mother's death."

We talked about how intense feelings are when you're thirteen, how things are often black and white. She saw then that the pain was her way of fulfilling her vow to herself. I asked her if her being unhappy is what she thinks her mother would have wanted for her, and she said of course not, that her mother would have wanted her to be happy. I asked if she was willing to talk with her thirteen-year-old and revisit that vow and see if she'd be willing to make a different choice. She was silent for a few moments as a stillness settled over her body. When it felt right, I said, "Whenever you're ready, go ahead and stand up there and pull on the sword and see what happens."

She did; the sword came out of the stone and her pain was gone.

We talked after the craniosacral session and she said that she estimated that she'd spent over $10,000 of her own money on top of all the insurance payments trying to get that pain to subside, that she'd seen probably forty different practitioners. I asked her if any of the practitioners had ever asked her to speak with the pain, to get its side of the story, why it thinks it needs to be there. None had. The first few years out of medical school I wouldn't have either. The methods and messages of medical training are very consistent. But by the time I saw Debra, I had learned that physical ailments don't just happen to you in a vacuum: there are usually reasons why the body is doing what it is doing (though not always, of course, as nothing relating to health is one hundred percent). But getting the body's side of the story is an angle that is definitely worth exploring, especially when your problems are resisting all the treatments you've been trying. Your physical feelings are packed full of information. Debra's experience with the healthcare industry over the previous fifteen years, with everyone trying their own particular approach to getting the pain to go away … all without talking with it … is a direct result of the world view that practitioners, including myself, are taught in their training.

Mike was a single man in his early thirties. He came in with a headache that had been present off and on for two years. He'd seen neurologists, his CT scan was normal, and he'd tried nearly a dozen different medications, all without any lasting relief. He'd seen a naturopath and had allergies ruled out. When he described his headache to me, it did not sound like the classic migraine or like a muscle contraction headache or chronic sinusitis, the three most common types of headaches. I asked him if he wanted to try the craniosacral therapy, which can be helpful for headaches in its own right, combined with dialoging with the headache to try to get a sense of what the headaches might be about. Like Debra, he was a bit skeptical but agreed to try it, since he'd seen the specialists, had taken the tests, and had tried the drugs.

He took off his shoes and got up on the exam table. I listened to his cranial rhythm from his feet, as I can often get a sense from there of where in the body the rhythm might be restricted. As I listened and assessed, I talked him through a simple centering exercise that encouraged him to focus his awareness into his body. Any time you focus your awareness, you are technically in a state of hypnosis. I found early in my craniosacral therapy experience that I did not need to do a formal hypnotic induction as long as the person was able to focus inwardly and listen to their own body/mind/energy.

With Mike, we were able to take turns speaking with him and with his headache. When he gave voice to his headache, we were both surprised to find that it was quite angry (and profane). With your indulgence, I'll quote the headache verbatim.

"So, Mike," I asked, "Can you let your headache borrow your voice? I'd like to hear its side of the story."

"Sure." Then the headache just mumbled some profanity.

"Headache," I said, "sounds like you're pretty angry."

"You bet I am."

"Why are you so angry?"

"Because here I am bustin' my ass for Mike and all he wants to do is annihilate me."

"Is that right, Mike? Do you want to annihilate your headache?"

"Yes, I want it gone."

"Well, headache," I asked, "why are you here?"

"Mike knows damn well why I'm here" it growled.

"Is that right, Mike? Do you know why you're having these headaches?"

"No, I don't have a clue."

"Well," the headache jumped in, "do I have to spell it out for ya?!!"

"Please," Mike responded.

"Okay. M-I-K-E H-A-T-E-S H-I-S J-O-B!" It literally spelled it out.

"Is that true, Mike," I asked, "do you hate your job?"

"Yes, I do."

"How long have you had it?"

"Two years."

All this while, I'd been working on Mike's neck and head. Restrictions were releasing. We spent some time exploring what he'd rather do for work instead. I saw Mike a month later. He had changed jobs and his headaches were gone. He was able to stop all of his medications, which weren't working anyway.

He told me that on many occasions, he wished that he had a different job. But nothing in the job itself was bad enough to motivate him to go to all the trouble to search out new jobs, arrange interviews, and do all the other work that goes into changing jobs. But, once he understood his headache's side of the story, once he knew what it was trying to do for him, he found the motivation to do the work necessary to change jobs. And he was much happier for it.

After Mike's visit and follow-up, I gave his story quite a bit of thought. I saw him several years ago, soon after I added craniosacral therapy to my practice. At that time, I could not reconcile his experience with the prevailing conventional medical model, in which I was still fairly ensconced. For Mike, his headache was trying to get his attention, and it wouldn't be easily pushed aside by medications, even some very powerful medications. Some part of Mike really wanted him to have a more satisfying job, one that better used his talents and encouraged him to keep growing. That part was somehow able to generate the sensation of a headache when it wanted to, powering through the medications, and then stop the headaches when it wanted to. He was not conscious of that part.

The part that generated the headache seemed to have an intelligence that could see the bigger picture of his life and also somehow control his body. This was an intelligence deeper and different from the intelligence in his conscious mind. The conventional medical model makes no reference to such a deeper intelligence. The idea that an illness, such as a headache, could have our best interest at heart was not discussed in my medical school. As physicians we often see a person's illness as a threat to them. The tools of conventional medicine are generally aimed at correcting the physiological, microbiological, or biochemical imbalances that occur when someone is sick. So we have medicines to lower blood pressure, blood sugar, and cholesterol; we have antibiotics to kill bacteria, fungi, and now a few select viruses; we have medications to suppress the immune system, replace hormones, kill pain … the list goes on.

But, as Deepak Chopra[33] points out, the physiological expression of the disease is generally not the cause of the disease. Trying to interfere with the physiological expression generally does nothing to change why that imbalance is there in the first place. The closest examples of treating the cause we have in conventional medicine are antibiotics. Notice that, unlike your allergy, arthritis, blood pressure, cholesterol, or blood sugar meds, you take them for a short time and then you're done with them. But even taking an antibiotic doesn't really address why you got the infection at that time. Sometimes infections are another way your body tries in order to get your attention or secondary to something else that is suppressing the immune system.

When I saw Mike, I was still greatly influenced by the conventional medical perspective that illnesses were bad and my job as a physician was to wipe them out. The idea that a person's disease could be a message from a deeper knowing, which was trying to get that person to change direction in their life, was fairly novel to me (this was the early '90s.) How often was that the case in my other patients, I wondered? So many people are experiencing health problems that are resisting treatment as vehemently as Mike's headaches did. How many of them have a deeper intelligence trying to get them to make meaningful changes in their lives and we're just missing the message? My gut sense told me this was happening more than we (in medicine) knew.

Back then, an awareness was slowly growing in me that there could be a different way to work with people with chronic health problems and that I had a whole lot more to learn. Over the years of doing this kind of work, I've observed that each and every one of my patients has this deeper intelligence. And I believe that you do, too. You could save yourself years of searching and thousands of dollars in unnecessary and ineffective treatments if you could learn to access and consult with it. (I didn't have the seven tools formulated when I saw Debra and Mike, but practicing them helps you do just that.)

Like Mike with his headache and Debra with her stabbing back pain, there just might be an important message for you in your physical symptoms, a message that will help you get your life back on track. Learn to listen to your body as best you can. If you ever feel stuck, find a practitioner who can help you listen. You may need to ask your body worker to help you listen to your body rather than just fix your body like a mechanic. Craniosacral therapy, some forms of chiropractic, yoga, soma body work, Hellerwork, Rolfing, Feldenkrais, and massage therapy are examples of body work that can potentially be done in a way to help you listen to your body[34]. I often use the body sweep when I want to listen to my body.

Body Sweep

There are several good ways to practice listening to your body. One of my favorites is the body sweep. This is often taught in birthing classes to help the woman prepare for labor. To begin, get yourself into a comfortable position, sitting or lying, and take a few slow quiet breaths. As you breathe, just gently bring your awareness to your toes. Feel whatever sensory information is coming to you from your toes. Are they warm or cold? Do you feel your socks or sheets touching them? Try feeling all your toes at once and then tune into one toe at a time. Then move your awareness into your feet. Again, note whatever sensory information is coming to you from your feet. Then move your awareness into your ankles, your shins and calves, and your knees. Keep your awareness in each area as long as you need to in order to get a good sense of what is going on there. See what physical sensations are there. Then look to see their emotional correlates, if you can (more about feeling both the physical and emotional simultaneously later). Move your awareness into and through your thighs, hips, buttocks, and pelvis. Take as long as you need. Once you get up to your pelvis and abdomen, you can feel what is on the surface of your body and you can let your awareness go inside and look around. Even if you don't know any anatomy, let your awareness move around inside your belly and just see what you see, feel what you feel. Move up into your chest. Feel your breathing, feel your heart beating. Just be curious, see what is there. Move up your back and into your shoulders and down into your upper arms, your elbows, your forearms, your wrists, and hands. Again, feel all your fingers at once and one finger at a time. Then move your awareness into your neck and throat. Take your time, feel whatever is there. Move up to the base of your skull, where your head and neck come together. Move up into your face, your tongue, your lips and cheeks, your nose, your eyes, your ears. Just feel what you feel. Make a mental note of it. Move your awareness into the inside of your head and just look around. Move to the top of your head, feel what you feel. Then bring your awareness to your skin all over your body. Once you feel that, gently move your awareness out into the room and see where you stop and the room takes over.

I like to practice the body sweep several times a week, often when I'm going to sleep. It is a great way to inventory the day and resolve any unfinished business (especially when you bring the rest of the seven tools to whatever you find). It's also a great way to let your body know that you're listening and that you care about what your body has to say. If you've ever had the experience of really being heard, you know how helpful that is. The body sweep is one way to give that benefit to yourself. Also—and this is very important—my patients bodies start using smaller symptoms to get their attention once they are listened to regularly. This approach to healing is very good preventative medicine.

Once, I sat down to do a body sweep with the goal of hearing as much information as I could from each part of my body. I started at the very tip of my big toes and listened as closely as I could. It felt like I was listening to each cell layer, one at a time. About an hour later, I wasn't even to the first knuckle of my big toes, so I stopped. I left that exercise amazed by how much information is stored in my body. I know now that when I listen on a gross scale, I'm missing a tremendous amount of information that is going on behind the scenes. Most of the time, you don't need that much fine-grained knowing in order to get the message that your body is trying to put forth, but it is pretty cool knowing that it is there and you can listen if you choose.

Whenever you exercise or practice yoga is another time to practice listening to your body. Feel how your muscles feel, how your joints feel. When you get into a posture, does that bring up any memories or emotions?

While getting a massage is another great time to listen in. Most massage therapists have seen people experience deep emotional releases while getting worked on.

Intentional movement is yet another excellent awareness exercise. Put on some really great music, like some Mozart, then get still inside and just move the way you want to move. Pay attention to the feelings that come up inside as you move. Follow the music, follow the feelings. Be the watcher, be the music, be the movement.

As long as we're talking about ways to listen to your physical feelings and your body, I'd like to give you an exercise that is good for increasing your awareness of the information that comes in through your five senses. I like to practice this awareness exercise when I go on walks. I start by becoming as aware as I can of everything I can see. I look around as I walk and make a mental note of as many details as I can. Then, while continuing to do this, I start to become aware of whatever I'm hearing. I will listen carefully and make a mental note of all the sounds that I can hear while still observing visually. Once I get comfortable with that, I'll start to become aware of whatever I can smell. Again, I make a mental note of it while also seeing and hearing whatever I can. Then I'll start to pay attention to whatever I'm feeling with my skin. The temperature of the air, my feet touching the ground as I walk, the clothing. I'll make a mental note of that while continuing to observe with my eyes, ears, and nose. If I get sensory overload or my mind starts to wander, I just start over.

The bottom line: you can practice awareness of your surroundings, sensory information, and inner experience at any time. When you are making yourself breakfast, when you are shaving, driving, typing on the computer; there is always an opportunity to practice awareness no matter what you are doing or what is going on around or inside of you. And your body is with you most of the time, unless you are very good at Astral travelling, so you have a constant source of information you can consult whenever you wish. Pay attention to your body, listen to your body, trust what is coming to your conscious mind through your body; these are great windows into your inner workings.

You will be amazed at your life changes once you practice listening to your physical feelings and your body.

Emotional Feelings

Emotions are a fascinating topic. We know they are very important. Marketers know that we are much more likely to be motivated to act based upon our emotions than upon our rational thoughts. But what are emotions? How would you define them?

In the body/mind/energy schematic, many experts categorize emotions as part of the physical: emotions are physical, chemical changes in your body. But I'm not convinced that seeing emotions that way tells their whole story. Of course there are molecules of emotion, as Candace Pert[19] points out. Whenever you have an emotion, there are hormones, neurotransmitters and other chemical messengers that carry out the Consciousness of the emotion in the body. Using the same line of reasoning, you could say that thoughts are physical because there are also molecules of thoughts: neurons interacting in your brain and such; and energy is physical because there are molecules of energy too.

The bottom line: your thoughts, feelings, and energy all have their representations in your body in the form of some kind of chemical change or holding pattern in your fascia. Remember, the body, energy, mind and contents of the mind are all just correlates of each other: any movement on any of those four arms of the mobile will set the whole mobile in motion. When one changes, they all change simultaneously. Science interprets all of its findings through the physical because that is where it is focused.

The quantum mechanical model for mind/body/energy interrelationships put forth by Amit Goswami, PhD[35] and reviewed in appendix C is a very elegant and formal way to think about physical and emotional feelings, but how can you use that information to be healthy with your feelings, to get the information that they are bringing you? We have to be pragmatic in clinical practice, so I find it useful to think of physical feelings as information coming to the conscious mind from the body and emotional feelings as information coming to the conscious mind from the unconscious mind. But, again, this is a simplifying assumption that makes physical and emotional feelings easy to conceptualize but is not the whole picture.

That physical feelings and emotional feelings are two ways of experiencing the same thing is another way of thinking about them. Watch your feelings carefully and see if you can prove to yourself that whenever you have an emotional feeling, it is also getting expressed in the body somewhere; and that whenever you are feeling anything in your body, there is an emotional correlate to it. One does not occur without the other. We miss this interrelatedness sometimes because we are more aware of one over the other at any given time. When your physical feelings are really intense, you might not be aware of how you are feeling emotionally; and, when your emotions are very intense, you might not be aware of how they are being expressed in your body. But start watching, and I think you'll agree that both are always happening together.

From a completely different perspective, some people interpret the word "emotion" to mean "energy in motion." These different views of emotions arise because body, mind, and energy are correlates of each other and different authors tend to emphasize one aspect over the others. So if you ask, "Do emotions come from the body or from the mind?" the answer is "yes."

Emotions are very influential no matter how you think of them. PET and functional MRI scans indicate that emotions inform our decisions and choices more potently than does rational reasoning, even in educated and/or self-described rational people[36]. Become aware of your emotions and how they influence you and you can gain conscious control of your creativity and health.

Many of us are oblivious to some of our emotions, at least some of the time. But that does not save us from them. Repressed emotions continue to exert their influence; they just do it from behind the scenes. Hidden or repressed emotions are a big part of the unconscious mind that Dr. Bargh[29] suggests that we have to come to terms with. Clues to repressed emotions often show up in the body as physical symptoms. They can also show up as blocks in the flow of your energy, as persistent thought patterns, as recurring issues in your relationships, as the accidents you have, or in the way you act out in your life. All of these things are important sources of information about how you work inside.

To get the most benefit from your emotions, you need to approach them in a healthy way. One of the most important foundational concepts toward that end states that an emotion, any emotion, by itself, is neither good nor bad. It just is. This is of critical importance to your healing. We make a big mistake with our feelings, whether physical or emotional, by rating them as "positive" or "negative."

This may sound like a radical idea to you, but there is no such thing as a negative emotion. Sure, you're going to like some feelings and not like other feelings, and there are good reasons for that; but the feeling is not the problem. The feeling is just information. We talked about this in the example of how to use the seven tools to find and change limiting beliefs in Chapter Two, now I want to go into more detail. The feeling is not the problem, but what you do with it often is. You can relate and work with it in healthy ways or in dysfunctional ways. Nearly everyone who comes into my office has a dysfunctional relationship with their feelings to some degree. This is very common and I see people who have been stuck in their disease for decades because they are blocked to the information coming to them from their feelings.

For most of us, the dysfunctional relationship with our feelings starts at a very young age. Toddlers have very strong emotions and they are usually very good at acting them out. This makes the adults around them uncomfortable, and they give the toddler the message that how they are behaving is not all right. The adult might say something like, "Aw, come on, it's not that bad." Or, "You're okay." Or, "Get a grip on yourself." Or even, "If you want to cry, I'll give you something to cry about!" Most of my patients learned how to repress or deny how they are feeling or that they are somehow wrong for feeling that way.

From the behavior perspective, the adults are correct. As toddlers grow and become contributing members of society, they need to behave in legal and respectful ways. But there are better ways to teach them. The dysfunction with our feelings starts when we learn to control our behavior by controlling our feelings. When you were little, how often did you respond to the way adults were treating you by squashing down your feelings inside? Imagine how it would have felt if, instead, your parents looked at you and said, "However you are feeling is understandable. Can you tell me about it?" Or even something to the effect of, "However you are feeling is okay, but you still need to treat your sister with respect." When we are little, it is much easier to get into control of our actions by repressing our feelings than it is to learn to just let the feeling be and control our behavior. Controlling behaviors by controlling feelings is the most common dysfunctional trait I see in my patients.

Here's why it's a problem: health implies wholeness. Wholeness means having free and full access to all aspects of yourself. You can't be healthy and fragmented at the same time. When you are cut off to your feelings, you are cut off to parts of yourself. You can't be healthy and have repressed or denied aspects of yourself.

In addition to how you may have been trained as a toddler, there are generally good reasons why you repress or don't want to feel certain ways. If you are like most people, you don't like feeling uncomfortable. But, so often, in order to heal from a trauma or chronic health problem, you need to explore your repressed and denied parts of yourself: you need to feel the discomfort, the pain, the abandonment, the abuse ... whatever it was. Do this kind of exploration in the presence of someone you feel safe with—find a good therapist.

But here is a common misunderstanding and even a reason some of my patients have avoided looking at their feelings: you don't need to feel these things just to be traumatized all over again. You feel these things to see what conclusions you drew your first time through the experience and see if those conclusions are still valid from a higher perspective. In other words, you explore your repressed and denied aspects in order to reframe any limiting conclusions you may still be carrying from those experiences. You feel your feelings to find your present truth and align it with higher truth.

You can't go back and change what happened to you, but you can free yourself from any deleterious influences those experiences are causing in your life now and from this moment forward. That is how you claim the freedom that is your birthright. For example, if you were abused as a child, that abuser has hurt you enough already, your abusers don't need to keep hurting you by causing you anxiety, depression, or dysfunctional relationships today. Your healing is always possible, you can always get to know yourself better, and you can always move more into your personal power. But you may need to learn how to be comfortable feeling uncomfortable in order to use your feelings to do this kind of healing work.

Don't worry, we all have inside of us the equivalent of a circuit breaker. You already know how to repress these feelings—chances are they have been repressed for years—so if things get too intense, you will just shut them down again. You can trust that aspect of yourself. Its goal is to protect you. As you work more deeply with your feelings, the part of you that protects you from your painful feelings will learn to trust that you are strong enough to feel what seemed devastating in the past. The protector will let it through if you keep approaching the feelings with a gentle hand. Keep in mind that, whatever you have gone through so far in your life, you have already survived it; so looking at it again won't actually kill you, even if you feel it might.

But if your capacity for painful feelings is too small, your circuit breaker will trigger a shut down as soon as you get started on your inner exploration. This makes progress difficult. To expand the horizons of your explorations, you may need to raise the threshold for shutting down. Practice sitting with the discomfort you are feeling for just a moment longer, one more breath, open to receiving just one more new insight. The next time, you sit just another moment longer … and so forth. Building your capacity to feel your repressed feelings is like starting to exercise when you are out of shape. Start with little baby steps and give yourself encouraging pep talks. By sticking with it when the going gets hard, your abilities grow.

When you first start listening inside you might be surprised at the level of physical pain that you feel. This is the pain your body has been generating to get your attention but that you've had tuned out. It often subsides as you are able to open to listening to it and to any other information coming from your body. The more you listen to your pain, the more your inner wisdom learns to trust you. As your inner trust grows, so will the amount and depth of information your inner wisdom will share. Listening to and honoring all the feelings, emotional and physical, coming to you is one of the most important steps to true healing.

Train yourself to be comfortable sitting with your discomfort. Use your discernment. I've been talking about the discomfort that is due to traumas in your past. If your discomfort is due to actual tissue being damaged, move right to tool seven: right action. Do whatever you need to to take care of yourself. I hope you know what I mean.

Your primary goal when exploring painful feelings from the past is to see what conclusions you drew from your first time through those experiences. They are exerting their lingering influence on your life because of those conclusions. Change those conclusions and you free yourself from the limiting influences of those experiences. You can keep the strengths and gifts from them.

Open and listen. Sit with however you are feeling in this moment and just be. That is my most frequent prescription. That is my most commonly assigned homework. Listening and accepting are skills that get better with practice. How you are feeling right now is information. Whether the feeling is coming from your body, your energy, or your mind, it is a clue to whatever is happening inside. If you like the feeling, most likely what is happening is working for you, is consistent with your deeply-held belief systems. If you don't like the feeling, chances are something inside is not working for you. Something is out of balance. The feeling is a messenger bringing your conscious mind information about the imbalance. It is not the problem itself. Thinking that feelings are the problem is a very pervasive and damaging confusion in our culture. Therapies that work only on the level of changing feelings keep you stuck.

So many therapies and so many addictive behaviors are aimed at getting you to feel one way in preference to another, without first exploring and understanding why you're feeling the way you do. Focusing on the level of feelings is too superficial when you're working for real healing. Forcing your feelings to change without dealing with their underlying cause will not give you the life-long transformation you seek. Feelings are messengers, not the message. By listening to and accepting the feeling just as it is, you are able to receive the message that your feelings are carrying. No matter whether they are emotional or physical feelings, becoming aware of them, receiving their message, and taking the appropriate steps will give you the transformation you seek. These are skills that get better with practice. The feeling will change once you get the message and respond in a healthy way to it: once you've received it, the messenger doesn't have to keep bringing you the same message over and over.

"You shall know your truth and your truth shall set you free." This is a most powerful law of Consciousness. If you only learn one thing from reading this book, learn how to become aware of your truth, acknowledge your truth and be kind to yourself that you are experiencing your truth. The only way I've seen anyone free themselves from an affliction is by dealing with the truth of it. Repressing it, denying it, sugar coating it, exaggerating it, or putting any of a number of other spins on it will not free you from it. Spin doctors don't heal, they obfuscate. So often, to know your truth, you need to face your discomforts. So be kind to yourself. If dealing with these feelings and issues were easy, you'd have done it long ago and wouldn't be in this situation now.

Healthy Relationship with Feelings

Learning how to be comfortable feeling uncomfortable is an example of how to be healthy with the feeling of discomfort. To be healthy in general, you must be healthy with all of your feelings. So now I would like to show you how to apply the skills of awareness, acceptance, and compassion to each and every moment of your day, no matter how you are feeling. Your feelings come in all sorts of shapes, sizes, colors, and flavors. You naturally like some feelings and don't like other feelings. But don't let how you feel about your feelings keep you stuck. The goal is to receive their message without them pulling you off of your center.

When my patients first start paying attention to their feelings, they often notice that they don't like most of them, or that many of their feelings are very uncomfortable. You are much more likely to repress feelings that you don't like than those that you do. That is just human nature. So, once you start waking them up, all the painful feelings that have been waiting in the wings start stumbling out onto the stage of your conscious mind first. Eventually they even out, so exploring your feelings does get easier over time. Once you're balanced with your feelings, you will probably like about half of them and not like the other half. But, ultimately, when you are truly healthy with your feelings, how you feel about your feelings won't really matter to you: those feelings will just be more information, too.

A healthy relationship with your feelings is based upon "Rule Number One and the Three 'A's."

Rule Number One says, "All feelings are valid." You never have to say to yourself, "Oh, I shouldn't be feeling this way." The fact is you are feeling that way. Better to explore it. Instead of negating or questioning the validity of your feeling, take your awareness deeper and notice what that feeling is about. What triggered that feeling? What world view would have created that feeling from that trigger? Your feelings are continuously bringing you information about how you operate inside. When all is said and done, all of your feelings are of equal value.

Feelings are innocent messengers. The message is not the messenger's fault. Whatever is in your mail is not the letter carrier's fault. It's not good form to chop the head off the messenger just because you don't like the message. Yet we do that to our feelings all the time. We like these kinds of feelings so we do things to create them and we don't like those kinds of feelings so we do things to avoid or repress them. Managing feelings is addiction. I like this definition because it points right to the treatment: learn to be in the moment with however you are feeling, free to choose what you say and how you act. More about addictions later.

So, if feelings are the messengers, how do you receive the message? The three 'A's do that.

The first A is for awareness, which you recognize is the second of the seven tools of healing. We went over the body sweep as a way to practice becoming aware of physical feelings in your body. Now you're ready to take your awareness a step further. Every physical feeling has an emotional and energetic component to it. In this next exercise, we'll practice becoming aware of the emotional component.

Take a moment and put your awareness into your right hand. Notice any physical sensations that are coming from your hand. Is it touching anything? Can you feel the air temperature? What position are the finger joints in? Now become aware of the emotional tone in your right hand. This is hard to describe. For now, just look for any other kind of feeling coming from your right hand. Now put your awareness into your left hand. Again, notice any physical sensations coming from your left hand. See if you can identify how it is that your left hand feels different from your right hand. They really ought to feel different. One has had a right hand experience of your life and the other a left hand view. One is dominant, the other assistive. Most people can feel the difference even if they can't describe it. This practice can be done with any paired structure in your body: your ears, knee caps, feet, elbows, whatever.

The next step in opening to your emotions is to look at any physical pain you are having and see what emotions that pain brings up. This is easy when you hit your thumb with a hammer or hit your head on the corner of the cupboard door. But try it with your headache or your heartburn or with an arthritic joint. So, for example, if I want to listen to my back pain, I first become aware of the pain, where it is in my back, I note its intensity and quality—is it achy, sharp or grindy?—and then I put my awareness into my solar plexus and just sort of let my awareness sink down into it and see what I notice.

For me, the most common feeling I get when I do that is grief. I can then sense into the grief and just be with it in an open-hearted way. I often go to a time when I was an infant. My mother started having pain from ovarian cysts shortly after my birth and by the time I was six months old had surgery for them. She had a long convalescence (she always referred to that surgeon as a butcher) then got pregnant with my little brother. My father worked full time and my mother was home with my toddler brother and infant me. I know that during those first few months after her surgery, every time she cared for me, I caused her pain. One of my foundational beliefs has been that my very existence is a bother to the people around me. I have learned many such things from my back over the years. As I apply the practice of the seven tools to my back, it is getting better.

Another word for practicing awareness is mindfulness. John Kabat-Zinn[37] has done an excellent job discussing the virtues of mindfulness. He presents many ways to practice it and I highly recommend his work. Many forms of meditation[38] are also exercises in awareness. Some are mental exercises in concentration, and those are very useful, but others stress awareness more.

But of all the awareness practices I've come across, the best is to just be aware of your body. It is feeding you a constant stream of information. You will be in an excellent position to heal your life if you can just learn to hear that information, interpret it correctly, and then act accordingly.

For many reasons, our culture tends to raise people with low emotional intelligence[39]. When parents focus on controlling the child's behaviors that result from their powerful emotions, when children are shamed or ignored or praised[40], when children are constantly given the message to repress rather than learn about their feelings, they grow up distant from themselves, cut off from their bodies. This happens to children of both genders so both genders have difficulty being healthy with their feelings. But when it comes to the awareness step, I find in my practice that awareness of feelings is often less of a hurdle for women than it is for men.

Many men in our culture get trained from an early age to ignore their feelings and soldier on. Do what needs to be done. Keep a stiff upper lip. Don't show your vulnerabilities or others will take advantage of them. Be mission-driven. Forget how you feel about it. Weakness is shameful. Sensitivity is a weakness. Such messages for men come loud and often. While women get unending unhealthy messages from society about body image, men get their unhealthy messages concerning their feelings. No wonder clogged up hearts are more common in men. Perhaps these pent-up emotions, along with testosterone, explain why more men in our culture have explosive anger problems than do women.

The foundation of your healthy life is a healthy relationship with your feelings, no matter your gender. You can take supplements until the cows come home, but if you remain dysfunctional with your feelings, your health will continue to elude you. The first A, awareness, moves information from the not-known into the known. With practice, everyone, including men, can get very good at being aware of how they are feeling.

Once you are aware that you are feeling a certain way, the second step, the second A, is to acknowledge the feeling. Allow the feeling to be. No need to change it, nothing to fix. Your job is not to fix your feelings; your job is to be kind to yourself, no matter how you are feeling. Give it a name. Admit the truth to yourself that you are indeed feeling that way. (You will recognize this as the third tool.) No judgment; all feelings are valid. Acknowledging the truth of how you are feeling cuts through denial, repression, rationalizations and other evasive maneuvers you've learned over the years. It opens you to your own personal truth in that moment. Once you acknowledge your truth, it can set to work setting you free.

Many people harbor a fear that if they acknowledge an unwanted part of themselves, it will move in, take over, and never change. In fact, the opposite is true. Repression, denial, and pushing things away are forms of attention. Your attention directs your creativity. So, by resisting your truth, you are inadvertently creating more of what you are resisting. This is the basis for the saying, "What you resist persists." But, when you work with the truth of what you don't like about yourself or your life, you stop creating it and are free to start changing it.

The third "A" is ask. Ask the feeling to take you to its roots. Look the feeling right in the eye, tell it you see it, you know it's there, then ask it to take you to its roots. Where did that feeling come from? What's behind it? When did you first ever feel it? Be curious. Why that feeling now? Why not some other feeling? Curiosity is a powerful way to focus your creative Consciousness.

Then get centered and grounded and trust your first impression about the answers that come. (This step is critical. Many of my patients have difficulty hearing what they know at first. If this happens to you, please be patient with yourself: trusting what you know gets better with practice.) You may have a memory of an earlier experience that led to the conclusion that set a certain belief in your worldview, or you may just go directly to the belief itself. If you have a memory of a particular experience—like when I tuned into my back pain and had the memory of being a six month-old baby lying in a bassinette, wanting my mother, casting my awareness around, and finding no one—then look at that experience and see what you concluded from it. What was your take-home message from that experience? (Oh, like maybe, "I am in this world alone, no one can be depended upon, therefore, I have to do everything myself.") Chances are, that is the belief that has been influencing you down through the years.

Once you see the conclusion or belief, then you run it through the three 'A's just as you did with your feelings, only with a minor variation. You've already done the first A: you are already aware of the belief, as the feeling just led you to it. So you move on to the second A: fully admit your truth to yourself that you have been holding that belief.

Here is where you have to be careful. This step is a common trap for many of my patients. Once a belief comes to light, it is only human nature to try to fix it, especially if you can clearly see that the belief is not true. But, once again, you must admit your truth to yourself before you can free yourself from its limitations. And that truth is that you've been holding on to that belief, that belief has been in your unconscious mind shaping your world view and influencing what kind of life you've been able to create, even though the belief itself may or may not be true. Once you fully admit the raw, naked truth to yourself, you are ready for the third A.

Look the belief right in the eye and ask it, "What would my heart say about this belief?" or, "Is that belief true from a higher or spiritual perspective?" Is the conclusion you drew at the time the only one that could have been drawn or, knowing what you know now, would you draw a different conclusion? For most of my patients, just seeing the belief and looking at it through what I call "spirit eyes" is all it takes to get the belief to shift and change and align itself with a higher truth. If not, then continue to practice being kind to yourself that this happens to be your truth at the moment, and the kindness will eventually align the belief with higher truths. Once the belief shifts, different feelings start to get generated. For example, things that used to get you all riled up don't faze you anymore. Fears ease. Tolerance grows—for yourself and for others. You've probably already experienced this kind of shift at some point in your life. We often call them "Ah, ha!" moments.

George is a woodworker who owns his own small shop. He is a real artist with his work and specializes in custom furniture and cabinets. He works mostly with wealthy people as clients. Even though he is amazing at what he does, if he ever gets behind and is late on a delivery, his clients often get impatient and yell at him. He wants to do a good job and keep his customers happy, and their response to him greatly increases the stress he feels.

Through the craniosacral work, he was able to see that he's had issues with low self-worth that have impacted his business. He was able to see the experiences he had as a child that led to his limiting conclusions about himself. He had great parents: they never belittled him or put him down; he saw that he had used his heightened artistic sense of self-awareness to be really judgmental toward himself. He'd always had unreachably high expectations of himself and had always fallen short in his own estimation. This inner process had started at a very young age and the small child concluded that he just wasn't good enough. Interestingly, this inner message always came from himself, never from his parents.

Once he saw this pattern and all of the conclusions he'd drawn because of it, he was able to take a more reasoned look at himself and see many of his amazing talents and strengths. He started to value himself more. He was also able to connect with an innate sense of worth that was independent of his talents and abilities. Shortly after those sessions, he got behind on an order, called the client to explain, and the client was very understanding and reasonable. They worked out a modified schedule for the project and everything went smoothly. He was amazed. The new pattern continues to this day. So often when we make changes to deeply held beliefs, those changes are reflected back to us as changes in how we are treated by others. It's like magic ... or mirror neurons[41] ... who knows?

What I've just described to you is an elegant and effective method for using your feelings to uncover and then free yourself from beliefs that are holding you back and/or creating dysfunctional patterns in your physiology. To summarize: become aware of how you are feeling; admit to yourself the raw, unadulterated truth of your present experience; ask the feeling to take you to its roots; even if the belief is clearly off-base, admit to yourself your own personal truth that you've been holding that belief as if it were true; see how the beliefs or conclusions behind the feelings look from a higher or spiritual perspective; just be kind to yourself about the whole thing. Your own kindness toward yourself works your inner transformation. Compassion is the alchemist.

However, many of my patients find this process too cumbersome or too intellectual. There are too many steps to remember in the heat of the moment, when they are in the trenches with the bullets flying and the poison gas clouds rolling, like when they're home with little children. A much simpler path to the same destination is to simply ask the feeling, after you've acknowledged it, "Okay, feeling, how do you want me to be with you right now?" (The wording of that question is very specific and deliberate—notice it has nothing to do with doing. It is one of the most powerfully healing questions I've ever witnessed people ask themselves.) The vast majority of the time, the feeling just wants what you want: to be heard, to be treated with respect, to be able to tell its side of the story. Practice giving your feelings that level of consideration and they will automatically walk you through the steps that allow you to both get the message they are bringing and respond to that message in a healthy way. "How do you want me to be with you right now?"

Have you ever had the experience of really being heard and understood? I did once. Until my youngest brother came along when I was nine, I was the middle of three boys about a year and a half apart. When we were really little, we all three took baths together. As we got a little older, we took them one at a time and we had a family rule that you would clean out the tub when you were done in preparation for the next bather. When I was eight, we were visiting my dad's parents in St. Joe, Missouri for a couple of weeks. We loved to play in the woods across the street and would get covered head to toe with dirt.

One evening my younger brother took the first bath. Then it was my turn. I went into the bathroom and the bottom of the tub was covered in dirt. I came out and asked my younger brother to please clean the tub. He said he did. I said he didn't. I asked one of my parents to go look to see if they agreed that he had not cleaned the tub. They told me to just go do it. From my perspective, my younger brother was always getting away with stuff. This was just one more example. This was too great of an affront to my sense of justice. I stood my ground. My dad was embarrassed in front of his parents so he got very angry and started yelling at me to do as I was told and just clean the tub. I stood my ground. At that point, my grandma got up, took me by the hand and said, "I don't like sitting in other people's dirt, either. Come'on, I'll help you rinse out the tub."

In contrast to all the times in my childhood when I was just told what to do no matter how I felt, this incident sticks in my mind as one of the only times that I was heard, acknowledged, and helped. Even today, over fifty years later, as I sit and remember how that felt, I get more calm and centered and open inside. Imagine being able to give that same kindness and consideration to all the different parts of yourself that are clamoring with unmet needs. In that little moment, my grandma gave me a great gift that has stayed with me all my life. You can give the same gift to yourself.

There are many different questions you can ask of your symptoms, but over time, I've found that asking "How do you want me to be with you right now?" is often so much more helpful than other kinds of questions. The "why's" and "how's" make themselves known as the feeling or belief is allowed to just be in the presence of a compassionate observer (you!).

As I've already mentioned, I'm not a post-modern, extreme relativist. I believe that kindness towards oneself and others is intrinsically better than abuse of self and others. I believe all sentient beings are created equal, stuff like that. I also believe that there is a higher truth. I see it arching over us like the dome of the sky. At the same time, you have your own structure of interpretation, your own set of lenses through which you view the world. Whenever your personal structure of interpretation does not line up and harmonize with the higher truth, symptoms get generated. Those symptoms are really just attention-getting devices, intended to motivate you to explore your beliefs and get them lined up with higher truths. If, instead, you take herbs or vitamins or drugs to quell the symptoms, they will either persist, come back later, or come back as some other symptom. You may have even experienced this already on your healing path. I've observed that the more my patients' structures of interpretation change to line up with higher truth, the healthier they get.

Ann has been working with me off and on for years. When she first came in, she had a fairly conventional view of medicine and healing. But she was open to options and had been having some health issues that weren't responding to conventional approaches. Her weight was creeping up over the years, as was her blood pressure. She is intelligent, well educated, and fully capable of doing her own reading and research.

She knows how to eat well, and when she does, she loses weight and her blood pressure normalizes. But she couldn't seem to always eat well. Something always happened in her life to de-rail her self-care. Over the years, she tried many different approaches, yet the pattern of making some gains then backsliding persisted.

Her father passed away and she had a strong sense that his presence was still with her. She felt that, once he died, he saw the errors of his ways, so to speak, and, through this sense of connection, was able to resolve much of the unfinished business in her relationship with him. One of her daughters faced very serious health challenges of her own, and Ann was able to stand up to one of the largest children's hospitals in the country and advocate for her daughter to achieve a successful resolution. Ann's mother is an extreme narcissist and is in a nursing home in need of constant care (Ann's mother needs constant care, too). All of Ann's siblings have bowed out and left her to care for her mother alone. This remained one of the major stressors in her life. Working together over time, she practiced the tools to deal with stress, to work with anger, to help her in her marriage; she branched out from conventional medicine and has seen naturopaths, chiropractors, acupuncturists. She has done a tremendous amount of work on herself; yet, despite it all, her weight problem persisted.

She knew she was blocked; she could sense that much. But she couldn't see what that block was. She recently came in for a visit because her brother and his family were coming to town and she was worried that her anger towards him about abandoning her to her mother would boil up and ruin their relationship. She was able to admit that she didn't want to visit her mother, either. But her mother had systematically driven everyone else away. Even Ann's daughters didn't go visit their grandmother because of the way they were treated when they did. I asked her why, if she felt so strongly about it, did she continue to visit her mother? At first, she said it was out of guilt. But when she thought about not visiting her mother, she quickly realized that she didn't feel right about that either, and not out of guilt. She realized that taking care of her mother, no matter how her mother slammed her for it, was an important part of who she was.

She was able to see that her brother was just being who he was, which was much like his mother, and she could accept that. Her anger eased. Then she got on the treatment table for some integrative body work. She was able to feel the block that kept her from eating the way she knew worked well for her. By sitting attentively with it, she was able to see that it was a deeply held belief that she didn't deserve to be happy; she didn't deserve autonomy or any free agency.

Children of narcissistic mothers generally were never given the basic foundation needed for good self-esteem. Even during the newborn time of their lives, their mother remained the center of the universe. They are often raised to serve their mothers as their only reason for existing and are generally led to believe that they are never good enough at it. Many grow up thinking that if they could just be good enough kids, then their parents would be better parents. As these children move into adulthood, these beliefs keep sticking their foot into the isle to trip them up. This all came clear to Ann in that moment.

A deep belief of not deserving, whether it be deserving to be happy, deserving to be financially comfortable, or even deserving to have this life, is a fairly common finding in people who have chronic illness. Even though Ann had been working on herself for years, she had not yet been able to admit the truth of this belief to herself. Without admitting the truth of it, it had not changed, no matter what she thought and learned intellectually. Her sense of not being worthy was expressing itself as her excess weight. She could force her weight to normal temporarily, but as soon as her resolve fatigued or she got distracted by life circumstances, her weight went right back up.

These kinds of life patterns are important clues. If you are trying to make changes in yourself and those changes only last as long as you put lots of energy and attention into maintaining those changes, chances are you are bumping up against a deeply held belief that you might not consciously know you hold. But, with practice, anything that is in your unconscious can be accessed consciously. Carl Jung puts it this way, "One does not become enlightened by imagining figures of light, but by making the darkness conscious."

You know how to be conscious. You know how to be enlightened. Your life circumstances—including your health issues—are there to help you live what you know. Being healthy with your feelings is an important part of your healing. Let's go into more detail about how to do that.

There have been many proposed systems for classifying feelings. I like to keep things simple, so I ascribe to the four primary feeling theory. This theory is very similar to the three primary color theory. All the colors that you see can be made by the proper mix of the three primary colors. As for feelings, all the feelings you have can be created by the proper mix of four primary feelings. That's the theory, anyway. Some theorists see seven primary feelings, others twelve, and so forth. But splitting hairs too finely makes things more complicated than they need to be. All you need to do is figure out how to be healthy with your feelings. How those feelings fit into some academic schemata is fun to think about but if you get caught up in too many details, you risk missing the boat.

The four primary feelings are:

- Mad
- Sad
- Glad and
- Fear

This grouping might not be proper grammar, but the simple rhyming makes them easy to remember. Each word stands for a category of feelings. "Mad" stands for anger in all of its amplitudes from mildly piqued to fully enraged. "Sad" is for grief and depression, again, in all of their intensities. "Glad" is for everything from happiness to ecstasy. And "fear" is for anxiety to shear terror.

Some people don't like the simple "four primary feeling" theory because they look at "mad, sad, glad and fear" and say that three of the four are negative. I have not found that dividing my feelings into positive or negative has been very helpful. I used to do that. I then focused on the feelings that I believed to be positive and tried to avoid, ignore, deny, or repress feelings I judged to be negative. I got very good at it; it just didn't work to help me grow. Sometimes the negative feelings would erupt like Mount St. Helens; other times they would be determining how I treated other people without my knowing they were doing that. As I mentioned earlier, if you are also using a positive-negative classification for your feelings, please try to see past that. Try seeing them as equal messengers.

There are so many things you can do with your feelings once you are having them. You can feel them. You can put them to words. You can act on them. You can judge them. You can analyze them. You can ignore them, repress them, or deny them. You can project them and assume others feel the same way. You can transfer them. I found that I could even "head them off at the pass": I could censure my feelings before they even got to my conscious level of awareness. So, of all these things you can do with your feelings, how many of them do you think are healthy?

Becoming healthy with your feelings is quite an accomplishment. It takes practice, courage, and commitment. Many of the ways that we stay dysfunctional with our feelings are very subtle. Many were learned at very young ages and have decades of practice behind them. Remembering "Rule number one: All feelings are valid" is of utmost importance. Feelings are messengers. The feeling itself is never the problem. Feelings are information, they are neither good nor bad, positive nor negative. They just are. Your job is to be kind to yourself no matter how you are feeling, then get the information that is embedded or encoded in the feeling.

Feelings bring information to your conscious mind about what is going on. If there is a biochemical imbalance in your body, a feeling will be generated. If there is too much inflammation, a feeling will be generated. Any conditions in the environment, such as air temperature, amount of light, whether or not it's raining, etc., will generate feelings. Whenever you relate to anything—whether to another person, a pet, an idea, a thought, a movie, or book—feelings will be generated. In fact, every experience you have, every bit of information that comes to you through your senses and thoughts, generates a feeling in your mind. It is as though all of life gets translated into feelings in your mind. Therefore, if you can learn to get the information carried by your feelings, you can get the information coming to you from your entire life.

There is a river of feelings constantly flowing inside of you. And though it is always changing, never still, never the same twice, there is always a sense of familiarity about it. You need to learn how to navigate this river to get through life healthfully,. Perhaps that is why, in Herman Hesse's *Sidhartha*[42], Guatama ended up working on a river ferry boat. In mythology and dreams, water often symbolizes emotion.

To be healthy with your feelings, you need to be healthy with each one of the primary feelings. Some skills can be applied equally to all four but each of them also needs to be approached slightly differently. The same skills that help you be healthy with anger may not work as well with fear, for example. Let's go through each primary feeling individually and look at what it takes to be healthy with it.

Anger

Mad stands for anger in all of its range, from slightly piqued to full-on rage. Anger is often profiled as a "negative" emotion, as destructive. But remember, all feelings are valid. They are innocent messengers. "Positive-negative" is a judgment and judging yourself or others is always hurtful. So, if you have been employing that way of categorizing your feelings, please temporarily suspend that and see how this other way of being with your feelings works for you.

I would like to make one caveat here, before we get too far. If you are having such powerful feelings, like anger outbursts, catatonic depression, panic attacks, or PTSD triggering, that you cannot control your behavior, or cannot focus on anything else, you may need professional help. You might need therapy, acupuncture, supplements, and even medications to give you a leg up so that you can start to make in-roads into their root causes. Once you make real, significant changes in foundational beliefs or abusive circumstances, you can often stop the medication or supplements. Think about them like a shoe horn: they make the job easier but you still have to put your foot in the shoe and push. Then, once your shoe is on, you don't walk around all day with the shoe horn in your shoe.

When you are perseverating on feelings and can't stop, you need techniques to break the cycle. Dialectical behavior therapy[43] gives you several such techniques. If you decide you need professional help, I recommend that you look into DBT or some other techniques that help you bring down the intensity of your feelings enough that you can actually have a conversation with them.

But I think that you'll find that, as you get more adept at hearing your feeling the first time and using Rule Number One and the Three 'A's, it won't need to repeat itself over and over in your mind. Then you won't need suppressive or interventional medications or techniques and can focus your energies on getting the messages and working with the messages.

But now I need to give you a second caveat. Please be mindful of any technique you use to work with your feelings. Remember, many of them treat the feeling as the problem, and they work to get you to feel one way in preference to another, distorting your ability to experience the truth of your present moment. As a result, you miss the chance to get the message. Find a therapist who will help you deepen your understanding of your truth. With these caveats, let's take a look at anger.

Most of us fear anger because so many of the examples of its expression are destructive: the man taking the shotgun into McDonalds, the wife-beater, the driver exhibiting road rage, the person obsessed with revenge and such. But does anger inevitably have to be destructive? Fire is the element that symbolizes anger. The dramatic effects of fire are when a house burns down, when a forest burns down, when a bomb explodes. These are the well-publicized destructive uses of fire. But what about the fire that heats your home, cooks your food, or turns your internal combustion engine? We get a great deal of good work out of the energy of fire when it is contained and channeled. When it breaks loose and is uncontrolled, it can be destructive.

The same can be said of anger. Anger is a powerful force that can change the world for the better when it is contained and channeled in a healthy way. Note that "contained" does not mean "repressed." As long as the fire stays inside your oven, your furnace, or the cylinders of your car's engine, it does beneficial work. As long as you use your anger to motivate you to do things to make the world a better place, it does beneficial work. Anger is a potent messenger, letting you know that something is out of balance in your life.

So what triggers your anger? I don't mean specific things like someone cutting you off in traffic or your daughter piercing her belly button. Look at what is going on in and around you in general when you get angry. I bet you'll see that something is going on that you don't want to be going on, whatever that may be. Anger is a normal, natural, healthy response at these times. Anger is also a normal, natural, healthy response any time you or someone or something you care about is being treated with less than love. Anger can also persist from hurts and abuses from the past. How do you let anger deliver its message so that it can go home?

Since anger arises any time you see something going on that you don't want to be going on, the first issues to explore are your wants. Are they reasonable? Is it reasonable to expect other people to behave a certain way all the time? Is it reasonable to expect that the air that you breathe and the water that you drink be clean and unpolluted? Is it reasonable to know what has been added to your foods so that you can make informed choices about what you eat? Is it reasonable to have your human rights honored? Is it reasonable to have access to healthcare and education? To law enforcement? To economic opportunities? You probably have plenty of wants. Getting clear about their reasonableness helps you decide how to prioritize your energy and activities, how to pick your fights. One of my favorite bumper stickers says: "If you're not outraged, you're not paying attention." The trick is to use your outrage to make the world a better place. I recently saw another great bumper sticker: "Don't agonize; organize."

If your wants are reasonable, and something's going on that goes against your wants, chances are you or someone or something you care about is being taken advantage of, discounted, ignored, or even outright attacked. Once you are clear that your wants are reasonable, then your anger becomes a call to action, a call to do something concrete to make the world a better place. There are several examples of people or groups who have used their anger that way: Gandhi, Mother Theresa, Martin Luther King, Jr., Mothers Against Drunk Drivers (their acronym even says it), and millions of other people who work tirelessly to solve problems and improve conditions all over the world but rarely make the headlines. If your wants are reasonable, then do something effective to manifest those wants. This would be the seventh tool, Right Action.

Then there are those times when you might think your wants are reasonable but, when you look at them carefully, they actually violate laws of nature and/or Consciousness in some way. For example, when you want your spouse or partner to be different that they are, you are, in reality, wanting to be in charge of something over which you have no jurisdiction. How do you heal these kinds of wants?

When you find unreasonable wants, look at the beliefs underlying them. There is a good chance that some of those beliefs are not in alignment with higher truth. When the beliefs get realigned, the wants change and the anger resolves. Remember, you can align your beliefs by first bringing them into the light of your conscious mind (you do that by following your feelings back to their roots) and asking the belief: "are you really true?"

Buddha is credited with saying something like: you are not punished for your anger, you are punished by your anger. If that is true, what does it mean? I've interpreted it to mean that it is okay to get angry but the anger shouldn't stick around. "Holding on to anger is like grasping a hot coal with the intent of throwing it at someone else; you are the one who gets burned." Buddha said that, too. Anger needs to flow and move on. Use the seven tools.

Be aware of your anger, listen carefully to it to see where it is coming from and how it got generated. Then look at your wants and expectations and, if they are reasonable, do whatever you can to remedy the situation. Anger says you are not supposed to live with unreasonable wants on one hand nor in untenable situations on the other. Responding to the situations that generate your anger in a healthy way can go a long way to help you live conscious and free.

Many people I've met who have dysfunctional relationships with their anger grew up in households with a rage-a-holic. A rage-a-holic, as the name implies, is someone who uses rage to manage all their other feelings. They also use their anger to manipulate and control those around them. Rage is their default setting; it is the first feeling to which they go. A rage-a-holic needs their own ecological niche. If you happen to get angry around them, they will out-rage you in order to boot you out of their territory, shut you up, and stay in control. You can just imagine the child trying to learn how to be healthy with their anger in such an environment. How often are they heard, acknowledged, and helped?

Many children in that situation quickly learn to transpose feelings that ought to be played in the key of anger into the key of anxiety. The rage-a-holic is okay if you're anxious around them; just don't let your hackles rise. Many of my patients with anxiety issues find that the solution to their anxiety is to learn how to be healthy with their anger. People who have no access to their anger are often doormats. They do not know when they are being abused. They often have to wake up to their anger then learn how to be healthy with it in order to stop the abuse and regain their sovereignty.

I've also seen people who have dysfunctional relationships with their anger who grew up in families where everyone had to be nice all the time. They were often shamed for any displays of anger. When you get a minute, look up "nice" in the dictionary. It comes from the Latin root "nescius."

"Ne-" is a negating prefix and "sci" is the subject of "scire." Scire means "to know" and is the Latin root for science, and conscience. So "nice" means "not knowing" or, more bluntly, being an idiot. Obviously, that is but one meaning of "nice" and not how it is frequently used today, but think about it in terms of when you are "being nice." What are you doing to yourself inside, especially if that is not how you are really feeling at the time? Right. You are stuffing some part of yourself, and, as you now know, that is an idiotic thing to do.

Contrast that with being kind. You can be kind without selling your soul. When you are being nice, you are compromising yourself in some way. People who are brought up to be nice are often fragmented, cut off to entire aspects of themselves. Learning how to be healthy with their feelings, no matter what those feelings are, helps them find their wholeness.

It may be possible to eventually adopt a world view that allows you to transcend anger all together. The Dalai Lama[44] says that he has not been angry in over thirty years. He strikes me as possessing a great deal of self-knowing and integrity and I have no reason to doubt that what he says is true for him. And he, and certainly his culture, gets treated with less than love on a regular basis. I think he is a living example of how the adept use of compassion, the fourth tool, can grasp the message of anger and put the inciting situation into a higher perspective before the seeds of anger even have a chance to be sown.

What can you do when someone else's anger is being directed at you? First, remember that how someone responds to you is giving you information about their structure of interpretation and inner workings: they don't know you; they only know their impression of you. Next, look at what feelings are generated in you because of their anger towards you. Ask those feelings to take you to their roots and see what aspects of your own structure of interpretation they relate to. Are those beliefs still correct from a higher perspective? While you are doing this inner work on yourself, also take a good look at your own actions. Have you done anything to hurt or abuse that other person? Have you acted with less than love toward them? If so, what was that about? Is there anything there that is asking to be healed?

If the other person is a rage-a-holic, chances are, no matter what you say or do, they will get pissed off. Don't take that personally. If the angry person is prone to violence, then do whatever you need to do to protect yourself. I have had some patients who have had very difficult times getting out of abusive relationships either because the abuser threatens their lives if they try or because they get out of one abusive relationship and then just get right back into another one. You may need to use your creativity, deep knowing, and all the social support systems available to you in order to get out of an abusive relationship. My patients have shown me over and over that the diligent practice of the seven tools helps them heal whatever abusive relationships symbolize to them, and then they stop getting into them.

I know that last statement will anger some people, because they will look at it as blaming the victim of a domestic abuse situation. I don't see it that way. I have not yet met anyone who consciously chose to be in an abusive relationship. While I've met some who consciously chose to stay in them, for their own reasons, I don't think any sane person consciously goes into a relationship knowing full well that they are going to be abused.

On the other hand, I've met several people who have gotten out of one abusive relationship then started a new relationship with someone else who seemed completely different than anyone they've been with before. In the beginning, everything goes great, and then, once they make a commitment, it is as if a switch is thrown in their partner, and they become abusive. My patients didn't see it coming. How do you explain that? How do you ever know someone well enough to know for sure that they will never abuse you? You don't. What determines who you are attracted to and who is attracted to you? Most of us do not live at the level of conscious manifestation whereby we can wake up one morning, say to ourselves, "today I'm going to meet my soul-mate and live happily ever after" and have it be so. For most of us, who we meet and fall in love with is all part of our unconscious manifesting as our fate.

Some people give up after a few such experiences with abusive relationships and lose trust in their ability to ever have a loving, intimate relationship. I've worked with some of these people and, when they heal whatever is inside of them that relates to abusive relationships, whether it was the latent effects of their own abuse, self-esteem issues, family patterns, or what, then they get into healthy, loving intimate relationships. So, for me, if you find yourself in an abusive relationship, it is not about blame.

It is not about being a victim. It is about information, about healing deep inner wounds, about knowing in your heart that you are lovable, and about treating yourself that way. We'll talk more about this when we go over how to use relationships to get to know yourself better.

In summary, denying, repressing, rationalizing, sugar-coating, or ignoring anger will only come back to bite you in the long run (or in other places). Losing control and acting it out unconsciously will generally bite you even more quickly. No need to fear your anger. No need to label it as bad. Learn how to receive and trust the message within your anger. Trust that your anger is there to help you. Let its fire energize your healing (and maybe even the healing of your entire community).

Sadness

Sadness and grief are very similar feelings. Grief is the normal natural feeling anytime circumstances change or you lose something important to you. If you look closely, you'll see that whenever you come to a crossroads in your life and choose one of the roads, you grieve the loss of the road not taken. These are universal experiences. We've all known grief. There are different levels of it and different stages, as was pointed out by Elizabeth Kubler Ross[45] (who's work I also highly recommend). Since sadness and grief are inevitable, the question I want to explore with you is how to be healthy with them.

Where anger is often a call to do something to make the world a better place, grief generally asks you to just be with yourself with kindness. For example, let us say that you've just gone over to your best friend's house to be with her because she just got the news that her mother passed away. How would you be with her? You can't fix the situation. How would she react if you tried to cheer her up? You could make some food for her, or clean her house for her, but she really needs you to just be there with her and for her. What your best friends need from you in their time of loss is exactly what you need from yourself any time you are grieving.

If you are being with someone else in their grief, it is a perfect time to practice open-hearted kindness towards them. When you are grieving, it is a perfect time to practice open-hearted kindness towards yourself. Both are equally important. So many people I meet are incredibly loving and kind to others while the thought that they could extend those same considerations to themselves has never entered their minds.

Just sit with sadness, really let it in and experience it, listen to it and hear its story. You may fear that it will swallow you up or that it is more than you can bear. Just notice what is going on inside yourself and give yourself a hug. Getting frozen and stuck in your sadness, or any feeling for that matter, is much more likely if you resist it, try to push it down and not feel it, distract yourself with busyness, or take medications to avoid it. The effort you put into avoiding your feelings just empowers them.

Sometimes, your grief may exceed your ability to sit with yourself in kindness. These times of feeling overwhelmed are very uncomfortable but can be incredible turning points. Seek out someone you trust. Find someone who can listen to you without getting all wrapped up in their own discomfort. I hope that you have such people in your life. And, when the opportunity arises, be that kind of person for someone else.

If you feel totally buried in your grief, get professional help. Medications used appropriately can be a big help but, in my opinion, should never be used alone. If you are taking medications to help you with sadness, depression and/or anxiety, please also work with a good counsellor or advanced body-worker if at all possible. Grief is not a Prozac deficiency disease. Drugs are your ally, your helper, not the cure. They can help you get the job done but you still have to put your foot in the shoe and push.

The only people I've met whom I've felt really needed antidepressants and anti-anxiety medications in order to function were reared in a uterus awash with psychoactive drugs. Other people may have an inborn error of their methylation pathways that cause lower levels of serotonin, norepinephrine/epinephrine, and dopamine that can lead to mood swings and depression. There are blood tests that can tell you if this is an issue for you. I would strongly recommend that you consider getting yourself tested if depression, anxiety, mood swings, and alcoholism tend to run in your family. A methylation problem, while you are born with it, can be easily treated by taking the methylated forms of folate and vitamin B12, both of which are available over the counter.

Everyone else I've worked with could eventually work their perceptions around to change their biochemistry and alleviate their chronic depression. The right drug at the right time in conjunction with the right kinds of other support can make these changes of perceptions more likely to happen. Of course, not all sadness and loss leads to depression. More about depression later.

Every so often, I see a person who is very aware of how they are feeling. They know full well why they are feeling the way that they are, but every time they try to sit with the feeling just as it is, they shut down inside and can't seem to get to the underlying belief system. Certain feelings can be so powerful or they've been with you for so much of your life, that when they come up, you can't see out of them. It is very much a case in which you can't see the forest for the trees. How do you shift such a situation? How do you receive the messages the feelings are carrying yet retain enough perspective to be able to change the underlying false or limiting beliefs and not get pulled off your center or have your circuit breaker thrown by the intensity of the feeling?

First, develop enough self-awareness to know when you are that overwhelmed. One clue is that you've had this same feeling dozens of times before and it still hasn't shifted. Another is that these feelings have been with you as long as you can remember. Another is that, whenever the feelings come up and no matter how prepared you think you are, they still pull you off your center. These are all clues that you most likely have some deeply-held beliefs that are a foundation of your world view yet are untrue or limiting and are holding you back and asking to be changed.

The next step is to get curious. What are those deeply-held beliefs? What did you go through that led to their formation? How do they want you to be with them right now?

Practice filling yourself with a sense of open-heartedness. Feel that open-heartedness spreading all throughout your body. Whatever image works for you. Tap into your ability to be kind and caring and let that feeling fill your whole being. If you are spiritual, feel how much God or spirit loves you. That open-hearted space often has a sense of quiet and peace associated with it, too. Once you get that feeling all through your body and mind, and know that you are surrounded by love, then turn and look at one of those feeling states that reliably cause you so much trouble. What does that feeling look like from this open-hearted perspective? Breathe into it.

Please note that you are not trying to feel open-hearted instead of however else you are feeling. (I tried that, too, and it didn't work.) You are trying to construct a container of open-heartedness that gives you the support and room you need to explore the deeper meanings of your feelings. You are erecting an inner platform, a point of view, of open-heartedness upon which you can stand while you are feeling however else you are feeling. Stand on that open-hearted platform as long as possible. If the other feeling starts to get too strong again, practice putting it on hold for a moment, get back into the open-hearted space, then turn and look at the feeling again. This gets better with practice. Compassion is a perspective, a point-of-view, from which to view the truth of how you are feeling. It is not a substitute for the truth of how you are feeling.

Each time you come back to the feeling, give yourself a little pep talk: "listen up. You can do this, you can look at this feeling, you can hold on for just one more breath … one more breath …" Before long, you will be able to stay with this feeling a bit longer before it becomes overwhelming. Eventually you will be able to get all the way to its roots. Resolving a feeling is like draining a swimming pool. The plug is at the bottom and you have to dive all the way down to get to it. Diving in then turning around before you get all the way to the bottom only means that you're all wet. You'll have to do it again if you want the feeling to resolve.

Sadness and anger often dance together. They are often layered one on top of the other in a person's psyche. Some people put the anger on top so that when they work down through it, they find a hidden lake of sadness underneath. Others put their sadness on top and can only feel their anger once they learn to really sit in kindness with themselves. It makes sense that very often the same situation would generate both feelings in us. As you learn to just be, you will see that you frequently have several different feelings at the same time.

Happiness

Happiness is the feeling that most of us are striving to feel as much as possible. Contentment, satisfaction, fulfillment, joy, exhilaration, and ebullition are feelings that fall into this category. Rarely does someone come into the office with the chief complaint: "I'm too happy and I want to do something about it." So, in medicine, we spend most of our time focused on alleviating the other three feelings, trying to help the person experience more of this one. But trying to avoid some feelings while creating others is addiction. Trying to make yourself feel happy when the truth of your moment is that you just don't is as unhealthy as stuffing, repressing, or denying any other feeling.

Happiness ebbs and flows just like all feelings. I think we crave happiness because we confuse it with that sense of deep, inner peace and tranquility that we know is our birthright and natural state, that inner peace the search for which drives all of our efforts to heal. Happiness is a state of mind, a messenger, it comes and goes depending upon circumstances. Your deep, inner peace and tranquility is a state of your soul. It is just who you really are, once you dig down through all the false beliefs, effects of domestication, wounds, and other stuff of the mind that obscure it. Your deep, inner peace is not dependent upon your circumstances. The person with a good connection to their inner peace can still find it no matter what is happening to and around them. You can fully experience your inner peace and have full access to all of your feelings at the same time.

We think we are searching for happiness in our lives but we are really searching for that inner peace that can only come once we know who we really are and fully accept that. We like feeling happy and we hate it when it goes. But feelings have to flow. Messengers come and messengers go. Otherwise your house would fill up with UPS guys. You might think that would make you happy, but only until you had to buy all the groceries.

Feeling happy and being in that place of deep, inner peace can feel very similar at first. But once you connect with your inner peace, you will be able to feel how solid it is, how immutable. It is your foundation and your thoughts and feelings are just wisps flitting around above it. Once you find your inner peace, there is little confusion. Seeking happiness won't necessarily help you find your inner peace; this is a trap many fall into. True healing leads you to your inner peace. Then happiness becomes just one more color on your emotional palate, to appear on the canvas of your life as circumstances dictate.

Your feelings can help you deepen your understanding of your inner processes and of your place in the world. We've already explored how feelings can lead you to your unconsciously held beliefs. If you don't like a feeling, chances are the belief underlying the feeling is not working for you on some level and is trying to get your attention so that you can change that belief. When you are happy, that is a clue that the belief or part of your world view that is up at that time is working pretty well for you.

One caveat: feeling happy means only that the current situation is bringing up feelings that are congruent with major parts of your dominant world view; it does not necessarily mean that the beliefs are true or in alignment with higher truths. For example, a bank robber might feel a very strong sense of satisfaction after the successful completion of a heist. All that means is that that part of his belief system is working for him. It is not necessarily working for the highest interest of him or of the rest of creation. The sociopath's sense of happiness and contentment is totally divorced from the higher good. But, assuming you are not a sociopath, most of the times when you are feeling happy and content, those are times to celebrate and give thanks.

There is the old saying that "ignorance is bliss." Yet walking around in a blissful state of ignorance is not likely to be healthy for long. Even though you like feeling that way, explore and learn from your feelings of happiness just as diligently as you would from any of the other feelings that you wished would go away. Don't just take happiness for granted. Look at what is going on in your life and inside of yourself when you feel happy. Keep your awareness working.

Fear

The last of the four primary feelings is fear. When you look around at how our society works, at least how it is portrayed in the news, you could easily conclude that fear is the major motivator for most of what we do. You might even conclude that society trains us to be fearful starting at a very young age. Perhaps this is because fearful people give their power away and there are many powerful factions in our society that want you to give your power to them. For example, our economy would collapse if advertising didn't work. And advertising works better if you are afraid of ring around the collar, bad breath, or what your neighbors might think if you have a dandelion in your front yard. Marketers and politicians know to appeal more to your emotions than to your reason, and fear is one of your emotions they appeal to frequently.

But you claim your power back as you heal. You claim your power back from anyone who has abused you, from any situation in which you feel like a victim, and from anyone who wants you to do what they want you to do beyond what you agree to. To claim you power back, to heal, you must be healthy with your fear.

Fear is the most common block to my patient's continued growth. So, in order to overcome your blocks and keep growing, you must learn how to be healthy with fear. To expect fear to go away is unreasonable. In fact, we have a word in English for the absence of fear: foolishness. "Fools rush in where Angels fear to tread." We also have a word in English for doing what we need to do even in the face of fear: courage. Mark Twain put it this way: "Courage is resistance to fear, mastery of fear, not absence of fear."

David Hawkins, in *Power vs. Force*[46], reports on the results of his twenty years of research on human Consciousness. He was able to assign a numerical value to the different levels of human Consciousness. The number represents the amount of energy available at each level. Any level below two hundred is weakening to the soul and any level above two hundred is strengthening. Interestingly, courage comes in right at two hundred. Courage is the watershed between living a weakened, powerless, blocked life and living a strong, growing, empowered life. To keep growing in your personal understanding, in your ability to learn from life's lessons, in your ability to live your power and come into your full potential, you must develop courage and learn how to be healthy with fear. I'd like to describe what I've learned so far from both my own fears and from helping my patients with theirs.

"Fear is a wonderful servant but a terrible master." I don't remember where I first read this, but few sayings about fear are truer. If fear is functioning as your servant, it is informing you, keeping you from doing foolish things, and encouraging you to prepare for the future. But when fear becomes the master, when it reaches over and grabs the reins of your life out of your hands, you are a victim; you are trapped. I have never witnessed anyone heal and remain a victim at the same time.

The difference between servant and master can be subtle. Often a refined sense of awareness is required to detect the difference. If you are aware of your fear and can hear what it is saying to you and you are able to take that information into advisement but are still able to make your own decisions and choose your own actions informed by your higher knowing, fear is probably still serving you. When it makes the decisions for you, regardless of other information or the consequences of the actions it drives you to take, fear is being your master.

But even keeping fear as your servant is not the best or healthiest way to relate to it. Anything you do out of fear to keep yourself safe and prepared can also be done out of self-respect. You can exercise because you fear that if you don't you'll get flabby and have a heart attack, or you can exercise because you listened to your body and it asked you to move it and you respect yourself enough to take good care of yourself. Even if you were doing the exact same exercises, which motivation would give you the better result? Which motivation stimulates your body to make the healthier chemicals?

Fear can also be looked at as an acronym that stands for "Forgetting Everything's All Right." I first saw that on a bumper sticker and it just rang so true. I like this acronym better than "False Evidence Appearing Real" since the evidence might be real but the problem lies in our interpretation of the evidence. But maybe they are just two ways of saying the same thing. I like the first because, when I feel fear, it reminds me to ask myself, "What have I forgotten? How is it that I'm really all right despite what is going on right now?" It helps me to remember that all things are well on the level of my soul. My life might be in eminent danger, but my soul is immortal.

Realistically, though, most fearful situations are not that drastic. Like Mark Twain said, "I am an old man and have known a great many troubles, but most of them never happened." Unless you are living in very harrowing conditions, Twain describes how most of our fears work most of the time. Most of our fears we do to ourselves; underneath it all, we really are all right.

I used to fret and worry about every little thing all the time. Then, several years ago, I was handed an incredible gift in the form of a question one of my patients asked me during the course of a conversation. She asked, "You know what worrying is, don't you?" I said, "What?" And she said, "Worrying is praying for what you don't want." At that time in my life, I was exploring how thoughts became things, how our thoughts are creative, so the first thought that popped into my head when she said that was, "What's the point of that?" And ever since then, I haven't worried.

The timing couldn't have been better. My daughter was in Argentina for a year-long exchange program and, a month or so after that patient said that to me about worry, Argentina's economy collapsed. Suddenly the banks were all closed. My daughter's debit card stopped working. There were riots in the streets. I called her and asked her if she wanted to come home. She said that she wanted to stay there and experience how the people worked things out. I said, "Okay." And I didn't worry about her. I knew in my gut that she was okay, that she was resourceful, that, if she changed her mind, she would call. I was watching my inner responses to her situation and was amazed by how calm I stayed. And she was fine. She stuck it out. Argentina got back on its feet, and she learned a great deal from her experience.

Once I saw how, by fretting and worrying, I was using my creative energy to create and maintain the biological stress response in my body, it just made perfect sense to me to stop doing that. A lightbulb turned on in my head. And, just like the belief I had formed that exercise would hurt me, something inside shifted. Now it's not as though I have to remind myself not to fret; the fret just isn't there. It doesn't come up in the first place. Once a part of your world view shifts, once an unconsciously-held belief aligns with higher truth, the change that follows does not need your attention and energy to maintain it. It becomes who you are. Your goal with fear ought to be the same as with any other feeling: you want it to deliver its message and move on.

Fear is a major trigger for your fight, flight, or freeze reflex, also called the stress response[47]. You have a stress response hard-wired into your physiology because it has been incredibly successful helping organisms survive intense, life-threatening situations. It is a very primitive reflex; even amoebas have their version of a stress response. Your unconscious will often assume the most threatening situation first and ask questions later. To repeat a classic illustration: imagine you are walking down the sidewalk at dusk and catch a glimpse of a big snake out of the corner of your eye. How are you likely to react? Most would startle and jump. Then, after you collect yourself for a few seconds, you look again and see that it is just a piece of rope lying there. Your body reacted to your perception of the situation, not the reality of the situation. And it will generally respond to the most threatening interpretation of your sensory input because that is what it needs to do to keep you safe.

When new situations present themselves, if they are threatening, you often have to react before there is time to think. So you are hard-wired to react to the worst-case scenario first. You are not broken for doing that, you are only broken if that is all you do, if you don't reassess the situations and adjust your response accordingly.

Our stress response is designed to work in the old jungle we used to live in, where many of the threats we faced could lead to imminent physical harm. But, to your brain, a threat is a threat, whether it is real or imagined, whether it is physical or psychological. So, even though most of the threats we experience from our modern jungle are in the mental arena, our bodies still respond in the way that they were designed to respond.

The stress response is designed for emergencies, like when a tiger wanders by. Most of these emergencies were short-lived. Because of all the changes that happen in your physiology during the stress response[48], you cannot live in the stress response long term and stay healthy at the same time. Physicians now estimate that somewhere between seventy to ninety percent of patient visits are for stress-related illnesses. It just naturally follows, then, that to be healthy in today's world, you need to figure out how to be healthy with stress. Being healthy with fear goes a long way towards keeping stress from making you sick.

Practicing the seven tools of healing is a powerful way to literally make yourself impervious to stress[49]. You can find and change the underlying beliefs that determine how you interpret your experiences, so that they don't look stressful in the first place. This is essential because, once you are stressed, your body reacts within milliseconds—much too quickly to stop and breathe or to tell yourself to think positively. The stress response releases cortisol, which stays in your blood stream for about three hours. So you only need three or four stresses per day to essentially spend the entire day in the stress physiology. If you do this day after day, your health will suffer.

Practice the seven tools and how to be healthy with your feelings to find out for yourself how to be healthy with your fears. I'm speaking here mostly about your inner psychological fears. If you are living in a war zone or with an abusive person and your life or health are constantly being threatened for real, you also need to evaluate what steps you can take to change your situation. But, even in times of extreme danger, you can use these tools to keep fear serving you rather than the other way around. Use them to take a look at your life and remind yourself how you are really all right. See yourself having your fears. See what those fears have been doing to you all this time and be kind to yourself about it. Open your heart to yourself that you are in a situation that generates these fears. Ask the fear how it wants you to be with it right now. But most of all, trust yourself. Trust what you know.

Summary

These are just some basics about feelings. The topic is complex. The bottom line, though, is that feelings are messengers. They are bringing information to your conscious mind so that you can know how you work inside then make better-informed choices for yourself. Practice putting yourself in the perspective of compassion and then turning to explore your feelings, physical and emotional: see them for what they really are. Admit the raw naked truth of them to yourself and follow them to their roots. Notice any tendencies or desires you have to make your feelings be different than they are. You can heal your whole life using the information you skillfully receive from your feelings.

Thoughts

Just as you can become aware of your feelings, both physical and emotional, and follow them to their roots and receive their messages, you can place your awareness on your thoughts. Just as you can watch your body, you can watch your mind. At first, this might feel kind of freaky, like Ted Nugent or something coming out of the psychedelic sixties … but you really can watch your mind thinking thoughts. And, with practice, you can learn to direct your thoughts in a way that serves you best.

When I first start working with people for whom these are novel concepts, most have assumed that their awareness is their mind and their thoughts. They have to look fairly carefully before they can see that there is an awareness beyond their thoughts, an awareness that can be aware of their conscious mind. But it is there. That always raises the question, "if you are not your mind, if you can watch your mind, then who is doing the watching, who is doing the directing?" This is a great question to ponder.

I have my opinion, of course, but I'd like you to come up with your own answer for yourself as we go along. (Hint: it is not your brain.)

What are thoughts? How do they work? What influences them? What do they influence? To start answering these questions, we must first talk a little more about the mind.

One quality that makes living matter different from non-living matter is that living matter has an ability to sense the environment and respond to it. If you touch an earthworm, it responds, if you touch a sea anemone it responds, if you reach in with a microprobe and touch an ameba, it responds. If you touch a rock, it doesn't respond, at least not in any way that we know how to perceive. This is not to say that a rock is any less an expression of Consciousness than any other part of the Universe, just that the rock does not have mind as we understand it. This ability to be sensate is what we call "mind." The mind is that perspective of the divine substance that is subjective, that can take in and process data, make conscious sense out of the data, decide how to respond and send the appropriate orders to the body. Thinking is when your mind is processing data.

The mind thinks. That is what it does. (Getting it to stop is actually a very focused and intense meditative practice.) And the mind thinks quickly. Some experts estimate that we think on the average of 600 thoughts per minute. This makes for roughly 864,000 thoughts per day, depending upon how much Starbucks® you've had.

We do not need to go into great detail about thoughts here; philosophy, psychology, and Eastern tradition texts go into more detail than you'd ever want to know[50]. Simply put, thoughts can be conceptualized as the medium of exchange the mind uses to manipulate and process data. From this view, the mind uses thoughts to organize, sort, and otherwise manipulate data similarly to the way our society uses money to organize, sort, and otherwise manipulate human life energy.

The mind will start taking in and processing data, using thoughts, about whatever it is focused upon. (So which aspect of you gets to choose where the mind is focused?) In this way, thoughts both result from, and then represent, where you are focusing your attention. Your creativity flows where you focus your attention, so thoughts are also an indication of where you are aiming your creativity. This is why many people say that thoughts are creative. But the way that I understand it, Consciousness is creative and thoughts are more an expression, reflection, or indication of how Consciousness is flowing through you at that moment. In other words, the subjective aspect of Consciousness gets translated into thoughts on its way to getting expressed by you in the material world.

To put this idea into Quantum Mechanical terms, using the model presented in appendix C, you are represented by a potential function that is in Consciousness, outside the laws of time and space. This potential function has many aspects to it, one of which is the subjective. When your potential function collapses to create the "you" that is experiencing this present moment, the subjective aspect of this function gets expressed in the realm of time and space as your thoughts. In contrast, the objective aspect of your potential function would collapse as the electrical activity in your brain that represents that thought (along with all the other biochemistry going on in your body in that moment).

So your thoughts are simultaneously a determinant of what you can create and a result of what you have created. Beliefs, as we will see, are just patterns of thoughts that remain fairly stable in your mind. Because of this, they exert a much more powerful influence over your creative flow that do fleeting thoughts. More about beliefs later.

Your mind is thinking anyway, and your thoughts influence what you are able to create in your life, so, you might ask, why not think about what you want? And this is exactly what many of the leaders in the manifestation movement teach. But there are some big problems with this advice: you have two kinds of thoughts: those that you choose, which I call volitional thoughts; and those that just flow when you are not volitionally choosing, which I call automatic thoughts. About ninety percent of the thoughts you will have today, you also had yesterday. On top of that, most of us spend most of our day thinking about what we already have or, if we think we're thinking about what we want, we're really thinking about what we don't have (and what is that creating?). So the question arises: "what is the best way to direct and control your thoughts?"

First let me define what I mean by "control." You control a process in your life when you have total say over it from its very inception forward: you, the source of your volition, has total creative license over the entire project. There are many aspects of yourself and your life that, though you do not control them, you can exert some influence upon them. Sometimes exerting that influence feels like you are in control. When you can only influence something, you can alter it, direct its flow, repress it, or do other work on it, but you don't consciously ask whatever it is to be there in the first place. Feelings are one such aspect. You can influence your feelings in all sorts of ways once you have them, but you didn't ask those feelings to show up.

Control of your thoughts is theoretically possible but is a tall order. Take a moment and watch your mind thinking thoughts. I think you'll see that if you want to think about a specific thing, like your favorite animal at the zoo or what you want to do for the weekend, you can (volitional thoughts). But if you just sit and watch your mind, thoughts just flow (automatic thoughts). Harkening back to the river metaphor, we even call the way your mind just flows "stream of consciousness." Your thoughts are much like your breath. You can control them when you focus on them, but, when you don't, they just flow on their own.

Since thoughts become things[51], here's the shocking news: the thoughts you just think to fill in the gaps when you are not consciously directing your thoughts have just as much influence upon the life you are creating as the thoughts you are directing. Just like most of the breaths you breathe in a day are automatic, so are most of your thoughts. Your automatic thoughts are determined by your world view, the rack of lenses through which you view the world: your unconsciously held beliefs.

To control your thoughts, you basically have two choices: you can practice and practice staying aware of and consciously directing every thought you have, which is the practice most self-help gurus teach, a process that is akin to consciously choosing every breath you take in a day; or, you can do the work to align your world view with higher truth and let your automatic thoughts flow from that truth. If your automatic thoughts are flowing from higher truth, they are already the best thoughts you could be having in that moment, even if you were creating them consciously. So, I bet you can guess which option to direct your thoughts I hope you choose for yourself.

Using the exact same process you use to be healthy with your feelings, you can watch your automatic thoughts, become aware of them, admit the truth of them, get curious about where they are coming from, ask them to take you to their roots, and you will be able to bring to the light of your conscious mind the unconsciously held beliefs that spawned those thoughts. You can then admit to yourself your own personal truth that you have been holding onto those beliefs and ask whether or not those beliefs are really true from a higher perspective. Perform each of these steps with as much kindness toward yourself as you can muster. Used this way, those stream-of-consciousness thoughts become important clues to associations that you've made and beliefs that you hold and are yet another pathway to finding and changing your unconsciously held limiting beliefs.

Many self-help techniques teach you to control your thoughts by not thinking certain thoughts. But then you experience the consequences of an interesting property of your mind. Since thoughts are how the mind manipulates information, if you are trying to not think about something, you have to think about it first in order to not think it. By telling yourself not to think about something, you are unwittingly thinking about it, which focuses your creative powers on what you don't want to think about. So practice thinking about what you want, don't not think about what you don't want.

Let me illustrate with an example borrowed from Susan Ford Collins in *Our Children are Watching*[52]. So ... don't think about this pretty crystal bowl with two scoops of ice cream in it. And don't think about the hot fudge sauce pouring smoothly over the two scoops. And don't think of the white, fluffy whipped cream with nuts on top. Did you think about it? But I asked you not to. The unconscious mind does not hear the word "not." To effectively use your thoughts to focus your consciousness on creating change, you need to learn how to stay out of this trap. Do just that by compassionately watching your thoughts and applying the seven tools to them.

The practice of thought control is very powerful since thoughts consciously direct your creativity. Meditation is the classical awareness exercise for gaining control over the mind[38,53]. There are many different ways to meditate and if meditation is something you'd like to try, I encourage you to look around and find a technique that feels right for you. In general, the practice of meditation is to learn to watch your mind (and everything else) with the ultimate goal of transcending your mind and connecting directly with pure undifferentiated Consciousness: your core or Atman in the Vedic model (see Appendix A). In the process, you learn a great deal about all the different aspects of yourself, seeing each for the illusion that it is, and peeling it back to expose the next layer of illusion until, ultimately, you get to an aspect of yourself that is not an illusion, something that is actually as it appears to be: your Atman, your soul, your divine self. As you can imagine, this can be a lot of work. Save yourself years of frustration and find a teacher that you trust and work with that person.

> *To enjoy good health, to bring true happiness to one's family, to bring*
> *peace to all, one must first discipline and control one's own mind. If*
> *a man can control his mind, he can find the way to Enlightenment,*
> *and all wisdom and virtue will naturally come to him.*
> *—Buddha*

I think this process is just as true for women. Male preference aside, let's take a closer look at what Buddha is saying here. To enjoy good health and true happiness, one must first discipline and control the mind. So Buddha is confirming that learning how to think the right thoughts are important for your health. But what is the best way to discipline the mind and what aspect of you is doing the controlling? Many different answers to these questions and many different ways to do this practice have been devised over the centuries. Traditionally, most of these practices either require years of sequestered intense dedication or they don't work. This is a big problem for those of us who want to keep our day jobs and become enlightened at the same time.

From what I've witnessed as my patients walk their healing paths, I would recommend that you discipline your mind to focus on the following:

- the practice of what to have faith in,
- the practice of awareness of your truth,
- the practice of fully accepting your raw, unadulterated truth,
- and then the practice of letting your inner love be in control of your truth.

With this practice, your health challenges (actually any experiences in your life) function as stepping stones and guideposts on your path to enlightenment. Practicing the seven tools of healing turns your life experiences into these stepping stones and can be used in the middle of your hectic day.

You can observe your thoughts. You can even observe yourself thinking your thoughts. (You can even observe yourself observing yourself thinking the thoughts that you are observing, but don't get too carried away.) When you become aware that you are thinking thoughts that are not supportive or are counterproductive, I suggest that you simply clear a place in your heart and put those thoughts in there; that you say to yourself something to the effect of: "Here are those thoughts again. I can see them. I am choosing to have compassion for myself that I am thinking these thoughts and for all that has happened that has led up to me thinking these thoughts." Practice the Three A's as discussed and you will then start observing new thoughts that are arising out of that place of compassion. Very much like feelings, thoughts can also lead you to deeply-held limiting beliefs.

So far, we've established that:

- you are creative—and not just creative in terms of being artistic, though that is certainly creative—you are creating your life, moment by moment, as it flows along
- your creativity is always on
- your thoughts are simultaneously aiming or focusing your constant stream of creativity and, at the same time, are an indication of how you have been aiming and focusing your constant stream of creativity
- you can control your thoughts when you focus on doing so
- by following your automatic thoughts back to the unconsciously held beliefs behind them, you can use the seven tools of healing to align those beliefs with higher truths, which will then direct your automatic thoughts from that truth

Manifesting

As a human being, every thought you think counts, from the fleeting thoughts of a momentary distraction to your deeply held belief structures. You are not merely a separate individual but are a living, breathing, contributing part of a seamless whole. At the level of Consciousness, there is only one; your own personal expression of Consciousness is as a drop of water in the ocean, or, as Rumi[54] put it, "like a grain of salt in the mountain, still un-mined."

Because of this, you can be thought of not just as an information receiver, taking in information through your five senses, but as simultaneously an information transmitter. You don't just receive information out of the ethers; you actually transmit information back, encoded in the frequencies you emit. This process is a very real two-way communication. This is one way that you can create circumstances that appear to be coincidences. We are all excellent manifesters, some are just better at manifesting what they consciously want. As you heal, you will gain more conscious control over your manifesting and the opportunities you need will seemingly appear out of the woodwork. Perhaps you've already experienced this or witnessed it happening for your friends.

You attract that which is consistent, harmonious, and most in alignment with the preponderance of the contents of your mind: both conscious and unconscious. You may consciously want to create a change in your life but there may be contradicting or negating beliefs in your unconscious. You want something different in your life, so you think about that with conscious thoughts but then unwittingly push it away with other unconscious thoughts—there is some belief or other aspect of yourself that won't allow it to be. If this is happening to you in your search for health, you probably feel like everything you try isn't working. Use the seven tools to follow your thoughts and feelings back to their roots, looking for conclusions that you may have drawn that are contradicting your desire for health or whatever else you are trying to make manifest.

Personal Responsibility

I truly believe that we are creative in this way, but I strongly recommend that you apply this concept to yourself and others with wisdom and compassion. I'm not convinced that, as individuals, we have full control over all aspects of our inner and outer workings. We seem to have two conflicting higher truths: on the one hand, we create our lives moment to moment; on the other hand, bad things—that no sane person would ask for—happen. Both are true. How do we resolve this conflict?

I don't claim to have all the answers, but reminding myself about the real meaning of personal responsibility helps me with this contradiction. We often think responsibility means that we caused something. But it is better to think of responsibility as the ability to respond to all that influences us. You didn't cause the economic collapse and the loss of your job and house, but, potentially, you can choose from a range of different ways to look at and respond to these experiences. The way you ultimately view and respond to the events in your life depends upon what you believe. The same could be said if you are dealing with diabetes, high blood pressure, heart disease, cancer, fibromyalgia, or any other health challenge. Use the seven tools to align your beliefs with higher truth and believe what would help you the most.

Regrets

When you look back, you might see how a decision or a choice you made led to being in the predicament you're in now. Living with regrets is difficult and unproductive. Here are some things that help me during such feelings. Remember you have always done the best you could with what you knew and how you felt in any given moment. Having regrets for past choices and actions, or even wondering why something happened to you, is a great time to practice compassionate, accepting awareness of what is. Ask the qualities of your heart to rise up and be present with the qualities of your mind. Ask yourself, "what is possible if I choose to source my thoughts and beliefs from my true authentic self?"

The power of thought and the potential that we can control it have spawned huge resources of information about positive thinking. Positive thinking is useful as long as you are not using it to deny what is. Forcing yourself to think positively is not really necessary for, as you continue to practice compassionate accepting awareness of what is, your inner love will gently gain control of your mind and your thoughts will just naturally trend toward understanding, kindness and peace.

The Energetic

Just as you can watch your thoughts and feelings and get information about yourself from them, you can also learn to be aware of your energy.

The concept of energy is not included in the conventional medical model. What follows is my understanding of it.

The energetic view of a human being has an interesting history in Western culture. For over fifteen hundred years, it was a major tenet of Galenic[55] medicine but got discarded in the 1600s, as more physiologically-based medicine started to replace Galen's ideas. But energy has remained an important part of Traditional Chinese medicine (chi), Ayurvedic medicine (prana), and most forms of herbal medicine practiced around the world.

Since the 1600s, in the West, the concept of a vital life energy keeps getting rediscovered. Hahnemann[56] discovered it when he developed the practice of homeopathy. Palmer[57] discovered it when he developed chiropractic. Southerland[58] discovered it when he developed cranial osteopathy and Reich[59] discovered it and called it "orgone" just to name a few.

The nature of this energy is confusing. In physics, energy takes the form of four primary forces[60]: electromagnetic force, gravity, and the strong and weak forces. Each of these forces (with the possible exception of gravity, which may turn out to be more a property of matter/space/time than a force—the jury is still out on that one, in my opinion) propagates at the speed of light and decreases exponentially over distance. They are also measurable with scientific instruments.

The energy that healers speak of does not seem to have these properties. The body obviously works with a kind of energy recognized by physics: it generates its own electromagnetic field that can be measured by ECGs, EEGs, EMGs and the like, and it has gravitational attraction that is not debated by conventional science. This is also not the energy that I'm referring to here. So far, there are no generally recognized machines that can measure this kind of energy, sometimes referred to as subtle energy, though some believe that is what is being detected by Vega machines[61], Rife machines[62], Kirlian photography[63], and the like.

There is also some confusion among energy workers between this energy and Consciousness. Consciousness does not diminish over distance. In other words, in studies of intercessionary prayer[64], the effects were just as strong if the person doing the praying was in the other room or on the other side of the planet. Consciousness also seems to propagate instantaneously, not at the speed of light, as near as we can tell. This energetic perspective is a manifestation of Consciousness, just as is every other aspect of reality, but Consciousness per se is not what is being referred to by this perspective. Consciousness is much greater and all-inclusive.

So what is this "energy", if it is not part of physics as we know it and it is different from Consciousness? Some people can see it, many others can feel it. It is recognized all around the world and down through history (with the last four hundred years of conventional medicine as the anomaly), so we might assume that there is something useful to this concept. All I can speak to, in an attempt to answer these questions, is my own experience of it.

Remember, Spinoza[15] said that who we really are is a mystery. If we look at that mystery for physical characteristics, we find them as the body. If we look at that mystery for mental characteristics, we find them as the mind. I see this phenomenon we call energy as a third independent perspective, a third way of looking at our mysterious divine substance. Your body is made up of stuff of the earth, the matter/energy of physics. Matter and energy in the traditional sense (not the energy we are taking about in this section), are just two sides of the same coin: $E=mc^2$; m is mass and c is a constant, the speed of light. Your mind is the bridge that connects this matter/energy with Consciousness. I experience this other phenomenon we are calling vital life energy managing information.

The basic packet of life as we know it on this planet is the cell. Your body can be thought of as a community of cells that have thrown in their fates together, specialized, and committed their individuality to the benefit of the whole (see Bruce Lipton's *Biology of Belief*[8]). The human body is made up of an estimated 50 trillion eukaryotic cells and well over 500 trillion bacteria and yeast, and over 5 quadrillion viruses, give or take a few. To put this into perspective, there are only 7 billion people on the planet. There are somewhere in the neighborhood of 70,000 times more cells and 700,000 times more bacteria in your body than people on the planet.

Imagine what your day would be like if you had to get up each morning and phone the other 7 billion people to find out what they had planned so you could make your plans to fit in. That amount of information exchange would more than swamp our current telecommunications capacity (and you think you get a lot of emails now!). Societies need other ways to inform citizens about how to fit in than just verbal communication. And they have them. There are non-verbal expectations, customs, laws, schedules, and such.

The body is no different. It has several different ways to manage the information needed to get all of your cells to work together. It uses the nervous system to send some information around, it uses hormones and prostaglandins and cytokines and other chemicals to transmit some information around. But my sense, from doing body work, is that the information required to efficiently and effectively coordinate the activity of so many cells far exceeds the carrying capacity and response times of the nervous and chemical systems.

So enter the concept of group consciousness. This is a fascinating topic that is just starting to get explored by some serious researchers. It's the old "wherever two or more are gathered ..." We have neurons in our brains that are being called mirror neurons[41]. Their job is to detect this group consciousness and help us know how to modulate our own responses to fit in. People who are very charismatic, the life of the party, and comfortable in groups may have highly functioning mirror neurons. People who never seem to know the right things to say or who stumble over themselves in social situations, with autism perhaps as the far end of the spectrum, have less efficient mirror neurons. Napoleon Hill[65], way back in the 1930s, talked about the "group mind" that forms when several people, in a spirit of cooperation, come together to work toward a common goal as being greater than the sum of the individual minds in the group.

Well, imagine the group consciousness that could be generated by 50 trillion individuals. It is an overarching superstructure of information that permeates the body. Each cell can tap into it to know how to plan its day. There is good evidence to support the idea that this information is stored holographically in the body[66] (though that is another topic). This cellular group consciousness, this information blueprint for the body, is how I conceptualize what is meant by this energy perspective.

Certain conditions can interfere with the flow of this information and many treatments are specifically directed toward this energy. Food contributes to your energetic body as well as to your biochemical body. So do herbs. Homeopathy and flower essences are also primarily energetic treatments. Acupuncture, Reiki, therapeutic touch and craniosacral therapy, to name a few, are therapies that work directly on energy and how it flows.

Energy can also be directed by consciousness. When asked how they can do so many amazing things with their bodies, yogis often respond, "I can direct the flow of prana in my body." How can western medicine even interpret such a statement without a concept of this vital life energy? Many yoga traditions teach pranayama exercises[67] to learn how to work with this energy.

You can also increase your energy awareness when you practice tai chi[68] or chi gong[69]. As you do your practices, stay very present with your inner experiences. Not only feel your body moving, feel your energy flowing, feel your breath. Again, be the watcher, see how all the aspects of you—mind, body, energy—respond to the exercises. Use these techniques to listen to your energy and any disturbances in it rather than to just force your energy to be a certain way. A block in your energy is just as much a symptom and clue to an imbalance as is a block in your biochemistry. Use compassionate accepting awareness of your present energetic moment to receive their message, then the blocks will naturally release.

To those who can see and/or feel this energy, it is just as real as the body or mind. It has many of the qualities of electromagnetic energy, such as frequency, current, and voltage but cannot be detected by electrodes and such. If body and mind are just two sides of the same coin, energy is the third side. It is a distinct and irreducible perspective on you. It is subtle; in fact, many energy workers refer to it as subtle energy. But you can learn to sense it and work with it if you can't already. Energetic blocks are just information and can be listened to using the same skills you learned to listen to your thoughts and feelings.

Here is an exercise I use in my beginning craniosacral classes to help the students start to feel this energy. Hold your arms straight out to your sides like you're greeting the sun in the morning. Now cock your wrists so that your palms are facing each other. Take a few slow gentle breathes, get yourself grounded and centered and put your awareness into the palms of your hands. Keeping your awareness in your palms and being curious about what you feel, slowly start moving your hands closer together as if you will end up palm to palm in front of your sternum, like a Chinese greeting. Most people can feel a transition about two feet out from the body. There is often another transition felt when your hands get about eighteen to twenty four inches apart. By the time your hands get eight to nine inches apart, you may feel a mild springiness or pushing back or repulsion of your palms, as if you're holding a head-sized nerf ball. This repulsing feeling often gets stronger as you bring your palm all the way together.

Different people feel the transitions or boundaries in different ways. For some, it is a change in temperature; for others, it may be a change in a buzzing sensation in their palms, others may feel it as a small zone of resistance that their hands move through. What you feel gets better with practice. The keys are to get centered, grounded, and calm inside so that you can put exquisite awareness into your palms.

Here is another good exercise to practice feeling energy. If you have a partner, you can practice scanning each other's energy. Start by having one person lie down while the other person gets calm, grounded, and centered, focusing their awareness into their hands. Most people hold their hands about three to four inches above the supine person's body as they gently scan from the feet to the head. Again, you may feel regions of cold or heat, areas that seem to pull your hand in or push it away, areas that feel calm and other areas that increase the sense of buzzing in your hand. Just be open to whatever you feel. Feeling energy is one thing. Interpreting the meaning of what you feel is another.

Your vital energy body, as some energy workers refer to it, has its own organization, or what could be thought of as energy anatomy[70]. There are many versions of energy anatomy and getting into all of their subtleties is not necessary for you to be able to start to feel your own energy, listen to it, and get the information you need in order for your energy to go back into balance.

Beliefs

Becoming aware of your beliefs, and then changing them to line up with higher truths, is the most important practice for your healing. Your entire world view, how you see yourself and the rest of the world, can be distilled into beliefs that you hold. Beliefs serve two very important functions. First, beliefs act as the lenses that you, your conscious sense of self, look through as you peer out at the world and, also, as you look inside at your own inner workings. Second, beliefs are the determinants of which aspects of Consciousness you are able to bring forth in your life. Change your beliefs and how you see the world changes; change your beliefs and what you are able to create changes.

You are consciously aware of some of the beliefs that you hold. But the vast majority of them are held in your unconscious, working behind the scenes: all you see are their effects in your life. Those effects will be whatever you experience as:

- how your body is functioning,
- how you are feeling,
- how your energy flows,
- your actions,
- your personality,
- what you like and dislike,
- the quality of the relationship you are having with yourself,
- the quality of relationships you have with others,
- the people you are attracted to and vice versa,
- your career choices,
- how much wealth you can create,
- and so forth.

If you are dissatisfied with any of these effects, don't get caught in the trap of trying to make the effects be any different than they are. Rather, listen carefully to them in order to trace back to the underlying beliefs, bring those beliefs into the light of consciousness, and get them aligned with higher truth. The effects will then change.

Most techniques currently available to help you change yourself and your circumstances focus on trying to change the effects themselves. Or they may be sophisticated enough to tell you what you should think, feel and believe in order to work the change. But they generally do not show you how to get yourself to just naturally think, feel, and believe that way, which means that you get into a perpetual tug-o-war within yourself. Avoid those traps.

Choose instead to practice compassionate, accepting awareness of whatever is in and around you. Admit to yourself the truth of your circumstances and how you feel about your circumstances, be kind to yourself about the whole scenario, and then ask your feelings to take you to their roots. This generally brings the belief or conclusion into the light of consciousness where you can then admit the truth that you've been holding that belief and then see if, in your heart of hearts, you still believe that belief is true. In most instances, being in that place of full, open-hearted acceptance, while connected to a higher perspective, is all it takes to get the old belief to change to a higher, truer belief. Once that happens, the world exerts a different influence upon you and you are able to bring forth aspects of your life that were previously unattainable.

If you employ other methods to change your beliefs, such as affirmations and visualizations, you may see changes in your creative flow for a while; but these techniques don't remove the old beliefs. You are just layering new beliefs on top of the old, with the risk that they can then bubble up to the surface of your life some time down the road.

Dreams

Dreams are arguably the most common way that your unconscious communicates with your conscious. Entire books have been written about dreams and their interpretation. All I want to say here is that dreams are a potent potential source of information about what your unconscious thinks about things. Remembering your dreams can be practiced and you can get better at it, if you put your mind to it.

What goes on in dreams often makes no sense in the light of day so dreams generally cannot be taken literally. But there is often deep symbolism to the imagery and circumstances. The same symbolism that appears in art, cinematography, and mythology can often be used to understand dreams[71].

Be aware of the feelings you are feeling in the dream, rather than the plot. The feelings help you unlock unconscious beliefs that are asking to be transformed. Use your attention to feel into the dream, bring the issues into your conscious mind, and then use the seven tools to align them with higher truth.

Actions

What you believe determines your response to your life. How you act in the world—the words you speak, the tone of voice you use, the body language you project, the choices you make—all spring from how you're feeling at the time. How you're feeling at the time is determined by how you are interpreting what is going on in and around you. And, as you know, how you interpret what is going on in and around you is determined by what you believe. All of your actions have your beliefs at their roots.

Because of this, you can also watch your actions in order to uncover hidden, limiting beliefs. And, as you may have deduced, change your beliefs and change your actions. The best way to change any behaviors that are causing you problems in your life, such as anger outbursts, emotional eating, or any of a number of addictions, is to find and change the beliefs at their bedrock. Be the observer. Listen to the tone of voice you use while talking with someone. Be curious. "What am I feeling that causes me to use these inflections and not those inflections? To choose to phrase it this way and not that way?"

This level of awareness is a noble aspiration, but in the heat of the moment, you just act. Sometimes you have to look at your actions in retrospect to see where they came from. But with practice, your inner observer starts to function more in real-time and you are then able to understand the messages from your actions as they are happening. Ideally, you want your inner observer to be so real-time that you are able to see how you are feeling but then be able to choose your actions independently from how you feel, if necessary. Be patient with yourself. For many of my patients, this skill takes time to develop.

Studies consistently show that actions stem from feelings, even in highly rational people[72], but there's the rub. You are legally liable for your actions; but have you noticed that you are not legally liable for your feelings? It's okay to want to rip somebody's face off; it's just not okay to actually do it. Rule number one (all feelings are valid) does not apply to actions. Not all actions are valid. Some will get you into trouble.

So, even though feelings drive your actions, feelings and actions follow different rules. For example, there is much you can do to manipulate a feeling once you have it, but you didn't ask it to be there in the first place. You don't control your feelings and most of the things you do to try are dysfunctional. Let the feeling be, experience it, and apprehend the message it has for you. But if feelings drive actions, then you don't control your actions, either, and that leads to problems. Anger outbursts, impulse buying, emotional eating, hitting your kids, and the list goes on.

You need to be able to choose your actions freely if you want to claim your birthright as a free being. You need some way to uncouple your actions from your feelings. How can you do that? Well ... I bet you can guess what I'm going to say: practice the seven tools, of course.

Years ago, while teaching people how to use the seven tools as a method for personal coaching, we were talking about these concepts and I'd written the expression of manifestation on the board like this:

Thoughts   Feelings   Actions   Results

We were discussing each word and each arrow in the expression. We started by defining what results we want, for example, to heal or resolve a particular health issue. What actions might lead to those results? The arrow between actions and results is actually made up of the laws of nature and the laws of Consciousness. How do you know that a given action will lead to your intended result? You don't for certain. All you have to go by are probabilities. But the more you know about how the world works, the better you can choose your actions. Science is attempting to understand nature so that we can have conscious control over it. We study psychology so that we can better predict human nature. We formulate laws of economics to better predict how to manipulate the economy, and the list goes on. None of these are exact disciplines, and the most successful people often study as much as they can and then trust their instincts as well. Spend some time contemplating the last arrow in the above expression and see what you judge for yourself.

The next step back in the expression states that our emotions lead to our actions. When I first saw this expression, I was curious that it states that our emotions drive our actions. Most of my friends, colleagues, and

I strive to live our lives rationally. But study after study of brain function support what marketers have always known: we are driven to action by our emotions, by our passions, more than by our reasoning[73].

Right away, this causes a dilemma. Your feelings are innocent messengers bringing you information. You don't choose your feelings. They just show up. If there is a solid steel push-rod connecting your feelings to your actions then you don't control your actions either.

So we were talking in class about how, if you ever want to step up and claim the freedom that is your birthright, if you ever want to control your actions so that you have some hope of ever controlling the results you achieve, the arrow connecting "feeling" and "action" needs to have a gap in it. You need to be able to let your feelings just be your feelings, so that they can deliver a true, untainted message to you while, at the same time, allowing you to be free to choose your actions.

In Eastern philosophy, that gap is called detachment. Detachment often gets misinterpreted in the West. It does not mean isolated or cut off from how you are feeling. Quite the opposite. It means that you are fully aware of how you are feeling, so fully, in fact, that you can clearly see how your feelings are influencing you and you are able to consciously intervene and choose how you act. Ideally, you want to be in conscious control of your actions while letting your feelings just be. True detachment requires a high degree of awareness and living in the moment in pure compassion and is therefore a much more challenging skill to develop than learning how to control your actions by stuffing your feelings.

Young children have very strong feelings and often act on them, making the adults in their life uncomfortable. Adults want children to learn how to behave appropriately in social situations and so often give toddlers the message that certain behaviors are not all right. Perhaps because the adults around us focused primarily on our behavior or perhaps because it is much simpler to control feelings than behaviors, most of us learned to control our behaviors by controlling our feelings. When you were growing up, how often did you hear something to the effect of: "I know you are feeling angry right now and that is okay. But hitting is a mistake. Please use your words to tell your sister what you need." I don't know about you, but I didn't get spoken to that respectfully when I was wigging out as a kid.

Like me, most of my patients learned to stuff their feelings when they were babies and toddlers. They learned to control their actions by controlling their feelings. But then they were left with dysfunctional relationships with their feelings. Most people with outbursts of uncontrollable behaviors are sitting on a powder-keg of stuffed feelings. To heal the dysfunctional relationship with your feelings that started so young, practice being fully aware of your feelings (tool two), fully experiencing your feelings (tool three), while compassionately watching yourself having them (tool four). This will detach them from your actions, like reaching up inside a player piano and disconnecting the tape from the keys. The tape can keep rolling but you are free to play whatever song you want.

One of the students in the personal coaching class pointed out that being able to choose our actions is an act of free will and that free will is a gift of grace. The extent to which we are able to create that space between our feelings and our actions is the extent to which we can claim our free will. So we dubbed that gap in that arrow the "Pause of Grace."

It just so happened that, at that time, the office where I was holding class had a photo in the bathroom of a mother polar bear holding a cub between her arms. The cub was sleeping peacefully, but the mom was looking at whomever was taking the photo, obviously through a telephoto lens, with a clear expression on her face saying, "Don't you dare take another step closer." The quote under the photo was something to the effect of: "No harm can come to whomever God protects." I kind of liked the image of God as a mother bear and wondered what it would feel like to be that cub, so calm and protected and totally unconcerned, nestled safely between those massive paws. I also thought about what that student said about our freedom being a gift from God and I came up with this affirmation that helps me separate my feelings from my actions and step up and claim my freedom: "I allow myself to be held in the Pause (paws) of Grace, fully free to feel my feelings and fully free to choose my actions."

This affirmation does several things at once. It reminds me that I'm loved and protected, and it helps me claim my free will, one of my birthrights. It helps me have a healthier relationship with my feelings and reminds me that I choose—and am responsible for—my actions.

So, imagine your self-talk goes something like this: "I practice compassionate, accepting awareness of what is. I allow myself to be held in the Pause of Grace, fully free to feel my feelings and fully free to choose my actions." The next challenge is to have the presence of mind to actually fulfill these affirmations in the heat of the moment. That is where practice comes in. Practice being the watcher. Practice kindness toward all of creation until compassion is your default setting, until it is where you just go automatically.

Try this: stand up, put your feet a little more than shoulder width apart, extend your arms down and out from your sides a little bit with your palms facing frontward. Roll your shoulders back, lift your chest with a deep breath in, look to the sky and say "I allow myself to be held in the paws of Grace, fully free to feel my feelings, fully free to choose my actions." If your palms start tingling, all the better.

With practice, you can insert your Consciousness between your feelings and actions, receiving the messages from your feelings, moment by moment in real-time, and choosing your actions based on input from your inner love. What a way to go! Until you get to that point in your personal growth, however, watching your actions can be used as another avenue of awareness into your inner workings, giving you more opportunities to align your structure of interpretation with higher truth.

Relationships

Relationships give you a rich and wonderful opportunity to practice awareness. I think of relationships as feeling generators. No matter whom you are relating to, whether it is the person checking out your groceries or your spouse of sixty years, feelings are being generated. Those feelings are messengers from your unconscious mind. In this way, relationships function just like mirrors: the person is reflecting back to you your interpretation of them and your current interaction with them.

Since no one ever really knows you … all they know is their own perception of you … how another person responds to you is giving you a window into their own inner workings. But how you feel about how another person responds to you is a window into yourself, showing you your own inner workings. That is how relationships are mirrors. Mirrors help you see yourself, but unlike the glass mirror, relationships are more symbolic than literal. For example, if you see someone being a jerk, that does not necessarily mean you are a jerk. Their jerkiness brings up feelings in you and those feelings are information about your own structure of interpretation.

I've seen relationships be symbolic mirrors in two ways. First, as we just discussed, relating to someone else brings up feelings. Those feelings are messengers bringing you information about your world view or other beliefs that you've formed. Then you can follow those feelings to their roots and open your heart to yourself, as you would with any feeling. For example, a coworker compliments you on how you look. Any number of possible feelings could come up. You might feel pleased and happy that someone noticed; you might feel uncomfortable as if they were trying to put unwanted moves on you; you might barely notice. However you feel depends upon your past experiences and any conclusions you have drawn from them. Follow whatever feeling you are having back to its underlying belief and see how that belief looks through spirit eyes. If it is a false or limiting belief, then be kind to yourself that you went through the experience that led to the formation of that belief; and be kind to yourself about how that belief has been affecting you over time.

The second way that relationships are mirrors show up in their patterns. How often have you ended a relationship with one person only to, at some later date, get into another relationship with someone else and sooner or later find yourself dealing with the exact same issues all over again? Patterns in relationships are information. There is a very good chance that there are inner aspects of yourself relating to each other in the same patterns you see repeating in your relationships,.

For example, let's say that the last three boyfriends that you've had didn't treat you with respect. Chances are, there is an inner aspect of you that is not treating some other aspect of you with respect. Or that you have a belief that you don't deserve to be treated with respect. Until the beliefs change and the inner patterns of relationships change, you will probably have difficulty forming a relationship with someone else that doesn't have that pattern in it. So relationships can be used to find and change deeply held limiting beliefs.

Unless you are being physically, sexually, or emotionally abused, I would generally encourage you to stay in your relationships and use the seven tools to explore and heal all the issues that come up. Moving from relationship to relationship without healing tends to perpetuate the same patterns over and over. More than one of my patients has described their multiple relationships as "same package, different wrapping paper". If you feel like that, you've got your own issues to heal; your partner is standing in as spirit's pawn to show them to you.

When you use your relationships to advance your healing, they often survive and get much better. Or, if they don't survive or have already ended, the next relationship can bring up other, yet unexplored issues, as the old issues have been healed. When both people in relationship are actively engaged in their own personal growth and use all of the feelings they experience because they are in relationship to get to know themselves better, just about any issue can be faced and healed. These tend to be very resilient healthy relationships.

A relationship doesn't have to be active in order for you to heal any issues that it was bringing up. You can heal unfinished business with people who have passed away, moved away, abandoned you, whatever. You have a memory of the feelings, both in your mind and in your body, which the relationship generated. The memory of a feeling works just as well as the actual feeling in the moment to guide you to the underlying beliefs. Then use the seven tools to align those beliefs with higher truth.

Surroundings

Your surroundings are exerting a constant influence upon you. Different feelings will be generated in you if it is cloudy rather than sunny, cold rather than hot, if your room is messy or neat. Be aware of these influences. The feelings that come up will help you get to know yourself, and you might be able to see how you can change your surroundings to help yourself. Then again, sometimes you can't.

Everybody complains about the weather, but nobody does anything about it.
—Mark Twain

Colors, textures, shapes, floor plans, furniture styles: every aspect of your environment influences you in some way. Artists, architects and interior designers are well aware of these principles. Landscape architects also make use of these ideas. The value of aesthetics to your health is not trivial. Urban planners have recently discovered that the simple act of planting trees in a neighborhood will decrease the crime rate there[74].

On one hand, it is worth your while, whenever possible, to create functional, efficient, aesthetically pleasing surroundings for yourself: in your home, in your yard, in your community, and in your work place; and on the other hand, keep an eye on how your surroundings, whatever they are, are influencing your thoughts, feelings, and actions.

Feng Shui is the study of how the environment influences you on all levels, physical to energetic. Several good books have been written on the subject[75], if you want to look into it more. Bottom line: your surroundings and the feelings that they bring up in you is yet another window into your inner workings.

Common Pitfalls in the Use of Awareness

We just went through an exploration of aspects of your life that are helpful to pay attention to: your physical body, emotions, thoughts, beliefs, dreams, relationships, environment and such. So now let's explore how to use awareness skillfully and how to avoid some of the pitfalls I've seen catch my patients over the years.

I cannot overemphasize the importance of awareness if you want to grow and heal and come into full possession of your creative abilities. Truthful awareness, the combined use of tools two and three, is the quickest route to your freedom that I've ever witnessed. If you have any kind of malady in your life that you want to be free of, know your truth of it and follow the rest of the seven tools on through to right action.

Watch for patterns. Reoccurring patterns in thoughts, feelings, actions, issues, or situations that you have to deal with are very important clues to deeply held beliefs that you are holding in your unconscious mind. These beliefs are exerting powerful influences upon you. Often the beliefs that underlie patterns are major foundational beliefs in your psyche.

All of the seven tools are skills that improve with practice. Awareness is a choice. At first you might forget to make that choice, but whenever you realize that you have become oblivious to the messages coming to you from your body or emotions or surroundings, just gently make a mental note of it and choose to bring your awareness back to whatever is going on in and around you in that moment. Over time, the listening and observing becomes more automatic. Get curious. Challenge yourself. Ask yourself, "I wonder how aware I can get?"

Another common word for awareness is mindfulness. If you are already practicing any mindfulness techniques or exercises, you are honing and improving your skill of awareness. Turn your whole life into one mindfulness meditation.

When you have a chronic health problem, your body is really talking to you. When you first start listening to it, you may feel like you are listening to a cacophony, a room full of people all screaming at once to get your attention. How do you sort it all out? You may have to say something to the effect of: "all right everybody, quiet down and line-up. You'll all get heard, but I need to listen to you one at a time." Another option would be to step back in your mind's eye and look at the whole process of your illness at once, try to see any possible patterns that could be clues to underlying beliefs that might be affecting your whole being.

Let's say that you are practicing awareness of what is going on inside of yourself and you become aware of something that you want to change— for example, about how judgmental you are toward yourself, or how hurt you are by what someone said or did, or that a conclusion you drew when you were five no longer fits your life. Take a moment and watch yourself. Remember, the first step to changing yourself is to start where you are. What do you do once you're aware of an aspect of yourself that you want to change? Do you start to work right away to force the aspect to change? Chances are you've been doing that to and with yourself for years. Since that approach to getting yourself to change obviously hasn't worked very well, the first inner processes you may want to use the seven tools to change is how it is that you put pressure on yourself to change. Notice that you have that desire to jump right in and make that aspect of yourself change, admit the truth of that desire to yourself, be kind to yourself about it, and see what your inner love suggests you do next. Use compassionate, accepting awareness to get the change to happen.

You might realize how much you hate the way you've been feeling, how you're sick of it and want it gone, like Mike with his headache. Or you might see how you've been fighting it, repressing it, resisting it, or trying to annihilate it. You might tell yourself things like: "I shouldn't be feeling this way." "I don't believe that anymore; that's not me." Or you might see how you try to rationalize how you are feeling, saying to yourself, "Oh, that was so long ago, I don't need to feel that way anymore." or, "I ought to be more accepting of people. I can be such a jerk sometimes," or, "That person doesn't know what they're talking about. I won't let them get to me." There are so many ways you can make your feelings be different than they are. But if you warp your truth, it cannot set you free.

We get caught in these kinds of traps because applying some sort of effort to how you are feeling, thinking, or acting makes sense on the surface. You know from the physical world that if you want to change the direction of something or get something to start or stop moving in the first place, you need to apply a force to it. A force requires energy. Using energy implies that some sort of effort is being exerted. So it just makes sense that you would take what you learned works in the outer world and apply the same approach to your inner world. Unfortunately, Consciousness doesn't work that way. Your creative flow goes wherever you focus your attention, whether it is your conscious or unconscious mind doing the focusing. If you focus on the problem, that is where your creative flow is going: into the problem. Focusing on the solution to the problem makes a little more sense. But, if you focus on having compassion for yourself that you have the problem, your creativity is flowing toward more compassion. Being compassionate is who you fundamentally are, as your divine self. Practicing compassion for what is, for all that is present in your life right now, therefore, is practicing being yourself ... and that is healing. At the same time, you are stepping out of your own way and making space for your inner wisdom to come up with a solution to the problem. (I use the term "inner wisdom" here but you could substitute "spirit", "God" or "the universe". Whatever works for you.)

Most of the time, when you make an effort to change, like going on a diet or starting to go to the gym more regularly, or accepting your parents for just who they are, those changes require ongoing effort to keep them in place. You might think, "maybe if I practice the new change long enough, it will become habit." That is the hope; that is the promise of so many techniques that are used in our society to help you change. We spend way too much time, money, and energy working too superficially ... and that does not make real lasting transformational change.

When you are working superficially, as so often happens, something in your life goes south and then all of your efforts tumble down like a house of cards. You may be struggling on so many fronts, trying to change so many aspects of yourself at once, that you just can't keep that many balls in the air; you may get tired of all of the effort, sick of the diet, you may start to rationalize to yourself that it's okay to skip the gym just this one time; you may be trying to keep the lid on your anger until, finally, you blow a gasket and erupt like an exploding pressure cooker. Or maybe the new change brings up a whole new set of problems of their own that you then have to deal with. Eventually, for whatever reason, you fall off the wagon. Any of this sound familiar? Watch how you operate: see if you can catch yourself wanting to change a behavior by working on the level of behavior. Einstein said, "No problem can be solved from the same level of consciousness that created it." Whenever you use your will power to force yourself to change, be careful that you are not setting yourself up for failure. Be watchful. Look deeply at what you are doing to change. If whatever change you make in yourself requires ongoing energy to keep the change in place, you risk fatigue and relapse.

The only changes you can make in yourself that don't require ongoing effort to keep in place are the changes to be more of who you already are. You don't have to exert effort to be your true authentic self. But you do have to expend a lot of effort to be anyone else. Perhaps this is what some people mean when they say that true healing is effortless. Becoming your true authentic self is healing. Once you get there, you don't have to keep exerting effort to stay there. But for most of my patients, getting there in the first place is a lot of work.

You cannot heal by forcing yourself to change, but something needs to change in order for you to heal. Compassion works the change; you don't have to force it upon yourself. Exert your effort towards practicing compassion for whatever is your truth in this moment. Ask yourself, "I wonder how I can love this present moment more?"

Not every effort leads to healing (though you can learn from whatever choices you make). Just as there are many different ways to look at any given experience and not all of them are enlightening or transformational, there are many ways you can work to change yourself and not all of them are healing. But your inner wisdom can direct you. Keep listening to how your gut is responding to your life. Trust that quiet inner voice when it makes a suggestion that causes your gut to relax. Practice following for yourself the advice that you give to your friends.

Here is a game you can try at a party sometime, I often do this in my stress classes. Pair up with another person. Choose a problem or challenge you are currently dealing with and describe it to your partner. Your partner then role-plays that they have that same problem and they are coming to you for advice. You role-play the person giving the advice. Listen to yourself, because there is a pretty darn good chance you will give your partner excellent advice about how to deal with that problem. This exercise works because you already have inside of you the answers to all of your questions; you just don't always know how to access those answers. But that is what you are learning by practicing the seven tools.

As you continue to watch yourself and see how you really work inside, you may uncover some ways that you have been hurting yourself. Don't fight with them. Don't make an effort to stop them just yet. Behind every behavior is a motivation. Behind every motivation is a belief. Follow the behavior back to the belief. Use your awareness to see the truth of what you believe. See where the belief came from: what experience you went through and the conclusions that you drew from that experience. See how that belief has been affecting you down through the years. Learn as much about it as you can. Once you change the belief, whatever was causing the self-hurting behavior will no longer be in you and the behavior will just automatically change.

Other ways to try to change behaviors have been developed. For example, behavior modification is a form of therapy that focuses solely on changing the behavior. It is often used for issues that involve the unconscious mind, such as sleep problems. It can control symptoms but it does not help you deepen your understanding of yourself or make lasting changes in your belief system. It may work temporarily for some behaviors, but there is a high probability that the behaviors will return or the same issue will reassert itself through a different set of behaviors. So be cautious if you are trying to change yourself by using approaches that focus on the behavior. You may be short-changing yourself.

You can use your awareness to watch yourself carefully, to see how you're working on the inside, to see how you respond to your environment, to your relationships. Your ability to heal seems to be proportional to your ability to be conscious. Awareness increases your consciousness. So practice the awareness exercises—like the body sweep and intentional movement—that we've covered in this chapter. Practice paying attention to your feelings.

Feelings are messengers bringing you information that allows you to uncover your deeper belief systems. Become aware of your physical feelings; notice that every physical feeling has an emotional feeling associated with it. Become aware of your emotional feelings; notice that every emotional feeling has a physical feeling or bodily response associated with it. Physical and emotional feelings are just two sides of the same coin. Remember that all feelings are valid, your feelings are just feelings, innocent messengers, not the problem. Receive the message in your feeling by the practice of awareness, acceptance, and following the feeling to its roots. Your actions are also clues to your deeper belief systems. Be aware of your actions, follow their motivation back to the underlying beliefs and see how those beliefs look through the eyes of your inner wisdom.

Years ago, I was assisting my favorite general surgeon on an inguinal hernia repair on a patient whom I had referred to him. His chief resident was also helping. As we were operating, the surgeon was quizzing his resident about all the different methods that have been developed over the years for the repair of these kinds of hernias (and there have been many). After the resident had listed off the seventh or eighth technique, the surgeon made an observation that struck me as particularly wise. He said, "When there are lots of different ways to try and get the same job done, that generally means that none of them works very well." He went on to say that when something works, people tend to gravitate towards it. He was speaking about surgical procedures, of course, but I was struck by how truly this observation also applies to all the other ways we've developed to help ourselves change.

Think about all the different kinds of psychotherapies that have been devised, or about how many kinds of diets there are, all the different systems of medicine, the different approaches to education, or how many ways we have to try to grow our spiritual life, for that matter. Some of the variety comes about because there is no one recipe for life that fits everyone, but I think we keep developing newer ways to do therapy, for example, because none of the ways we commonly use actually work all that well. If therapists were honest with themselves, they would admit that. Many years ago, Eugene T. Gendlin, Ph.D. did admit that to himself so he decided to study the people for whom therapy did work to see what he could learn.

Within a short time, he noticed that the people who responded well to therapy all exhibited a certain characteristic. He found that he could go into a Psych 101 class, describe that characteristic to the students, then show them videotapes of people having their first therapy sessions, and the students could accurately predict which people would go on to get a good result from their therapy and which ones wouldn't. Dr. Gendlin also discovered that this characteristic can be taught to people, so that they would get more benefit from their therapy. In fact, people who were really good at this skill could resolve their problems themselves and didn't even need a therapist. Dr. Gendlin discovered that the people who got really good results from therapy all had a particular way of listening to their bodies.

Dr. Gendlin wrote a book about his findings[76]. In this book he not only describes the research he did at the University of Chicago that led to his observations, he teaches you how to do that kind of listening for yourself. The book is called *Focusing*. I highly recommend it to you. Focusing is, essentially, listening to the body deeply enough to see how your inner wisdom is expressing itself through your body. It is getting the message your inner wisdom is trying to put across by telling your body to generate those feelings. Gendlin's work confirms that those who listen to and get the message from their inner wisdom are successful in their efforts to change and grow. I think Gendlin's ideas have real merit and fit seamlessly into the practice of the seven tools.

Your growing powers of awareness are going to reveal all sorts of things about yourself to you. Some you will like; some you won't. What are you to do with all of this information? As you might guess, your inner wisdom has a suggestion about that. As you walk your path of self-discovery, for each and every new insight, your inner wisdom says things like, "Just accept that about yourself; that is your personal truth at this moment. You might not like it, and it won't always have to be that way, but that is the way it is now. Accept it." And that leads us to the third tool—acceptance.

Chapter five

Acceptance

The process of Mastery, then, is one of acceptance. It is a quiet embracing of what is. It is a non-resistance. It is a gentle walking into the moment, knowing that it holds for us, always, what is best for us all ways.
—Neale Donald Walsch

Acceptance is the third tool. Awareness shows you the truth of your moment. Your inner wisdom then says: accept your truth, surrender to your truth, stop fighting your truth. You have probably been trained by society to skip over this step and jump right in and start to fix yourself. When they first come to see me, many of my patients have been in this trap for years. Acceptance is the key to this trap, it is a vital step in the change process. Acceptance keeps you from getting locked into a tug of war with your issues.

Your inner wisdom says, "accept what is. Whatever is already is. There is no sense in denying your truth or railing against it. Only after you accept what is can you change." Fighting what is just entrenches it (by focusing your creativity on it). Acceptance lets the messages from your life be delivered to your conscious mind. Acceptance stops any wars you may be waging within yourself or with spirit. Accepting your truth creates space around it.

For years, I used the word "surrender" for the third tool. I liked it because it was jarring and reminded me to question my deeply-engrained resistance to this step of healing. Growing up, my brothers and I evolved a social structure very similar to a pack of wolves. I was very competitive within that pack: when I was going after something I wanted, I was relentless. My gut reaction to the concept of surrender was "no way; I'm not a quitter." Surrender was the last resort once I'd been completely beaten down and had no fight left.

But then I saw that, when I am working within myself on my own personal growth and striving to understand the information my life is presenting to me, what I am fighting against is myself. I saw that when I'm fighting with the truth, when I'm fighting against the advice of my own inner wisdom, well ... to put it delicately, that's just plain stupid. In the setting of my own personal growth it is not really wise to keep fighting my truth until I have no other options. That just makes life a lot harder than it needs to be. (By the way, how hard does life "need" to be?) Calling the third tool surrender really got me to stop and look at what I was doing.

Healing is not about war, especially when we're warring inside of ourselves. Ultimately, no one wins a war. There are always casualties on both sides—and when both sides are in you, you get doubly hurt by the resistance and fighting.

But when you contemplate the word "surrender," you see it has other connotations. The act of surrendering implies that, on some level, the surrenderer has reached some degree of acceptance of what is; "to bow to the unknown, to honor our mysterious interconnectedness, to see that the only way to security was through surrender" as Lisa Jones put it in her wonderful book *Broken*[77]. Surrender has a sense of finality and unconditionality to it; it reminds us of our vulnerabilities—uncomfortable truths for most of us. This kind of surrender is not quitting, it is simply stopping the war we're waging inside of ourselves; stopping the resistance to what really is. The jarring nature of the word surrender was a constant reminder to me that there are times when surrendering is not quitting but an act of wisdom. But I didn't learn this quickly.

By the time we moved to our small farm in Snoqualmie in 1999, my back had been hurting off and on for over fifteen years. But I didn't accept that. I wouldn't accept any physical limitations. I saw my role on the farm as the mule (my wife is the brains), and I thought I ought to be able to lift and carry anything I wanted. I kept hurting my back over and over again until 2005, when a lumbar disk had a major blow-out and I lost the feeling in and use of my left leg. I had surgery to get the disk fragments off the nerves. Even after that, I still hurt my back a few times. Finally, I was able to accept that I had some limitations. I learned to listen to my back much more consistently, and I now use physics instead of brute force (which I like more, anyway: "Give me a lever long enough and a fulcrum on which to place it, and I shall move the world." —Archimedes). I can find that fine line between exercising my back enough to keep it strong and working it too hard and making it hurt again for a few days. Inside the peace of this acceptance lies the chance that I can work with my back in the right way and allow it to heal.

Admitting the truth involves saying, "it is what it is." Surrender stops the war you're having with yourself and within yourself. It stops the offense <u>and</u> the defense. This is a very important point. Through acceptance, not only do you not need to fight as much, you also do not need to defend yourself as much. You will just naturally find yourself feeling more safe and secure as you heal your life. Being able to see and accept your truth for what it is forms the foundation of your sense of safety in the world.

Seeing the present moment clearly and honestly helps you put perceived threats into perspective. Sometimes the threats are less serious than you've imagined and you've built up defenses that you don't really need. And sometimes they are actually more threatening and you're not doing what you need to do to take good care of yourself. For example, preparing for disasters, saving for retirement, learning new skills. Many people use denial to stay in abusive relationships in which their well-being is in real jeopardy. If you need to take action to protect yourself, you can use awareness and trust in your own deeper knowing to get clear about what that action needs to be.

Acceptance does not mean quitting. It does not mean things will never change. It does not mean losing. It does not mean resignation. It does not mean that you'll always be defeated. Look at the Germans and the Japanese now. Surrender allows for a course correction, creates an opportunity to re-strategize—hopefully in closer alignment with your inner wisdom.

Have faith that a better future can be had. Plan for a better future by envisioning it, setting goals, acquiring the needed skills and resources, and working your action plan. You can do all that, but if, at the same time, you are denying that the present is the way that it is, you are putting your creativity at odds with itself. Denial is a form of attention and your creativity naturally flows where you focus your attention. Denial is a great way to ensure that the way your life is right now stays that way. But surrendering to what is, acceptance of what is, admits the truth of the present moment and stops the denial. It frees your attention to focus entirely on creating a new future rather than on creating a future that is just more of the past and present.

Here is another way to think about admitting the truth of your present moment. Moving from where you are now—in need of some kind of healing—to where you want to be—healthy, wealthy, and wise—implies something must change. Let's assume that your inner wisdom can function like your own inner navigation computer guiding you on your course to wellness. If this is so, what information does your navigation computer need? It needs to know where you are going, for sure; this is loaded into the computer by the goals and intentions you set for yourself. But there's one more bit of information it needs: your starting location. Admitting the truth of your present situation is like entering your starting location into your navigation computer. If you put in the address of where you wished you were, your computer would plot you a path that might not do you any good. Admitting the truth of your present moment is not resigning yourself to the possibility that nothing will ever change. In fact, it is the opposite. Once you start from where you are, your inner wisdom can plot the surest path to your goals. The third tool gives you that.

Accepting the truth is critically important for the process of change. The truth has a peculiar property to it. Remember: "you shall know your truth and your truth shall set you free." Your truth is the surest path to your freedom I've been able to find. And free is one aspect of your true authentic self: Immanuel Kant[78] demonstrated that over 200 years ago and scriptures from around the world tell us that over and over. Therefore, becoming free is very healing.

In order to be free of any malady in your life, you must work with the pure, raw, naked truth it. Denying, repressing, sugar-coating, intellectualizing, analyzing, or wishfully thinking about your present situation blocks you from knowing the truth and finding your freedom. Those defense mechanisms actually keep you sick. Awareness will help you uncover what is; then acceptance will stop the war against what is and open the possibility for you to much more easily see the truth. We think that we gain our freedom by fighting, but, paradoxically, we also need surrender to be truly free: fight for your future, but surrender to the truth of your present moment. Using your energy to fight against the truth of your present circumstance just makes you tired and keeps you stuck. If awareness is seeing the UPS driver walking towards your door carrying a package, then acceptance is opening the door and letting the UPS driver give you your package. Acceptance is a crucial step in your healing process.

Self-acceptance is an invitation to stop trying to change yourself into the person you wish to be, long enough to find out who you really are.
—Robert Holden

Most of my patients, at some point in their struggles, have experienced the benefits of accepting what is, of relaxing into the present moment and stopping the resistance and the fight. Yet when they return to the office for help with the next issue on their list, they are often back to their old pattern of fighting what is. Most of my patients have a very difficult time seeing their truth for what it is and accepting it. Even after they've experienced firsthand the transformational power of surrendering to the truth of the moment, they often don't use it again until circumstances get so bad that they are forced to. What keeps us from using acceptance more readily?

There are many reasons you might fear using acceptance and surrendering to your truth. My patients often voice a belief that if they really let in the reality of their pain or their tumor or their addiction and stop fighting against it, it will never change. They fear that accepting the truth of their present moment will reinforce it and make it permanent. This fear is very strong in our fix-it, doing oriented culture, even though our experiences, time after time, tell us the opposite is true. We forget that there is a difference between accepting the truth of the present moment and prognosticating about the future. Accepting that you're in pain now says nothing about how you may feel five minutes from now.

To experience what I'm saying here, try this little exercise. Take a moment to get centered and aware inside. See how these two statements feel in your body: "I guess that I have to accept that I will always have this pain." What does saying that do to your energy level? To your sense of hope? To your level of pain? Now get centered and aware inside again and see how this statement feels: "I am in pain now."

Feel the difference? The first is defeating, weakening, hopeless. The second leaves the door open to move in any number of directions with your next statement or question. Any of the following puts you on the right path. "I wonder what primary imbalance is calling for my attention through this pain?" "I wonder how to transcend this pain and move on in my life?" "I can have compassion for myself for being in this pain right now." "How does this pain want me to be with it right now?" Whatever seems to be the best next statement or question for you in that moment will work. Surrendering to your pain sets the stage for you to be with it in a different way. This is true of just about any situation in which you find yourself.

When we truly embrace acceptance, that is when our
body exhales and we can begin healing.
—Kris Carr

Rarely are you able to change your patterns, beliefs, thoughts and behaviors until you first accept the raw truth of how you are. The first step of twelve-step programs serves the same purpose with respect to the problem that program deals with: acknowledging powerlessness in the face of that problem.

The second reason I see for resisting accepting our truth is a confusion about the right use of the warrior archetype. We know that people who fight their cancer generally do better than people who roll over and give up. People who stand up for themselves generally do better than door mats. Dan Milliman wrote an excellent book called *The Way of the Peaceful Warrior*[79], about his learning at the hands of his spiritual teacher. So which characteristics of the warrior are helpful for healing and which get in the way?

Tenacity or stick-to-it-iveness is an important trait of a warrior. We are told, "seek and ye shall find," as if there is no chance of failure; it's not, "seek and maybe you'll find." But often the seeking is not easy. Some tenacity really helps when adversity arises. Tenacity is helpful when you are sitting with your discomfort for just one more breath before shutting down or freaking out. Tenacity is important when you need to stick to the pursuit of your dreams against all odds. Keep telling yourself that healing is always possible, even for you. Stick to your practice of the seven tools through thick and thin and you will get there.

Every block to a person's personal growth that I've met so far in my practice has been fear. So bravery and courage are also helpful warrior characteristics. Courage is the ability to do what you need to do even in the face of fear. It is a choice, whether you make it unconsciously in the heat of the moment, or you are trained to make that choice. The healthy warrior has learned to have a healthy relationship with their fear.

Warriors are also good at what they do. Their life depends upon it. You might not die from most of your actions, but your life also depends upon them. However you act, you will experience the natural consequences of those actions. So being skillful is a useful warrior trait. Skill develops through focused practice. Practice the seven tools, hone the skills for healing as if your very life depends upon it. Because it does.

I'm reminded of a story that was told to me by Michael, one of my early spiritual teachers. He was in his late eighties when I met him in the early nineties. He grew up in Poland and, when he was a teen, the Nazis came into his home, lined his family up against a wall and shot them all except him and his older brother, whom they took to a work camp. He escaped and made his way to France, where he joined the underground resistance. He eventually became a pilot stationed in England.

One day, an old man from India showed up at the barracks and started talking to the soldiers about meditation and spiritual growth. Michael felt strongly drawn to him and started studying with him. The old man said that he was a master who had been charged by his own master to train fifteen students in his life. He had trained fourteen by the time World War II had broken out and was hoping that he was done. But he got the sense that he had to go to England to find his fifteenth student. So he walked from India to France, took a boat across the English Channel and found Michael.

He told Michael about when he was a small boy and starting his training with his master. One day they were bathing in the Ganges River when his master, an old man himself, suddenly turned on the boy, grabbed him, and held him under water. The master kept him under until he stopped struggling then pulled him to the surface. As the boy gasped in his first breath, the old man held him face to face and said: "that is how much you need to want God." Most of us wouldn't want to go through such an experience at the hands of our teachers, but sometimes you do at the hands of your own inner teacher. Like a warrior in battle, there are times when you need to walk your healing path as if your very life depends upon it. There may be times when you are as desperate for your healing as you are for the very breath of life itself.

Not long after Michael started studying with the old Indian master, he was in a dog fight over the English Channel and was knocked out by a piece of his plane that got broken off and hit him in the head. His plane flew on and crash-landed in England, braking his back. He was in a body cast for a year, paralyzed from the waist down. The day he got his cast off, he was lying in bed and his master was sitting by his side. The doctor came into the room with a wheelchair and said, "This is your new home. Better get used to it." Then the doctor turned and left. His master looked at him and asked, "Is that what you want?" Michael said, "No." His master said simply, "Then remember who you are." He got up and left. Michael said he never saw him again. When I met Michael, he was living on a sailboat docked in Lake Union in Seattle. He said that he had difficulty skiing but could dance and otherwise get around pretty well. He worked as a therapist with a special interest in people with para- and quadriplegia.

Remembering who you are is powerfully healing. It is healing. "Remember" is an interesting word. You can get some insight into its role in your healing if you look at its opposite. Most people think the opposite of "remember" is "forget." But etymologically, the opposite of remember is dismember. So to "remember who you are" is, quite literally as Michael did, to put yourself back together again, to symbolically re-attach your arms and legs, your ability to move and act and be effective in the world. Not everyone who has severed their spinal cord will walk again, but it is certainly known to happen. How do we explain that? The point of Michael's story is that remembering who you are, finding and being your true authentic self, is healing—not just for your psyche but potentially and powerfully for your body as well.

Sometimes your inner teacher, the inner choreographer of your life, asks you to face life-and-death situations. In those moments, the passion and intensity of the warrior are good healing characteristics, if they are aimed at getting to know yourself better. However, if they are aimed at controlling how you feel or controlling others, they will get in your way.

A good warrior is also able to assess a situation accurately and make his or her plans accordingly. There is no point in harboring illusions about the situation you need to respond to when your life depends upon it. That same skill can be applied to your healing. Accept the truth of your life in this present moment. See your life for exactly what it is, with no spin, with no repression or denial, with no sugar-coating. You can then choose your options based upon accurate intel. Acceptance is an exercise in self-honesty.

If you have had to be strong in order to survive, you might find acceptance a particularly difficult tool to use. If you had surrendered, in the usual sense, at the time of your abuse or whatever very difficult experience you went through, you might have died. Your strength is amazing. Your strength is incredible. Now it is time to bring it to bear on your healing. You may be reading books or seeing therapists that tell you you have to go back and re-experience what happened to you and feel all the feelings that may have gotten suppressed or not felt because of dissociation. My patients have taught me otherwise. Over and over I've seen people heal from past abuse by applying the seven tools to however that abuse is affecting them now, in their present moment. To go back and revisit what happened is to be re-traumatized again, just reinforcing the effects of the original abuse. If a person does start to have a memory of what they went through while we're working, we focus more on seeing what conclusion they drew, what was their take-home message from that experience rather than on the exact details of the experience.

Acceptance may fly in the face of every survival instinct you have. You may fear that you are going to feel worse than you do now. And that may well be true. Over and over I've witnessed that, as my patients start to address their abuse head on, their whole life gets turned on its head. But only for a while. Once they get through the feelings, and find that place of compassionate acceptance, they find their freedom from the chains of their past.

Or maybe you know that something horrible happened to you and you don't want that experience to define you, you don't want that life. You know it is there, but you turn away from it and work on creating a different life for yourself. If you use any repression or denial in your turning away, that will just serve to empower the effects of the abuse in your life. You might find that circumstances keep cropping up that recreate the abuse or recapitulate the feelings you harbor about having been abused. Acceptance will remedy that but, at the same time, acceptance makes the abuse real. You may fear that the feelings that will come, if you really let the abuse in, will overpower your life. Again, they very well may … but only for a while. Stay true to the practice of the seven tools and you will get through those feelings and find your freedom on the other side.

Even when my patients are able to be excellent healing warriors and are willing to fully just be in the truth of their situation, sometimes confusions still arise. You see, there are two truths—and one truth is probably not true and the other truth is usually not obvious. And this can be confusing.

First, you have your own personal truth: the truth about what beliefs you are carrying (which makes up your own personal world view and makes the world look the way it does to you). Your truth in any given moment is that you believe those beliefs. However, some of those beliefs may not be true.

If you do not make room for the possibility that you may be harboring false beliefs, then the instant you uncover them and see that they are false, you may quickly move inside to minimize them or discount them. This is a form of denial and only serves to entrench them. This is the voice of experience talking: I was stuck for years by this one. Once you fully accept that you are holding a particular belief, you can often see what you experienced that led to the formation of the belief and also how that belief has been affecting you down through the years. However, if you discount that belief too quickly, no matter how ludicrous it looks now, without acceptance and exploration, you miss an opportunity to deepen your understanding of yourself and potentially free yourself from limiting beliefs.

You have your own personal truth; then there is an over-arching higher or spiritual truth. Wherever your rack of lenses or system of beliefs don't line up with this higher truth, symptoms will develop. These kinds of symptoms are invitations to become aware of how your personal truth doesn't fit with higher truth and then correct or align your personal truth. Healing often includes inventorying the beliefs within your word view and aligning them with higher truth. I've observed that the more my patients' own personal beliefs match this higher truth, as revealed to them by their inner love, the healthier they are. This makes sense to me, as living in harmony with higher truth allows us to be more of who we really are.

Here is yet another place that I commonly see people make an error on their healing path. You've perhaps heard the saying, "don't should all over yourself." This is very important. When you are changing old limiting or false beliefs, allow the new belief that comes in and replaces the old one to arise from your heart's knowing, from your inner love, from your deepest wisdom, rather than from your ego, your conscious mind's desires, cultural expectations, or your judgments about how you are supposed to be. But this is easier said than done. Watch yourself carefully. Tie a red ribbon around the work "should" and if you find yourself telling yourself, "you should do this," or, "you should think that," or, especially, "you shouldn't be feeling this way," set off the alarms inside your head, pull out acceptance of what is and practice it as quickly as possible.

I was able to discern these tools over time, as I worked to help people connect with their source of intrinsic knowing. Acceptance was the next to last of the seven patterns I saw (faith was the last), perhaps because I was so entrenched in my "fix-it" mentality that I didn't think this step was important (I have personally experienced all of the blocks to acceptance we just talked about). So I know how it feels to have difficulty really seeing the raw truth of what happened to you, how you're really feeling, what you really believe. So, please, be patient—with yourself, with others, with this process—and give the tools a chance to work. Chronic illness challenges you to your very marrow. It is difficult to fully admit the extent of your disability, for example. But admitting the truth of your disability doesn't mean that you give yourself over to it and let it run your life. It just means that, instead of using your will power and personal resolve to fight your truth, you free them to find the roots of your illness and resolve them.

Practice having faith in whatever helps you the most. This could be having faith in a Supreme Being who, hopefully, is benevolent and compassionate. Or it could be having faith in your own competencies or in the skills and caring of others. Have faith that you can get better. Healing is always possible, you just don't always know ahead of time what achieving your healing will ask of you. But faith that it is possible can keep you going, keep you searching, keep you asking the hard questions and demanding honest answers from yourself.

Practice becoming aware of the truth all around you and within you. Use your powers of observation and discernment for this. Watch the information that comes to you through your five senses. Watch the thoughts that flow through your mind. Watch how you feel and see what you believe. Watch how your mind works. Watch your energy, its frequency, its intensity, its pattern of flow, or how it is blocked. See how your creativity works, how Consciousness works.

Practice your powers of acceptance, of admitting to yourself the truth of your present circumstances. Practice this skill not as a way of giving up and becoming passive but as a way of determining the starting point from which you will move, as a way of setting the stage for effective change. Admit the truth of how the world looks to you with your present set of lenses; this sets the stage for adopting different lenses.

Now that you are becoming more aware of 'what is' and surrendering to and accepting 'what is', what does the inner knower recommend next? Over and over, it says things like, "just be kinder to yourself about that," or, "give yourself a hug; hold yourself in your arms," or, "let yourself know that you're all right, that you're not alone."

Over and over in my practice, I see this as the inner love asking the person to practice a little kindness, a little compassion.

Which leads us to **the fourth tool — Compassion**.

Chapter Six

Compassion

I've been thinking about compassion a lot lately. I used to say, with a good bit of confidence, that the only thing I've ever seen really heal someone is compassion. But now I'm not sure I can be so definite. Compassion, as love in action, is very important for healing. In fact, I think that love is necessary for healing, but, in and of itself, is not always sufficient. There is a very good chance that there are people in your life who love you very much. I'm sure that their love is very important to you ... but has it healed you? Then there is learning to love yourself. This is what I see happening to my patients who heal: they come to an understanding where they truly love themselves. But is it the love that heals you or is loving yourself just one of the outcomes or consequences of healing? I think it may be the latter. Then there is the love that you give to the world. Evy McDonald, RN[80] credits finding that kind of love for her recovery from ALS (Lou Gehrig's disease), a condition that is thought to be one hundred percent fatal. The same question could be asked: is loving the world the cause of healing or the result?

And what about people who are so inclined, believing that God or Jesus heals them? Over six months ago, John and his wife were having dinner with the pastor of their church. It was dark when it came time for them to leave. John was looking for his glasses, which he needed for driving at night, and couldn't find them. All three of them searched all over and the glasses were nowhere to be found. He was going to drive home anyway and, just as they were leaving the house, the pastor said, "wait a minute, I'm feeling something." And he walked over and cupped his hands over

John's eyes. For the next few minutes, John felt heat in his eyes. When the pastor removed his hands, John could see perfectly without his glasses. John related this story to me recently and he still does not need glasses. Even to read. But what really astounded him and his wife was that, when they got home, he looked in his brief case, which all three had searched through more than once while at the pastor's house, and there the glasses were, right on the top. How can you explain John's experience from the conventional medical model? It is important to also note that John's vision has improved but he is still suffering from many other aspects of his life. So his eyes are working better from a refraction point of view, but his life is still not yet healed.

As I understand it, God's love is in and around and through us at all times, like water is to a fish. Yet, when someone is healed by it, we think it is a miracle. Obviously, something else, besides love, is also needed for healing. What could it be? Jesus said that even he could not heal someone unless they believed. I'm not sure he elaborated upon what specifically they needed to believe, and therein lies the root of two thousand years of confusion. The Christians I've talked to about these issues think that He was referring to believing in Him as the true savior. But, then again, there are so many Christians in need of healing that I'm not sure that's the right answer. Whatever the right answer is for you, whatever you need to create a healing miracle in your own life, your own inner wisdom knows. Practicing the seven tools of healing is a simple, reliable way to communicate clearly with your inner knower.

Compassion, by and of itself, is not sufficient to heal your life. But, nevertheless, it is a vital link in the chain of events that lead to your healing. As a way of looking at yourself, no other perspective is more transformational. What is compassion? What comes to your mind when you say the word "compassion?" Please take a moment to answer this question for yourself. This is not a trivial exercise. I often find that people haven't thought much about it, or they don't really know what it is, or they have a difficult time putting their conception of compassion into words.

Imagine that you're walking down the street and you come across a puppy with a hurt leg. How would you feel toward that puppy? For most people, that is compassion. Years ago, I was talking with a patient about compassion and she didn't have a good sense of how it felt, so I used the above puppy example. She looked straight at me and said, "That doesn't work for me. I hate dogs." Well, it takes all kinds to put the world together, so I asked her, "Do you have any friends?" (Now I know what you are thinking, but it wasn't really such a dumb question. Anything is possible. Even someone who hates dogs could conceivably have friends.) She did, and she generally liked them.

So I suggested, "imagine that you are over at your best friend's house and she just got word that her mother had passed away. How would you be with her? You can't tell her how to feel; she'd just get mad at you. You can't fix it. What would you do?" She said she'd just sit with her, let her talk if she needed or be silent if she needed. She'd just be there with her. She hit the nail on the head. Rather than doing, compassion is a way of being, a way to be a witness. An open hearted presence, unreserved kindness: that is compassion. Imagine offering to yourself, at every moment of your life, the same open-hearted presence, the same "just being" you would offer to your best friend in their time of need.

Years ago, I was working with a woman, a kind, intelligent, accomplished professional, who was astounded when, during a craniosacral treatment, she realized that the idea that she could have compassion for herself had never even entered her mind. How many other people are like her? Her experience points out how much work we have to do to heal our culture.

> *No healing can occur without compassion.*
> —Deepak Chopra, MD

> *Kindness and compassion are among the principle*
> *things that make our life meaningful.*
> —Dalai Lama

Ideas about health and healing in our culture have been dominated by the conventional world view. Surgeons are fond of saying, "to cut is to cure," and they have a valid point when your appendix is about to burst. And placing stents in coronary arteries has prolonged countless lives. Insulin, inhalers, anti-hypertensives, and other medications are always staving off the inevitable. But these approaches are just managing your physiology and symptoms. By themselves, they do not necessarily help you free yourself from limiting beliefs or deepen your insight into yourself. We need to expand our views of healing. Using conventional and alternative medical treatments can be very helpful and supportive, but even more so if you also learn whatever lessons your experiences are holding for you. Ideally, you want to do both. So, use whatever treatments you need AND open your heart of hearts to yourself and receive the information waiting for you there. If we could all increase our understanding and embodiment of compassion, we could heal ourselves and all that we've done to each other and this planet.

Once my patients use their awareness and acceptance to get to the heart of the matter, they are constantly guided by their loving, wise inner guidance to just have compassion for whatever is. Their inner wisdom says: "have compassion for how you are feeling and for the experiences you went through that led to you feeling that way," or, "have compassion for how that person is treating you and for whatever is going on in that person that is motivating them to treat you that way." The inner knower becomes your compassion coach.

> *The therapeutic effect of compassion is infinite and immeasurable.*
> —Bernie Siegel MD

Compassion is many things. People often equate compassion with empathy. But compassion is more than that: it is more active, in some way. Paradoxically, while compassion is the ultimate form of being, it is also love in action; it is an open-hearted presence; it is unreserved kindness. But mostly, and this is critical for the right use of compassion, it is not a feeling in the messenger sense. You may have noticed in the discussion about feelings that love was not one of the four primary feelings (mad, sad, glad and fear.) How could that be? Love is so important. Being filled with love from head to toe is about as good as it gets. Our society has a saying: "love makes the world go 'round." So how could it not be an important feeling? This question had me stumped for a long time, until I thought about love in a different way.

This metaphor helped me understand love better:

Your brain is encased in your skull, floating safely in a very protected environment, surrounded by a moat and stone walls. Think of your brain as the king or queen, sitting on their throne inside their castle. The only way your brain knows what is going on around it is through the sensory data that comes in, like messengers coming to the castle from the four corners of the kingdom. What if the king or queen said, "I don't like those messengers coming in from the north. I'm not going to allow them an audience."? If you did that, you'd be cut off to part of your kingdom. You'd lose touch with what was happening. A foreign army could be building up on your northern border and you'd never know it. Feelings, whether physical or emotional, are messengers. It is bad form to chop the head off the messenger just because you don't like the message. Yet we do that to our feelings all the time.

Your feelings are messengers bringing you information about your kingdom. Love is not one of the messengers because love is the kingdom. Remember: "we all have our own issues we're working on and our own way of working on them, but we're all just trying to do the same thing: we're all just learning how to love better." Many world religions equate God with love. Since God is everything, everything is love. You are love; I am love; love is what the universe is made of. It is the basic building block, the predominant vibration of Consciousness. Since you are a divine spiritual being, love is who you are. Learning how to love is learning who you are; being kind and compassionate is being who you are: the very definition of healing. Rather than as a feeling, per se, compassion, as love in action, is more properly thought of as a *perspective,* a very truthful perspective, a place from which to view however you are feeling.

I learned this the hard way. When experienced as a feeling, compassion feels wonderful. It is very enticing and seductive, even intoxicating. It is the siren's song, potentially an addiction, since it can be used to supplant other feelings that your life is contriving for you to feel. When I was first learning these concepts, I had the idea—I put the should on myself—that I was supposed to be in the spiritual bliss of compassion all the time. I wanted to feel only that and not be bothered by frustrations, anger, fear, tiredness, physical pain, and all that lowly stuff. You can guess how well that worked. In order to stay in that place of bliss, I continually had to push all those other, very real feelings, which were clamoring for my attention, aside and remind myself that I was an enlightened, blissful being. Before too long, I blew up, melted down, crashed, and was totally bewildered by it all, not to mention feeling like a total failure (and irritating my wife).

Then I saw it. Feeling compassion instead of all my other feelings was just another way to practice avoidance, repression, denial, and other forms of focusing my creativity on what I don't want. Even though compassion feels like a feeling and can even be a feeling for a few moments, you run the risk of using it to put off the inevitable and avoid the truth. You stay stuck if all you want to do is feel good all the time. The right use of compassion is incredibly transformational; the wrong use is quicksand.

Compassion is indeed very powerful and we long for it, but we need to arrive at it, give it, and receive it in the right way. Compassion is not a feeling that you are supposed to feel *instead* of all of your other feelings. It is how you feel toward yourself *because* of how you are feeling. It is you holding your arms open wide ready to give yourself a big hug. It is letting yourself be enveloped in those loving arms while you watch yourself having your life. It is a place to stand from which to view yourself having your feelings and experiencing your present moment.

Our inner wisdom guides us to have compassion for ourselves for however we are feeling, for whatever we are experiencing, every single moment, no matter what. No matter how anyone else is treating you, no matter how anyone else is judging you or reacting to you, even if they are your parents or family, you are worthy of kindness, you can be kind to yourself. Their behavior towards you might be important information that you may want to take under advisement, but how someone responds to you or treats you says more about them and their lenses and beliefs than it does about you. No matter what your present moment holds for you, you can be kind to yourself. That is the right use of compassion.

A practice that often helps me with this is to end every observation about myself with "…and I can be kind to myself about that." For example, if I'm feeling tension in my shoulders and a headache coming on, I can say, "Oh, there is tension in my shoulders … and I can be kind to myself about that. I wonder what part of me is sending out the orders for that tension to be there and what is it trying to accomplish by doing that?"

See compassion as a point of view, a <u>way</u> of experiencing your feelings, a heuristic method for getting to know yourself. It is a platform to stand upon from which to view your life.

When you are identified with the aspect of yourself for which compassion is the dominant perspective, such as your inner love (the fifth aspect of yourself in the Vedic model of a human being), you just naturally see things differently than when you are identified with your more limited or fearful aspects (generally parts of your conscious mind, your ego). I have noticed that the more I practice compassion for what is, the more compassion becomes what is—that is, the more compassion gets mirrored back.

Remember the story of June, the woman who had such a severe childhood and had learned to dissociate in order to deal with it all. Despite all that she had gone through, she remained kind and caring toward others. But it was not until she could extend that same level of kindness and understanding to herself that she was able to stay in her body long enough to be with its pain, to be open enough to hear its anger, and to be accepting enough of her present situation to start to change. That alone took months of practice on her part. The right use of compassion really does work wonders.

Try this practice: take as long as you need right now to go inside and put yourself in that place of compassion, put your awareness into your heart area and let it expand. Now look at how you are feeling, look at what is happening in your life. How does it look from this perspective? What new thoughts and feelings come up inside when you view your present circumstances from this compassionate place? When you view your life from the perspective of compassion, you often see the behind the scenes workings of things; you often see the reasons why people around you treat you the way that they do; you often see options that you didn't know you had.

Stephanie harbored a lot of anger toward her mother. She felt like her mother was always cold, distant, and judgmental of her. Her mother never had a kind word for her, had always been excessively strict and un-empathetic. As we worked on her anger and she was able to open her heart to herself for what it was like to be a sensitive little girl with a mother like that, she had a flash of insight about what her mother's life had been like when her mother was little. She saw that the abuse her mother experienced and how her mother had compensated for it led her to be that way. Granted, her mother could have used the experience of having a child to heal her own wounds, but good healing tools were not readily available to people of her mother's generation and earlier. Stephanie was able to not only open her heart to herself but also to her mother.

The insights she had during that session and the perspective of compassion allowed her to reframe her anger completely. Once she had those insights, she was better able to see her mother for just who she was, accept her for being that way, and not need or expect her to be any different. Usually what heals a (by then adult) child's relationship with their parents is to do just what Stephanie did: see their parents for just the human beings that they are and then not need them to be any different. The compassionate perspective often shows the adult child how to make this change.

When you view your present moment through the lens or from the angle of compassion, how you are feeling in that moment will change automatically; that cannot be helped. But you must continue to be mindful, continue to be the kind, understanding observer and just watch as compassion changes your feelings at its own pace. When compassion becomes your way of looking upon your truth, you can leave your truth alone. You can get out of the fix it mode and just be. The saying "let go and let God" captures this idea.

Practice compassion for what is, not instead of what is. Practice viewing your present moment through compassion instead of practicing trying to change whatever is happening in your feelings or body. Remember, you can spend your energy trying to change what has already been created or you can spend your energy changing whatever is directing your creative flow.

Compassion is the alchemist; compassion informs and directs the change that is in your highest good. You don't need to force anything.

Whatever you need to do in order to respond to the present moment in a healthy way (tool seven) will make itself known.

I cannot emphasize this enough, as I am not the only person who has been caught in this trap. Once you start to open up to compassion in your life, you are often tempted to stay steeped in it, oblivious to how you are feeling otherwise. We want to feel good. As one practitioner of a Buddhist path I spoke with about this put it, he thought he "needed to be shiny all the time." We don't want to feel pain, grief, depression, frustration, anxiety, loneliness, isolation, or rejection. (Seems like there are a lot more feelings we don't want than feelings we do, or is that just me?) Used this way, compassion becomes just one more way to avoid and deny how you are really feeling, and this keeps you stuck—just as stuck as if you had no compassion for yourself at all.

Remember, feelings are messengers; feelings are innocent. How you are feeling is not the problem, even if you hate feeling that way. There is something behind the feeling and that is the problem. If you don't let the feeling in and allow it to show you what is behind it, you are not likely to get to the root of the problem. You are not likely to uncover your truth and find out how to get free of the problem. As you practice compassion, please be watchful of this temptation. If you catch yourself really wanting to just rest in the place of compassion, I recommend you take a deep breath, admit to yourself what is going on, and choose to refocus your awareness into your body, see what information you are getting from your body right then. Admit the truth of it, and open your heart to it.

Something deep inside you tells you that it is possible to find inner bliss: that deep sense of peace and contentment that is independent of any of your earthly experiences. That bliss is what you are really searching for when you want to feel good, you long for it to the depth of your soul. You just can't find it by being dysfunctional with your feelings. Compassion, used skillfully, cures that dysfunction: compassion becomes your center. Practice compassion for yourself having your present moment and it will then make whatever changes you need to make inside in order to get your personal truth aligned with higher truth. This makes your next present moment better.

Once you see how Consciousness works, you will know that your compassion is for all of creation … and you are a part of creation. No one in the universe is more or less worthy of your love than you are; we are all equal in the love that we deserve; that is a spiritual truth. You are a whole, integrated being, and all parts of you are also part of creation. So this spiritual truth also means that all aspects of you, even those parts of yourself that you despise, fear, reject, and so forth, are also worthy of your love. Compassion is for all of you: every cell, every fiber, every vibration, every thought, every feeling, and every belief of your being. Even the ones that make you sick.

Compassion is a holistic practice, a unifying practice, a way to get very different forces or interests to work together. "Health" and "wholeness" come from the same root word. Thus health implies wholeness. Wholeness implies having complete and free access to all parts of yourself. You cannot be whole and be fragmented at the same time. Once you are healed, you will have unconditional acceptance of all aspects and parts of yourself. I don't know if consciously fostering that unconditional acceptance of self facilitates healing or if healing just allows for the unconditional acceptance of self to happen. But I do see the two going hand in hand in my patients all the time.

If you choose to practice unconditional acceptance of all aspects of yourself, I would recommend that you then pay very careful attention to the feelings that practice brings up. It may force limiting beliefs, self-judgments, and other blocks out of hiding and then you can use the seven tools to work with them. But I like to keep things simple. So, rather than use visualizations, affirmations, tapping, or any other technique to try to make yourself be a certain way, just practice compassion for what is and this will inevitably lead you to unconditionally accept and invite in all aspects of yourself. It will foster your growth toward wholeness.

Often practicing compassion is all that is needed to start the process of change. I call compassion the "the alchemist" because it takes a circumstance that feels like a lump of lead in your life and converts it into a lump of gold. The practice of compassion allows you to receive the spiritual gift hidden in every experience. The love steps in and finishes whatever change needs to happen once you open-heartedly accept your truth and stop pushing against it. You may have to start by practicing compassion for yourself for having control issues and how difficult it is to get out of the driver's seat and trust that a loving, wise part will take over and steer you in the right direction. You don't have to force it or fix it. Faith is very helpful until you practice compassion enough that you prove to yourself that it will indeed work the changes you are looking for.

Practicing compassion naturally invokes your deepest wisdom to call forth and create the best possible solution to your problem. That is why your ego-self does not need to be in the driver's seat. That is why you do not need to over-think things, analyze yourself, or get in there and fix anything. All you need to do is decide on your goals (hopefully in consultation with your inner knower), have faith, then practice compassionate, accepting awareness of your personal truth *in this moment*. This moment contains all the influences from the past and all the potentials of the future, so nothing more is needed. With enough practice, compassion becomes the genesis for the workings of your mind, the source of your thoughts and feelings, the choreographer of your creativity. This is when real change starts to happen. Have faith in the power of compassion and apply your will to the practice of observing your life through its lens: this is the surest path I've found back to inner peace, happiness, and fulfillment: to health. Let your heart lead the way.

Try this exercise: think of an issue that is challenging you right now, like how your supervisor at work is treating you, or tune into your body and see if there is any place of tension or pain, like in your neck or shoulders. Choose one of these examples to work with. Hold that example in your mind, think about it, see what feelings are coming up. While you are holding that example in your mind, clear an open-hearted place for yourself, perhaps by putting your awareness into your left chest and breathe expansion into that area. Now put whatever you are thinking about and how you are feeling into that open hearted space and just step back and watch. What do you notice about your example when you view it from that open-hearted perspective? Do you see anything about it you hadn't noticed before? What are you feeling in your body? Has it changed? Ask your example how it wants you to be with it right now, what it needs from you in the way of help. Bring as much kindness to yourself and to your example and to yourself having to deal with this example as you can muster. What happens to your body, what do you feel?

To put the discussion in energetic terms, what would you say is the dominant vibration or frequency in your heart? What would you guess is the most dominant vibration in God's heart, or the heart of the universe? How different or similar could they be? Once you begin to grasp the scope of compassion, you will see how one could say that compassion *is* your true authentic self. To view your life from that place of compassion or through the lens of compassion is to see the world in a true way. The compassionate perspective will show you your truth and your truth shall set you … FREE.

The more I see people work with compassion in their lives, the more in awe I feel. I've witnessed people find the simplest, most elegant, and workable solutions to their problems when they view their life from that place of compassion. The woman who had never thought to be kind to herself was completely astounded by the concept. She said it felt so good to finally get off of her own back. You take on how you were raised as if it is your primary language. You keep treating yourself the way you were treated without even thinking about it … until you hit a brick wall. Your thoughts and actions have ramifications and consequences. If you want to be healthy, you've got to start thinking and acting in healthy ways. Let the love in your heart heal your wounds. In fact, in all my years of practice, the liberal application of compassion is the only salve I've ever seen really heal someone.

Believe it or not, I used the metaphor of applying compassion like a salve before I heard of Martha Beck[81]. Her understanding of the power of compassion is amazing. And she's got a great way of expressing it. I highly recommend her work; I think you'll see how nicely it fits with the seven tools.

Relationships

If you want to have a healthy relationship with yourself, practice compassionate, accepting awareness of your personal truth. Then your self-relationship can be the foundation for all of the other relationships you have with those around you. Unless you've done the work to heal it, chances are the relationship you formed with your mother when you were a baby functions as the default foundation or template or archetype for all of your relationships. Occasionally, I meet someone for whom that relationship is wonderful, supportive, and strong. But, for so many of the people I see with chronic health problems, that primary relationship is very dysfunctional.

Your relationship with your mother sets the stage for three major themes in your life. First, you tend to expect the whole world to keep treating you the way that your mother treated you (and, as you now know from beliefs, these expectations become self-fulfilling prophases). Second, you tend to keep treating yourself the way your mother treated you. And, third, you tend to treat others the way your mother treated you. This was the hardest for me to accept when I first started working on my mother relationship.

But once you heal your relationship with yourself, once you step up and claim back the right to define yourself, others' opinions of you be damned, that relationship becomes your foundation. The relationships you have with others are so intertwined with the relationship you have with yourself that they can be viewed as mirrors into yourself. Your relationships can be used as another avenue for you to get to know yourself better and thus advance your healing.

Relationships are tricky, though. I think that the work required to have healthy relationships is probably the most difficult work we do. On one hand, how someone reacts to you … how they treat you, what they say to you … is a direct result of how you appear to them as they peer at you through their own structure of interpretation. So, within reason, how someone else treats you is revealing to you their own inner processes. And how someone else responds to you is outside of your jurisdiction. You cannot control others. I like this paraphrasing of the serenity prayer:

"God grant me the serenity to accept the people I cannot change, the courage to change the one I can, and the wisdom to know it's me."

On the other hand, perhaps as a result of hundreds of thousands of years of tribal life, we seem to be hard-wired to take personally what others say about us and do to us, as if their actions are a direct reflection on us. We seem instinctively to give others the power to define who we are in our own eyes. We often draw conclusions about who we are based on the way other people treat us. This definition is inevitably limiting and you need to free yourself from it in order to continue to grow. For most of my patients, a great deal of awareness and practice is required in order for them to reclaim the power to define themselves, independent of how they got treated by their parents, extended family, teachers, and society in general. But doing so is very healing. Stand up and claim your right to define yourself. Compassion for yourself as you go through this process is crucial.

Even though how someone responds to you depends upon their own belief structure, at the same time, how they respond to you gives you a chance to look inside and get to know yourself better. As we talk about relationships, please remember that they are symbolic mirrors, not literal mirrors. Just like any other sensory information, what goes on in a relationship generates feelings in you. Those feelings are messengers bringing you information about your own inner processes. See the discussion about relationships in the chapter on Awareness.

Learn to keep one eye on what is going on between you and the people you are relating to and one eye on what is going on inside of yourself as a result of what is going on around you. Then just take whatever feelings come up and apply Rule Number One and the three A's to them. (Quick refresher course: Rule Number One states that "all feelings are valid." The first "A" stands for "awareness" of the feeling. The second "A" stands for "acceptance." Accept the truth of your present moment—all that is happening to you and however you feel about it. The third "A" stands for "ask" the feeling to take you to its roots. No need to do anything to make it any different than it is. Just be with it and it will take you to its roots or it will resolve in its own way.) The feelings will lead you to your beliefs and then you can open your heart to them and get them aligned with higher truth.

Please keep in mind that relationships are complicated. Rarely are issues in them cut and dried. The wise person does not let another define them but takes others' opinions into consideration or under advisement when exploring their own inner workings.

Another way that relationships offer you information about yourself has to do with patterns that keep coming up in them. Patterns in your outer relationships are reflections of patterns in how different parts of you are relating to each other inside. If you find that you keep getting treated the same way in multiple relationships, there is a very good chance that you have aspects of yourself inside that are treating each other the same way.

Recognizing patterns in your relationships and then looking inside to see if you can find similar patterns in how you are treating yourself can be powerfully healing. But, as with all powerful ideas, this one can get twisted around and misused. I talk to a lot of people about using relationships as a way to look into themselves and I've encountered some people who are very sensitive to any hint of blaming the victim. In their intent, I'm right there with them. If you blame the person who got raped for being too suggestive or seductive or if you blame the person who got beaten by her husband for making him angry, you are not only adding another layer of wounds to an already horrific situation (the opposite of compassion), you are not seeing the dynamics of the situation correctly and will never get to the real roots of the problem.

If you get abused in a relationship, that is not your fault. You don't ask to be abused and the abuser is still responsible and legally liable for their actions. If you stay in an abusive relationship or find that you get into multiple relationships that feel really good at the beginning but then turn abusive, you will have to look at yourself and make some substantial changes inside if you are ever to break these patterns in your life.

Upon closer inspection, you will see that the "relationships as mirrors" way of looking at relationships is not blaming the victim, for two reasons. First, we are not victims. And second, there is no blame. Let me explain.

Since you don't consciously control everything in your life, the victim perspective makes rational sense and is easy to adopt. Children don't ask to be sexually abused by adults, people don't ask to get cancer, or to have their house burn down. "Shit happens" really does seem to be one of the highest truths in this universe. But I've never seen anyone heal from any of these experiences and remain a victim of them at the same time. "Victimhood" and "healthy" seem to be incompatible states that cannot coexist in the same person at the same time.

You have to find a way out of the victim perspective, no matter how logical being the victim appears to be, if you want to be healthy. Being a victim denies your divinity. Being a victim breaks the laws of Consciousness. If bad things just happen to us, how do we get out of the victim mentality? The solution lies in realizing that being a victim and being victimized are not the same thing. Being a victim is a way of seeing yourself, a way of identifying yourself; being victimized is an experience you go through. Being victimized can be a powerful experience, one that should not be ignored. Like any experience, it is an opportunity to deepen your understanding of yourself and come more into your power, both to heal from the experience of being victimized and also to change any patterns inside that could potentially keep creating such experiences.

There is no concept of blame in a world view that supports healing. Let me explain. We are all just learning (see Appendix B). It is not our fault if we don't know something, even if the information has been presented to us several times. You have your own timing and your own reasons for what you do or do not know. It is not fair for you to judge yourself for not knowing something and it's not fair for me or anyone else to judge you for not knowing something. You wouldn't go into a kindergarten class and blame all the students for not knowing differential calculus. At least, I hope you wouldn't.

If you have the kind of internal relationships going on that lead to painful external relationships, that is not your fault; it is your opportunity. The internal relationships are plenty painful in their own right; you are not consciously choosing to create more pain for yourself. The outer relationships just symbolize your inner relationships; your outer relationships are there to get your attention, to help you see your inner relationships and do something constructive to heal them. There is no blame, only invitations to heal. Your conscious ego-self is not responsible for your life, it is responsible to your life.

The inner aspects of yourself are relating to each other in your unconscious mind. If you knew about them, they wouldn't be unconscious. Just as your body can talk to you about issues that you've buried or repressed, your outer relationships are trying to get your attention, trying to get you to bring your painful inner relationships into the light of consciousness so that you can heal them. The healing comes through increasing your capacity to have compassion for yourself, all that you've gone through, and all that you are currently going through.

As you heal the imbalances in your life that are creating your symptoms, your relationship with yourself will just naturally heal. But you will most likely also come to a point in your personal growth where you want to work directly on your inner relationships. This can be an amazing part of your journey. Your inner life is a magical place. You have inside of you every character in your dreams, every character in mythology. You have a king and queen, a prince and princess, a troll, a toad, a witch, a jester, a sage, a fool, a pirate, a knight, a mad scientist, an angel, a devil, and even God. You also have inside an eagle, a whale, a bear, an ant, a fox, a rabbit, and every other aspect of nature. Mythology is the sum total of our cultural understanding of how these aspects relate to each other inside of us.

Some aspects of your inner life you will like, some you will not. Some you will welcome, some you will exile (or most likely already have). Some you are proud of, some ashamed of; some you celebrate, some you berate. There is a lot going on inside of you. I am reminded of a button someone gave me: "You may think I am lazy, but on a cellular level, I'm really quite busy." And that's just on the physical level. Every one of your inner aspects, as different and varied as they may be, thinks it has your best interest at heart. It may have gotten its start because it had a job to do for you at a particular age or during a particular experience. Now that you are older, have learned more, and grown, perhaps you don't need that job done anymore. For example, perhaps you've been through enough therapy and developed new and better ways to work with your feelings that your inner protector doesn't have to hide painful childhood experiences from your conscious mind anymore. You can face it, you can confront and accept the truth of whatever happened to you and apply Rule Number One and the three A's to whatever feelings come up.

Remember, all of you is on the same team. And teams work better when the members all work together for the greater good rather than fight against each other for their own personal gain. How do you have healthy relationships with all these different personalities, these different energies, these different needs, these different points of view? How do you get them all to work together?

Our language holds a clue to the answer. To review, "health" and "wholeness" come from the same root word. Health implies wholeness. Wholeness implies having full and truthful access to all of you. You cannot be healthy and fragmented at the same time. So, when you practice awareness of all the different aspects of your life that we discussed in Chapter Four, you come into your wholeness. Then, the practice of acceptance, as discussed in Chapter Five, opens you to the truth of your wholeness. Compassion tells us that every aspect of you, every cell, ever fiber, every inner quality is worthy of honor and respect. So the first step in having a healthy relationship with yourself is to choose to treat every part of yourself with honor and respect, even the parts that appear to be causing all the problems. This is a very important choice for you to make because it honors a law of Consciousness: you are worthy of honor and respect; therefore, through the principle of wholeness, every aspect of you is also worthy of honor and respect.

The next step is to hear every part's story. Don't assume. Ask the trouble-maker to tell you its side of the story. How does your life look from its perspective? How has it been serving you? What does it need? How can you help it? How would it rather be serving you now? How does it want you to be with it? Try to hold off making any decisions until every part of you that wants to has had a chance to be heard. Every part of you has a right to its day in court, so to speak.

Next, try to find a solution to the problem that honors all of you. This is decision-making by consensus. No part of you gets silenced, bulldozed, repressed, or denied. The needs of every part of you get taken into account. If you search hard enough or learn to listen to your wise, loving inner guidance, a win-win solution can generally be found to whatever problem your inner aspects are having with each other. Spoiler alert: this often results in all parts of yourself treating each other with honor and respect as well as having compassion for themselves and each other.

If you have parts of yourself that you have exiled but you then say to the universe, "I'm sick and tired of being sick and tired. I want to be healthy!" because health equals wholeness, what the exiled parts hear is, "Oh, good. She wants me back." They come running up only to find the door slammed in their faces. They stand outside howling and banging on the door, and we call this phenomenon "symptoms." Symptoms are often an invitation to invite in and integrate separated parts of yourself. Most of my patients are initially reluctant to do this because there are generally good reasons why they exiled those parts. The aspects might be crazy, scary, dishonest, angry, hurt, or hurtful.

Once you become aware of these distanced parts of yourself, the next step is acceptance. These parts need to be accepted just as they are. You can't say to that smelly part, "I'll let you in after you take a shower." Well, you can ... but it generally won't transform anything. Acceptance needs to be unconditional. Extending unconditional acceptance toward yourself in all of your complexity is an act of compassion. It will help you heal.

Start looking at your outer relationships as vehicles to help carry you further along your path of self-knowing. Start to watch your feelings as you interact with the people in your life. Let those feelings deliver their message, see the fundamental beliefs behind them. See how those beliefs look from a kind, wise, understanding perspective. Look for repeating patterns. See if you can find inner aspects of yourself that are relating to each other in a similar pattern. Use honor and respect, unconditional acceptance, and consensus to help your inner aspects work things out and get along better. See if your outer relationships start to change.

Responsibility

The topic of victimhood always brings up the concept of personal responsibility. As I've mentioned, I've never seen someone heal and remain a victim at the same time. You need to find and change the beliefs that make your experiences generate the feelings of victimhood. People who are healthy just naturally take personal responsibility for their lives. Whenever you feel like you don't have personal responsibility for your life, take the time to explore your feelings and see what beliefs are underneath. Many of my patients have used the seven tools to change their beliefs and transcend victimhood.

A major tenet of New Age philosophy states "you create your own reality." This is certainly one way to take responsibility for your life: you created it; it's yours; if you don't like it, create a different one. If only it were that simple. Did you ask for today to be rainy or sunny? Did you ask to get stuck in that traffic? Did the people in the Trade Towers ask for 9/11?

I have had difficulty with "you create your own reality" because whether or not it is true depends upon your definition of "reality" and which "you" you're referring to. If, to you, reality means your perspective or view of the universe, then each of us has our own reality because we each have our own unique structure of interpretation. You then do, on some level, create your own reality because your perspective is determined by what you believe and, with practice, you get to choose what to believe. That is a major premise of this book.

But if, by reality, you mean what happens to you, then you don't create that. There are forces in your life larger than your ego-self. Conceivably, you could create all that happens to you if you have already mastered all the laws of nature and Consciousness, or if you are God yourself. Years ago, I listened to an audio CD of Deepak Chopra talking about the higher self[82]. I remember him saying something to the effect, "You are not in your body...your body is in you. You are not in this world...the world is in you. And you are not even in this Universe...the Universe is in you." If your ego-self has merged with and is now indistinguishable from your higher self, then I guess I'm okay with you claiming that you create your own reality.

When I hear someone say, "You create your own reality" I'm always reminded of the story of Job in the Old Testament. Here's the sweet and condensed version. Job's sitting there, all his ships are lost at sea, all of his cattle have died, all of his family has died, he's covered from head to toe with boils, and one of his friends asks him what he did to bring all this on himself. Old Testament New Age philosophy. His answer, of course, was, "I'm the same in my heart as you are. I didn't do anything to bring this on." His friend even invokes the circular argument that "even denying that you've sinned is sin enough." Of course, we know the back story. We know that God is just letting Satan test Job's faith in him. If anything, Job could be angry with God for letting Satan toy with him like that. But Job doesn't even go there.

The story of Job is not about patience, as our society seems to think, it is about faith. Job never cursed God for his experiences and, in the end, was restored. (Though I don't quite know how he got his family back. There seems to be a discontinuity near the end of the book that perhaps was cut out during translation somewhere.) The point is, Job didn't create that reality for himself, unless you argue that, if you're going to be a super-good servant of God's, then you're going to get tested and He's going to let Satan toy with you and you're supposed to know that ahead of time when you're choosing to be such a good servant. You see how circular and ridiculous the justifications for "you create your own reality" can get?

We had a good friend who was in a head-on collision that was of her doing. The woman she hit was killed. Our friend believed so strongly that her soul and this woman's soul contracted before birth for this to happen that she felt no remorse or sadness about what happened. Perhaps her beliefs helped her stay out of pain and remorse, perhaps her beliefs kept her from deeply exploring her experience and learning from it, perhaps her beliefs are true. Who's to say? Unfortunately and tragically, sometime later, she did commit suicide. I cannot help but wonder whether or not repressed and strongly resisted feelings eventually caught up to her and were unbearable. Regardless of what is true, holding compassion in our hearts when we go through such horrendous experiences can only help.

What if the Book of Job is trying to tell us about an important aspect of Consciousness? What if we don't always create all aspects of our reality—and there is such a thing as divine intervention—and what if no matter what happens, we're supposed to keep the faith? Then where does the concept of responsibility come in?

We are creative beings and we do create much of our life. But most of our creativity is taking place unconsciously, most of the time. And sometimes cumulative forces can overpower our own creativity. The Jewish people in Europe did not ask for Hitler. So, for the purposes of a healing world view, responsibility does not mean that you caused it; responsibility means you have an ability to respond.

No matter what life puts in your path, there is some possible way for you to respond. Your job is to figure out what response is the most appropriate; what response is in alignment with your best healing. The response that is most in alignment with healing, that is most loving for all of creation, is often called "right action." This is the seventh of the seven tools. Practice the first six tools faithfully and the right way to act will make itself known.

Each and every moment, with every experience, you can learn more about who you are, about your personal power: how you hold onto it and how you give it away.

Community

The topics of relationship and responsibility bring up the idea of community. As humans, we are social beings. We've lived in groups of one sort or another for all of our existence as a species. In fact, one might argue that the loss of our claws and fangs, the development of our big brains, language, and tools are all direct results of being social creatures. And now, there is mounting evidence that participating in a healthy community has more influence upon your health than smoking, diet, exercise, and stress. In addition to your own direct relationship with spirit, participating in a healthy community is also a foundation for your sense of safety in life.

We've had examples down through history of the health benefits of healthy community and what happens to people when that community is lost. When the Europeans first came to the Americas, the indigenous people they found were so healthy that they spawned the concept of the "noble savage." The early explorers wondered whether they'd found a people who had not been kicked out of the Garden of Eden. Unfortunately, the Native Americans' community did not protect them from the European strain of small pox. When small pox passed through a Native American village, it could quickly kill nine out of every ten people. Imagine what would happen to our social fabric if nine out of ten of us disappeared. They quickly lost the protective element of their community and the rest is history.

Entire books can be—and have been—written about the effects of community on health[83]. Given what we've said about healing, what aspects of community might be particularly healing? There are so many varieties of community. What makes one supportive of its members' health while another might actually contribute to its member's diseases? The healthy community will have many of the same traits as does the healthy person: all aspects are being listened to, the needs of all aspects are being met. The best way to construct a community like this is for each member to adopt whatever belief structure they need to in order to act with unreserved kindness. Imagine a society in which every member is kind to themselves, to each other, and to the planet. Imagine a community that is governed by the process of consensus. (Democracy, as good as it is (assuming it even exists in practice), is still just a sophisticated way to do "might is right," with the will of the majority being the might. There is always a disenfranchised, unrepresented minority. Hardly wholeness.)

Healing work is generally not easy. Even though we have within us all that we need for our healing, we need each other to access and utilize it. That is another paradox of being human. We need to be seen and heard. If possible, surround yourself with people who can see you and appreciate you for being who you are; befriend people who can see your quirks and allow you to have them. Be the kind of person who offers that to others. Judgmental and repressive communities impede healing.

If possible, immerse yourself in a milieu of love. Surround yourself with people who are also actively pursuing their healing in a good way. Play to your strengths and find people whose skills complement yours. Not every family of origin meets these criteria. You may need to create your own community outside your family or try to find a good circle of friends. Just know that you are not alone.

We are getting to the point where we can no longer ignore the health effects of community. There are so many people in our culture who are working tirelessly to get healthy, all the while staying immersed in a dysfunctional community. Their efforts are reaping only mediocre results. Diet and exercise are only going to prevent so much heart disease and cancer. And healthy community may be the best answer we have to problems such as gun violence, crime, and addiction. We need to work consciously to create community. It may be difficult at first, but it will be a positive feedback loop. It takes healthy people to make a healthy community. Healthy communities raise healthier people. And off the spiral goes in an upward direction.

Summary

Compassion is quite literally at the very center of the seven tools of healing … for good reason. Compassionate, accepting awareness of what is true is the surest path to healing I've ever witnessed. Give that to yourself. Practice, practice, practice … as if your very life and the lives of the ones you love depends upon it; because it does. As you become more compassionate toward yourself, you give permission to those around you to be more compassionate toward themselves, and the seeds of health sprout and grow. The final three of the seven tools naturally follows from practicing compassionate accepting awareness of what is.

Chapter Seven

Forgiveness

The first four tools—faith, awareness, acceptance, and compassion— are the workhorses for the process of lasting, authentic, healing change. You will find that using them gets much easier with practice. These four tools do many things for you. They help you:

- To source your creative flow from love rather than from the messenger emotions.
- Have a healthy relationship with your feelings.
- Receive the clues from your life and reliably follow them to the treasure, which is your true, authentic self.
- Be able to stay healthy in the face of stress.
- Heal any addictions you may have.
- Heal many other health issues.

In essence, they help you heal your life, whatever that means to you.

To review before we jump into new concepts, here is how they work: on a foundation of choosing to have faith in whatever helps you the most, you practice holding a compassionate, accepting awareness of whatever is your truth right now; then you become aware of your next thought, feeling or issue; accept the truth of it; open your heart to it; and so the spiral goes … deeper and deeper into the understanding of who you are and how you work.

Every experience that registers in your mind generates a feeling. Every thought, everything you see, hear, taste, touch, or smell is associated with a feeling. All of the clues coming to you from your life get translated into feelings. This means that if you learn to work skillfully with your feelings, you can also work skillfully with all of your clues. Your feelings are just messengers from your deeper workings, the result of your thoughts or sensory information passing through that rack of lenses in your psyche called your structure of interpretation. How you are feeling is never the problem. Rather than working to control them, work to get the message and then use that information to know your truth and inform your choices.

Many self-help techniques teach you how to control your thoughts and make new beliefs to gain more conscious control over your creative powers. But you will most likely layer your newly desired beliefs on top of all of your old beliefs that are still in your unconscious mind. They will sit in there, lurking in the shadows, scheming and plotting, waiting for just the right moment to trip you up. You need to keep putting effort into maintaining the new beliefs in order to keep the old ones at bay. The second you have any chink in your armor, or get fatigued, or distracted, or life calls your attention to something else, you risk reverting back to your old patterns where you continue creating more of what you already have.

But when you connect your conscious sense of who you are to your inner wisdom, your thoughts and beliefs just naturally align themselves to your highest good and you don't have to control them to have the life you want.

The practice of the first four tools is an excellent way to naturally and effortlessly generate the thoughts and beliefs that free you from bondage; that give you the freedom that is your birthright. The last three tools follow naturally from this practice.

When you bring enough compassionate awareness to a situation, forgiveness just naturally happens. **Forgiveness is the fifth tool.**

Every major world religion teaches forgiveness. Forgiveness is crucial for healing, both for you as an individual and for us as a society. But even with all the talk and advice about forgiveness that abounds in our society, I find that many of my patients still have misconceptions about it.

Forgiveness does not mean that you condone what was done; it does not mean that you forget. If you were sexually abused as a child, for example, forgiving the abuser does not mean that what that person did to you is ever okay. And forgiving your abuser does not mean that you ever need to or ought to forget what happened to you or that you need to start having a relationship with that person. Forgiveness is not for your abuser. Forgiveness is for you: to lighten your own load, to help you with your own growth.

When you are hurt or abandoned or betrayed, who is being affected if you hold on to your feelings of anger, your resentments, or your desire for revenge? Generally, how you are left feeling after being abused is no skin whatsoever off of the abuser's nose. In fact, staying hurt and angry might just increase the enjoyment they experienced from hurting you. The best revenge you can inflict upon your abuser is to go on and have a happy, fulfilling life. You can do that by practicing the seven tools of healing. Follow your hurt feelings to their source, see the truth about how that experience is still affecting you, and be incredibly kind to yourself that you have all that going on inside. Once you have enough compassion for yourself having been hurt, the forgiveness just comes all on its own. Forgiving that person and that experience is for you, for your own benefit and freedom.

Forgiveness is essential; otherwise you risk loading yourself up with unresolved baggage. Like Gandhi said, "If we live by 'An eye for an eye and a tooth for a tooth' the whole world would be blind and toothless." If it is for you, if it is the guidance you receive from your inner wisdom, you could be the one to take the first step toward forgiveness. The past does not have to determine your future. Forgiveness allows you to let go of any deleterious influences from the past and move forward into the future your wisdom wants to create for you. You have the motivation: you're the one with pain and disability.

Just as the whole of creation, including yourself, can be viewed with compassion, the whole of creation, including yourself, is eminently forgivable. When you hurt someone else, make a mistake, or fall short of your self-expectations, you may have feelings of guilt, regrets, or self-flagellations. Don't beat yourself up about that. Those feelings are just information. Follow them back to their roots and be kind to yourself about whatever you find there. Holding onto and reinforcing those kinds of feelings is often what your ego does when it believes that you don't deserve or are inadequate. Any beliefs you hold that say that you are inadequate or don't deserve spiritual bliss and earthly comforts are false beliefs by definition, because you are a divine being. So forgiving yourself is just as important as forgiving others. Do that by practicing compassionate, accepting awareness of your truth.

I know there is controversy around the issue of forgiveness. Some people interpret the Christian doctrine as stating that only God can forgive you; you can't forgive yourself. They say that the teachings say you forgive others but all you can do is ask for forgiveness for yourself. This may be true to some extent ... for example, you can't force someone else to forgive you. In fact, what someone else thinks, feels, or believes about you is none of your business.

But as to the issue of self-forgiveness, I would say two things. First, the notion that you cannot forgive yourself is not how I've witnessed people's inner wisdom working with forgiveness. It is constantly coaching people to be kinder to themselves, to get off of their own backs about things, to lighten up toward themselves. When a person brings enough compassion to a situation, whether they were the abused or the abuser, forgiveness just naturally follows. And forgiveness arrived at through the practice of compassion is transformational and global. By transformational, I mean that when a person reaches that realization of forgiveness by way of compassion, their relationship with that issue is forever changed. Emotional buttons are no longer buttons, anger cools, the need for revenge wanes, tension patterns in the body change. By global, I mean that the forgiveness applies to all of creation; and you are a part of creation. Therefore, you can forgive yourself.

Second, and this is from a Judeo/Christian perspective, I'd say perhaps this is another instance where you, as a child of God, can have characteristics in common with your Father in Heaven. God is compassionate and so can you be; God forgives, and so can you. Limiting your access to forgiveness limits your access to healing. Why would any true tradition teach something that is counter to or that blocks healing? I think the difference of opinion around the issue of self-forgiveness lies in the interpretations of the teachings, not in the teachings themselves. If you are a Christian, forgiving yourself is in perfect alignment with Christian theology, except, perhaps, when it is interpreted by people who want to use that theology to repress and control you.

Generally, whenever you find yourself in a situation in which you have to ask others for their forgiveness or to forgive yourself, it is because you've made a mistake. Richard Miller, Ph.D.[84] suggested seven steps to remedy a mistake:

1. Empathize with the other. Put yourself in their shoes.
2. Look at the situation in such a way as to be able to take 100% of your own responsibility for it.
3. Learn from it.
4. Make amends if possible—"How can I make it up to you?"
5. Apologize.
6. Forgive yourself for the mistake.
7. Let it go and see if it happens again. (Don't do this step until you've done the first six.)

Please make note of step number six: forgiving yourself is a major step in resolving or effectively responding to your own mistakes. If you don't forgive yourself, how can you ever learn from your mistakes and move on in your life?

Forgiveness is truly a letting go. Once forgiveness has happened, that issue or experience, whether it is you getting hurt or you hurting someone else, is no longer a button, there is no emotional rise or charge. You know that your thoughts direct your creativity. If your thoughts are filled with images of revenge and vengeance, of anger and resentment, of self-deprecation, even self-hatred, you will continue to create life experiences that reinforce these thoughts and feelings. That is one reason why "Honor Societies"—cultures that put a high value on saving face and such—are at risk of forming long-standing family feuds[85]. Forgiveness frees. Forgiveness lightens your burden, finishes unfinished business, and increases your connection to love and wisdom.

Again, you do not have to exert effort to repress, deny, or ignore painful, angry, or unsupportive thoughts and feelings. Just view all these through the lens of compassion. When enough compassion has been brought to the experience, forgiveness just follows, like water overflowing a container. Each situation and person varies in terms of how much compassion that takes. The inner wisdom coaches people to keep practicing compassion until that point is reached. That the feelings of anger, the need for revenge, the need for self-flagellation naturally cease is a clue that forgiveness has happened.

Real forgiveness has the power to change your physiology. I feel this while doing bodywork on people. As they are more and more able to view their circumstances through compassion, they reach a place where forgiveness just makes sense and I feel the release in their tissues. It often feels like a big knot somewhere in their body unravels.

Forgiveness is essential for moving forward, for the healing of life's inevitable hurts and injustices. Without forgiveness, your emotional load builds up until you become burdened, even immobilized. You may feel overwhelmed and trapped. Just be kind to yourself about that.

Many people practice forgiveness as part of their religion but, here again, I recommend caution. Saying that you've forgiven or acting as though you've forgiven while you still have anger inside that has not yet found a peaceful place to settle in (whether you consciously know it or not) doesn't transform or free you. Forgiveness that is forced or contrived or mustered as an act of will does not have the same power to transform as does forgiveness arrived at naturally through the practice of compassion.

Just as the inner knower encourages you to practice compassion for all of creation (including yourself), it also coaches you to practice forgiveness for all of creation (including yourself). If all of life is a chance to learn more about yourself, and the Divine is the teacher, then, when something happens that you really don't like, forgiveness is admitting the existence of divine intervention in your life (a definition of forgiveness that I first heard from Carolyn Myss[86]). In other words, you could see the person who hurt you as spirit's pawn, doing what they needed to do in order to bring you that particular aspect of your curriculum.

I have to admit that I have a little bit of trouble with this kind of world view. I do not think that any child creates their own sexual abuse, even on a spiritual level. For example, one afternoon Sue came in for her regular visit. We'd been working on healing the residual effects of child abuse that she'd experienced at the hands of a neighbor. She was also a follower of Gurumayi[87], a swami in the Siddha Yoga tradition[88]. I'd met Gurumayi in person earlier, when she was in Seattle, and Sue and I agreed to ask her essence to come be with us in the room during the treatment. As we started the craniosacral therapy, I felt a great peacefulness fill the room. As Sue was working on her issues silently at the time, I decided to ask Gurumayi a few questions of my own.

I asked her how it could be God's plan that Sue should go through the sexual abuse she did as a child. She replied (and this conversation was going on silently inside my own head, mind you), that it wasn't God's plan that Sue get treated that way. But it was God's plan that human beings have free will; otherwise, we'd be no different, really, than the tall fir trees outside the window. In order for us to have free will, God has to let us make mistakes. But that's also why God created healing. Sue would heal from her abuse, and she would find inner strengths and resources that she didn't know she had. But to gain these skills and strengths was not "why" Sue was abused. She was abused because the abuser was living so far from his heart (and in her neighborhood). The abuser was unhealed; the abuser was confused: he had no clue about who he really was inside. He did not know how to live from kindness and respect. He thought he was his own wounds and acted from there.

Gurumayi showed me that most of the hurts in the world are due to people harboring this kind of confusion. She also showed me that all of the suffering caused by man's inhumanity to man is still better than humanity not having free will. Healing from the hurts is possible. Each of us learning how to overcome that confusion and find our true heart is possible. Giving up our free will is tantamount to giving up our divinity—and that is counter to God's plan. Sue would heal from her abuse by reclaiming her sovereignty and desensitizing her PTSD (and she gave me some good suggestions about how to help Sue do that). And the abuser would heal when he opened his heart, but that was the abuser's own healing path to walk; that wasn't up to us.

Your free will is a most amazing result of your divinity. You relinquish it at great peril to your soul. Since free is such an important aspect of who you are, and being who you are is healing, when you forfeit your freedom, you forfeit your health. Your freedom is your birthright; it is for you to explore, to use to find out who you truly are, underneath the assumptions, the domestication (as Don Miguel Ruiz, MD[89] called it), the wounding. There are natural consequences to every one of your free choices. So there is healing for when you screw up. If I am confused about who I am in my heart and I do something to hurt you, healing is possible (for both of us).

If you are confused about who you are in your heart and do something to hurt me, healing is possible. If we are confused about who we are in our hearts and do things to hurt ourselves, healing is possible. It's a great system, really. Ideally, if you choose to do so, your experiences will teach your head what your heart knows and then, ultimately, you will participate less and less in man's inhumanity to man (including toward yourself).

Without forgiveness, you risk spending an inordinate amount of time rethinking the past. You risk becoming overcome with questions. "What were they thinking?" "What should I have said or done instead?" Fantasizing about how things could have gone differently. You ask questions like: "what if my parents really could have seen me for who I am?" Thoughts get repeated over and over and over. Forgiveness is giving up all hope that the past will ever be any different. Forgiveness is acceptance of what was and is. There is no profit in railing against what is. Forgiveness frees you to redirect all of that ruminating mental energy toward creating a more appropriate future.

Forgiveness helps you transcend the concepts of guilt and fault. Forgiveness allows you to step into a healthy and true relationship with your responsibility, your ability to respond. The ability to respond is also right action, which is the seventh of the seven tools. Forgiveness prepares you for right action; forgiveness helps you take appropriate responsibility for your thoughts, actions, and life. Feeling guilty or finding fault are weakening levels of consciousness, according to David Hawkins M.D. Ph.D.[46], and keep you stuck, unable to see the truth of the situation. When you become aware that you are viewing life through the lenses of guilt or fault, practice compassion for yourself and ask to view your entire inner experience through spirit eyes.

Have you ever experienced really forgiving someone or something? When I'm working with someone with the bodywork and they reach a point where the light bulb goes on and forgiveness of whatever trauma we happen to be working with that session just makes sense (it sort of falls into place), I generally feel a palpable change in the tension patterns in their tissues. They often report feeling more relaxed, in less pain, lighter somehow. That is how forgiveness lessens the burdens that you carry. You may have noticed that forgiveness and acceptance are very closely related.

Both are *made easier by* compassion and, simultaneously, are *expressions of* compassion.

The idea that there is something worthwhile in every experience is found in every culture around the world. (Whenever a concept shows up in every major world tradition, I take that as a clue that this concept must be capturing some essential aspect of a universal truth.) Learning is always possible; healing is always possible. We can have faith, then, that the worth of the experience is there. Sometimes, we just have to look for it. As we are able to practice the first five tools, our clarity around whatever happened or is happening increases. We often start to receive the learning or healing that was embedded in the experience. Practicing the seven tools is an excellent way to do that exploration.

You don't consciously ask for most of what happens to you. On one hand, you can view your experiences as conscious feedback for what your unconscious creativity is up to: a wake-up call, a call to action to become more conscious of your creativity. On the other hand, some people prefer to see their challenges as gifts from spirit, the teacher presenting the next item of their curriculum. These views are complementary. On the third hand (did you know you have three hands?) many of the great world traditions explain what happens to you simply, if crudely, as "shit happens." Either way, as you run your daily experiences through the first five tools ... on a foundation of faith that who you are is enough, that healing is always possible, that you are loved and supported, practice awareness of the present moment in as much detail as you are able, accept the truth of what you are experiencing, both internally and externally, and open your heart to that truth and yourself in that present moment. As any necessary forgiveness falls into place, you start to find the gifts hidden in your experiences; you open to and receive the lessons that the present aspect of your life's curriculum is attempting to put across.

You start to appreciate the intricacies of synchronicity, as Jung[90] called it, to see just how incredible reality really is. You may even get a glimpse into the workings of the world behind the scenes, the genius and power of spirit moving in your life. Often in that moment, a chill will go up your back and you will be washed over with a feeling of awe. Have you ever experienced that? That moment when the light bulb goes on, when the blinders come off, when the pieces fall together, when events in your life are seen with crystal clarity?

Forgiveness frees a space in our hearts for gratitude
for this precious life that we all share.
—Madeline Ko-I Bastis

Chapter Eight

Gratitude

In those moments of epiphany, have you felt blessed, have you felt deeply cared for? Once you start to let in how truly supported you are in your life, you often feel humbled and grateful. This profound sense of "Thank You!" directed toward the universe or spirit is the sixth tool. I call it **Gratitude.**

In my office, when a person is working through a difficult experience in their life and they spontaneously reach that place of gratitude, generally after much exploration of their feelings and beliefs and much practice being very kind to themselves (along with treating any medical issues they have going on), I interpret the arrival of gratitude as an indication, as a marker, so to speak, that they've gotten the healing hidden in that difficult experience.

When you bring enough compassion to your particular situation and the forgiveness has had a chance to work its magic, the feeling of gratitude that grows in you is an indication that you've opened to, allowed in, and accepted the compassion that spirit always feels toward you. As another way to word it, once you are filled with this awe-inspiring sense of gratitude, you have ended any inner resistance or blocks you may have had and are open to all the love that is available for you. I've also seen that when people reach this kind of gratitude, they also naturally feel safer, which is another way to meet Maslow's second need: the need to feel safe.

Ideally, the kind of gratitude we are talking about here is a spontaneous happening, once enough compassion has been brought to a situation or experience. Many people have found that gratitude can be practiced by itself with some benefit (many therapists encourage their clients to keep a gratitude journal for example.) But, here again, I must advise caution. Similarly to compassion, gratitude can be used to cover up how you feel in the truth of the moment: gratitude feels really good. But if you focus on feeling gratitude instead of however life is contriving for you to feel, you risk getting stuck, missing important information about how you are working inside. Instead, focus your will to practice awareness of the present moment, accept the truth of the present moment, open your heart to yourself in that present moment, and the gratitude will come.

A gratitude journal can be a great way to practice awareness. But then take this practice further by continuing to run whatever thoughts, feelings, and beliefs that come up as you write in your journal through the rest of the seven tools. In a process that is very analogous to how you get to a place of forgiveness by practicing compassion for what is, gratitude arrived at through the practice of compassionate, accepting awareness, again, is literally transformational … and healing. I've heard hundreds of people say things like, "I wouldn't choose to go through that again, but I'm glad I did for all that I've learned and gained from engaging with it, exploring it, and working with it in a healthy way." I've heard people say that about car accidents, cancer, being raped, having fibromyalgia, or having any number of other serious illnesses.

I am currently working with Carol (not her real name), a woman who is healing her breast cancer. I go see her in her home, because traveling is challenging for her. Currently, her cancer has completely consumed the left breast, leaving a deep ulcerated crater. It has spread to the left through her arm pit, plugging all the lymphatic drainage from her left arm. As a result, her left arm is swollen so tightly that she cannot bend her elbow or get much movement from her fingers. It has continued to spread around under her shoulder blade, pinning it to her ribs so she cannot move it. It has spread deep to her ribs and is causing her left lung to fill with fluid that needs to get drained every two weeks or she gets very short of breath. The cancer has also spread to the right across her breast bone and into the right breast and is heading for the right arm pit.

She was first diagnosed with this eight years earlier and a biopsy at that time showed the tumor to be estrogen sensitive. As a child, she had watched her older brother wither and die from the treatments for his leukemia. She declined surgery, chemotherapy, and radiation and instead went to the Gerson clinic in Mexico. She stayed on the Gerson protocol for several years until she was exhausted by it. She then started seeing a local naturopath who gave her high doses of IV vitamin C and other vitamins and minerals, as well as other supplements.

Over the years, she has read as much as she could about nutrition and other natural treatments for cancer. She tried them all. She tried everything she could in the form of diets and supplements to cure her cancer. In the meantime, her relationship with her husband didn't change, nor did her relationships with her children. She tried to hold the house all together so that her condition didn't affect them much. She is half Italian and half Greek and used to going full tilt all day. She was always last on her list of priorities.

By the time I started working with her, her studies were leading her to look at the energetic/spiritual aspects of her life and condition, beyond diet and detoxification. She was studying mindfulness and reading John Cabat-Zinn[37], as well as Ekhardt Tolle[91]. Since then, she has also read Lissa Rankin[92] and Joe Dispenza[34]. We had long talks about the messages coming to her from her life, and I taught her how to use the seven tools of healing. We have used craniosacral therapy to listen to the cancer's side of the story. All the while, she has held an unwavering belief that she was going to survive this cancer.

I diagnosed her pleural effusion (the water on the lung) and arranged for her to go to a local hospital for drainage. I also encouraged her to listen to what the oncologist had to offer. The cancer treatment center drained her lung and the oncologist suggested taking an estrogen-blocking medication. She read up on this medicine and agreed to try it. She still declined any surgery, radiation, or immune-suppressing chemotherapy.

Her husband most likely has some form of Asperger's syndrome[94]. She has been terribly lonely in her relationship, as she could not seem to connect with him emotionally. Before she met him, she was head-over-heels in love with "the love of her life", who died weeks before their wedding in a motorcycle accident. She has been devastated ever since.

One of the first messages she got from her tumor, when she was able to ask it questions and receive answers, was "get a life." It was telling her that it was time to make herself and her self-care a priority in her life. Next, it went to work on helping her heal her broken heart. It showed her how she had chosen such a spouse because, unconsciously, she didn't want anyone to threaten the heart connection she had with her deceased fiancé, which she was still holding on to after twenty three years. After some of our sessions, she was able to have much deeper conversations with her husband and children. Her husband "miraculously changed", and they have had more emotional connection than at any other time in their relationship. He and the kids all started stepping up to the plate and helping her more, as well as spending more time with her. Her amazement at the everyday beauty that surrounds her has been growing every week for the past month or so. She is much less anxious than she's ever been in her life and says that she truly enjoys every day.

The session she just had the week of this writing focused on her inability to get herself to meditate. From all of her reading, she had decided that meditating was an essential step in her healing. Yet, try as she might, she couldn't bring herself to do it. She always found some excuse to stay busy. As we started her craniosacral treatment, I asked her to focus on the feelings that came up when she thought about sitting down to meditate. The first feeling she noticed was fear: she was afraid that she wouldn't be able to stop her mind. Again, from the reading that she had been doing, she had developed the belief that this was the critical element to successful meditation.

I know from my own reading on the subject that many teachers talk this way. I pointed out that the ability to truly stop the mind, transcend it, and experience Samadhi[95] generally took most meditators decades of training. I suggested that the first step in meditating is to just watch the mind doing its thing and asked her if she thought she could start there. There was an almost instant release of tension through her chest, where I was working at the time, and she felt a rush of energy all through her body, stopping in a thick, heavy feeling at the top of her head. She said that she could most definitely start with watching the mind. I pointed out that if she started watching her mind like she had learned to watch her body and emotional feelings, it would teach her what she needed in order to discipline and exercise it and, perhaps, eventually transcend it.

She felt the block to meditating completely gone and felt an opening and bubbling sensation in her left chest and axilla that she likened to how it feels when a plugged sinus opens. We then focused on the heaviness at the top of her head. As she sat watching it, it thinned and opened and she felt a powerful connection of her energy with what she described as an amazing energy coming in through the top of her head. I felt the cancer getting washed over with waves of love and sensed that it liked that, that it appreciated not being reviled, feared, and attacked. In my mind, I asked her cancer if there was anything more it wanted to teach her. I got a sense that this was enough for today. She suddenly felt awash with a tremendous sense of awe and a feeling of being deeply loved and cared for. She was filled with gratitude.

Our session had timed out and I had to get back to the office to see other patients, so I left her there in that state of flowing energy and deep bliss. I spoke with her today and she said that she stayed in that state for another forty minutes and that her left chest and axilla still feel more open and flowing.

By conventional medical statistics, she still has a long row to hoe for her cancer to be gone, though I am always open to miracles. But no matter what happens with her cancer over the next few months, the work she is doing is alleviating her suffering, her anxiety, her regrets, and her sense of never being enough. She has learned in her heart of hearts that she deserves to be cared for by herself and others. She is experiencing a happiness at a level so deep that her pain and disability are not blocking it. Her relationships with her husband and children are the best they have ever been: they are out of denial and she is being open and honest with them about her condition. She tried everything outside of herself to heal her cancer. I am sure that these things have been helping her. (For example, when she went to the ER for the first time to get her chest drained, the ER doctor ordered a chest CT scan and told her that he'd seen better CT scans on dead people. He was amazed she was up walking around.) But her cancer continued to progress and her life had not substantially changed. The last few months she's been working her internal processing and emotional healing in addition to what she was already doing, and her life has really been improving. I see the sense of gratitude she felt as a good sign, along with the cancer being washed over with spiritual love and responding with appreciation. She is not at war with her cancer. Only time will tell how she does, but the way that she is responding to her current situation is very inspiring.

So many people look outside of themselves for their healing and for the answers to their problems. They often don't look inside until the last desperate moments. I'm not sure why this is. Some of it is cultural: we are very outward and doing focused. Some of it is an important part of the drug companies' marketing plan. Some people just don't know to look inside. Others know but are stopped by their fears. If you know that you ought to be looking inside for your guidance about what treatments to follow, for how to heal your relationship with your feelings, and for how to correct your belief structures but are stopped by fear, apply the seven tools to that fear. When my patients go inside and peel back enough layers, all they find is a tremendously wise and supportive presence just holding them in love. I have yet to see anyone find that they are being chased around by the devil with a pitchfork. When it comes to looking inside for your true essence, you have nothing to fear but love itself.

Treatments that work from the outside in may be supportive and beneficial on that level but they are rarely healing. The healing comes from bringing what I call "the human factor" to the work you do in order to get better. C.S. Lewis put it very well when he said, "You don't have a Soul. You are a Soul. You have a body." Live as if you are soul. Let what your soul knows guide you. Live in a way that keeps your soul happy.

Gratitude grown from the practice of compassion and forgiveness fills your mind with supportive, freeing thoughts, beliefs, and feelings. You don't have to exert effort to make your thoughts this way. If you consciously choose just to think positively (assuming you still use that dichotomy, which I hope that by now you do not), you risk missing important information about yourself and the imbalances in your life that are asking for help getting back into balance. Practice the seven tools of healing and, as your personal belief structures start to align with higher truth, your thoughts will just naturally be positive.

This world really is an incredible place; things don't just happen to you in a vacuum. There is meaning, though at times buried deep, in every experience—whether you consciously asked for it or not. You can always learn more about yourself, no matter what else happens to you. Spirit works in amazing ways and the human spirit is so beautiful and resilient … the sixth tool—gratitude—is an acknowledgement, a recognition, even more: a direct experience of all these things.

Like June, who had such a horrific childhood, you may have concluded from your life experiences that things just go from bad to worse and then you die, but I would ask you to pause for a moment and consider what the wise people of all ages and cultures are saying to us about that. The idea that there are gifts for us in all of our experiences and that we are cared about and for by some force or entity that is larger than ourselves, can be found in Lakota Sioux traditional teachings, Christianity, Hinduism, Buddhism, Taoism, Toltec teachings … everywhere you look. But, perhaps no one has put this idea into words better than Fra Giovanni Giocondo.

Within Our Reach: Joy
— *by Fra Giovanni Giocondo*

Fra Giovanni Giocondo (c.1435–1515) was a Renaissance pioneer, accomplished as an architect, engineer, antiquary, archaeologist, classical scholar, and Franciscan friar. Today we remember him most for his reassuring letter to Countess Allagia Aldobrandeschi on Christmas Eve, 1513.

"I salute you. I am your friend, and my love for you goes deep. There is nothing I can give you which you have not. But there is much, very much, that, while I cannot give it, you can take. No heaven can come to us unless our hearts find rest in it today. Take heaven! No peace lies in the future which is not hidden in this present little instant.

Take peace! The gloom of the world is but a shadow. Behind it, yet within our reach, is joy. There is radiance and glory in darkness, could we but see. And to see, we have only to look. I beseech you to look!

Life is so generous a giver. But we, judging its gifts by their covering, cast them away as ugly or heavy or hard. Remove the covering, and you will find beneath it a living splendor, woven of love by wisdom, with power. Welcome it, grasp it, and you touch the angel's hand that brings it to you.

Everything we call a trial, a sorrow or a duty, believe me, that angel's hand is there. The gift is there and the wonder of an overshadowing presence. Your joys, too, be not content with them as joys. They, too, conceal diviner gifts.

Life is so full of meaning and purpose, so full of beauty beneath its covering, that you will find earth but cloaks your heaven. Courage then to claim it; that is all! But courage you have, and the knowledge that we are pilgrims together, wending through unknown country home."

"Earth but cloaks your heaven. Courage then to claim it; that is all." That is one of my favorite lines. I believe strongly in its truth. But it seems that, as free beings, it is up to us to create our heaven here on earth. There is an answer to human suffering. You can do your part to alleviate it by healing your life and then bringing that healing out to the world. Imagine how an aware, compassionate, wise person would run their business or raise their children or pass laws or educate. We don't have to continue to put up with a dysfunctional society. But a healthy society cannot be legislated and imposed upon the population. It can only be built from the ground up, from the inside out, by each one of us healing ourselves and then being our true self in our life. Practicing the seven tools gives you the awareness and perspective to be able to receive the gifts that are hidden behind every experience you have, to be able to find your true authentic self and then find the courage to live as your true authentic self. A heart filled with compassion, a mind nimbly able to forgive, and a life filled with gratitude are the real roots of happiness.

Gratitude is a feeling that just naturally grows as you receive the gifts buried in your experiences, as you realize that you are supported in your existence by that incredibly loving inner presence, as you are able to move into and live from your personal love and power. Gratitude increases your experience of joy in every moment.

> *To speak gratitude is courteous and pleasant,*
> *to enact gratitude is generous and noble,*
> *but to live gratitude is to touch Heaven.*
> —Johannes A. Gaertner

Chapter Nine

Right Action

When you learn how to apply the first six tools to whatever is happening in your life, you find your true authentic self. The seventh tool is how you bring your true authentic self out into the world. Healing has two parts: the process of finding out who you really are and then living in a way that is congruent and consistent with who you are. Remember, we are all learning how to love better. As your lessons progress, you will notice that certain things just fall into place: compassion is your heart filled with love, wisdom is your mind filled with love, and kindness is your action filled with love. That is right action.

Doing is always happening: the sap flowing, insects buzzing, synapses in your brain buzzing, your blood flowing. Life wouldn't happen without doing. But as a human being, besides the natural doing of your physiology, you also have volitional action, you have free will, you have conscious access to Consciousness, you are soul. You can make choices and act upon them: you are more than stimulus in, response out. You are more than genetically determined behavior.

So when I'm talking about right action, I'm talking about your volitional actions, those actions that you choose. You already know that you have the ability to respond to any situation. How do you know what is the right response? What criteria do you use to judge what is right and what isn't? How do you know that your actions will bring about the results you desire? Believe it or not, philosophers (and investors) have been pondering these questions for centuries and still haven't come up with good answers.

There is no recipe for the best way to act in any given moment. Ideally, your actions will be informed by your being, by your loving, wise inner guidance. When you are healed, your actions will come from your true being. Before that, your actions spring from that moment's best sense of knowing in addition to however you happen to be feeling. Therefore, your actions are another expression of who you believe yourself to be. They become one more aspect of your life that you can use to get to know yourself better, to release yourself from limiting beliefs and move closer to the truth. As your sense of who you are moves closer and closer to your true authentic self, your volitional actions move closer and closer to right action.

There are so many hidden determinants and different factors operating in any given situation, that, at times, outcomes appear to be completely chaotic. You do the best you can with what you know and how you understand things to work, but you cannot know for certain what the outcome(s) of your actions will be. The best you can do is your best (which you are doing all the time anyway). But even your best is still no guarantee of anything. But if you see life as a learning experience, if you can make the most of your mistakes, your judgment and choices will get better over time.

> *Good judgment comes from experience, and often*
> *experience comes from bad judgment.*
> —Rita Mae Brown

> *When you make a mistake, don't look back at it long. Take the reason of the thing into your mind and then look forward. Mistakes are lessons of wisdom. The past cannot be changed. The future is yet in your power.*
> —Hugh White (1773 - 1840)

You would probably feel completely immobilized if you had no sense whatsoever of the most likely outcomes from your actions. But you can make pretty good guesses if you have some understanding about the world. The woodworker takes time to understand the properties of wood so that she can work it and get close to the results she envisioned. The businessman takes time to understand the economy and marketing and human psychology so that he can take actions that get him close to his desired results most of the time. Parents try to understand their children. Children try to understand their parents. The better you understand the world around you, the better you can choose the actions that will give the best results. The entire discipline of science is for that very purpose. The disciplines of psychology, philosophy, economics, history, theology, (and the list goes on), exist to help you deepen your understanding of the world around you so that you can make better choices. The best possible action that you can take, the ideal action, whatever criteria you are using to judge, is called right action.

In many world traditions, right action is considered to be the action that results in the highest good for the most of creation. Because we are all one and we are all interconnected and interdependent, the actions that are the most loving for yourself are also the most loving for those around you and for all the world. So, when it comes time to act, all you really have to focus on is the question, "what action is most loving for me?" I know this sounds hedonistic and narcissistic and plays right to the "me" generation, but it's not, when you look at it carefully. Notice I said "most loving." What is most loving is often not what is the most fun, the easiest, the most rational, the most profitable, or even, in some cases, the most acceptable. In extreme cases, sometimes the most loving thing you can do is to lay down your life for another.

The ego or conscious mind has a difficult time getting clear about what is most loving. There are so many self-interests and competing priorities. Connect with your inner love; trust what it knows and what it says to you. Let it inform your actions as much as you possibly can. Let your words and deeds arise from your inner love, including, especially including, how you speak and act toward yourself. People connecting with their love and acting from their love become the stuff of great stories.

Do you have the patience to wait till your mud settles, and the water is clear? Can you remain unmoving till the right action arises by itself? The Master neither seeks or expects; she is fully present; she can welcome all things.
—Tao te Ching #15

Right action is based upon right understanding. In my practice, I've seen that practicing the first six tools leads to right understanding and then the person just knows how to act in the moment. If you place yourself under too many "shoulds," you will collapse under their weight, you will fall off the wagon, get fatigued, distracted, and discouraged. Your doing comes from some aspect of your being anyway, so why not have it be your inner wisdom? As you uncover and bring forth more of your true essential self, your actions effortlessly tend toward right action. Your actions naturally express who you are, and, in a kind of feed-back loop, support you in being that.

Of all the actions you choose to take, perhaps some of the most important relate to how you optimize your health. Many experts have their opinions about that. There are dozens of books that will tell you how to eat, whether or not or how to fast, more will tell you how to exercise, how to relax, how to behave at work, how to parent. The list goes on and on. You have no shortage of good advice. But what advice is right for you and your family? How do you get yourself to actually follow the advice you agree with? The answer? Listen to and follow the advice of your own inner knower. Practice the seven tools of healing and you will know how to eat, how to exercise, how to recreate, what to do for a career, how to handle stress, how to treat those around you, how to treat the Earth. Get to know yourself better and your actions support your strength and growth rather than wear you out and make you sick. You will naturally adopt a healthy lifestyle; you don't need to force one upon yourself.

I can't stress enough the importance of finding your own right action when you are in need of healing. If you listen to the stories of many people who have experienced miraculous healing—Norman Cousins and his ankylosing spondylitis[96], Louise Hay and her cervical cancer[96], Terry Wahl and her MS[97], Evy McDonald and her ALS[80], Byron Katie and her depression[98] ... there are so many more—the actions they undertook to get themselves better were all different; but if you look at their processes, they all did their own research, listened to their own knowing, and acted upon it—sometimes in the face of opposing expert recommendations. If you want to experience your own healing miracle, trust what you know ... then do what you know. "Remember who you are."

As an example of growing into right action, many of my patients who have healed their fibromyalgia followed what I've come to call the "butterfly metaphor". The caterpillar stage of their lives is generally before they get sick. So often they are go go go: being supermom, climbing the corporate ladder, living with the abusive spouse, putting up with the abusive boss. Then they get sick and their life comes to a screeching halt. That is the cocoon stage. If you open up a cocoon part way through, all you find inside is formless goo. That is how life feels to the person with fibromyalgia. Most people will try things to feel better: take vitamins, get therapies, and/or take medications. Most will take any energy they gain from those therapies and use it to try to go back to being the caterpillar. Then they just get sick again. I've had some patients who have been doing that for decades before they come in. But by practicing the seven tools, many of them have moved through the cocoon stage and are able to more readily be who they are, naturally, with no exertion and no awkward self-consciousness. They are much less stressed by life's vagaries. That is the butterfly stage: fulfilling the higher purpose of their life. They are able to fly free, a beautiful example of what is possible for all the caterpillars toiling away below.

That there is no recipe for how to act in any given situation is one of the biggest problems with healthcare advice these days. Most of the advice focuses on behavior—what to eat, how to exercise, how to feel—with little or no attention paid to the underlying motivations or beliefs in the person. "One man's meat is another man's poison." Recent studies have found that, largely due to genetic variability, no one diet is ideal for everyone[99]. So how can you make broad reliable statements about how to eat that are right for everyone? "One person's stress is another person's recreation." How can you make broad statements about exercise or stress reduction or work situations that are right for everyone? And we've already learned that the feelings are not the problem, that trying to make your feelings be any preconceived way is addiction, so telling yourself how to feel or how not to feel doesn't work if you want to get better.

Philosophers have been debating the question "how do we act?" for hundreds of years without good consensus. The advice I see people get from their own inner wisdom is something like, "let your actions rise up from your heart in each moment." It advises people to "trust what you know and act from that." Most of the time when you get in trouble for your actions, or act in harmful or abusive ways, you will see that you were acting from ignorance, distrust, or fear. You were acting when you were far removed from your heart. When you catch yourself in such a cycle, practice compassionate, accepting awareness of your truth, until the forgiveness just naturally comes to you. Sometimes the best way we can learn to live from our hearts is to pay especially close attention to all of the times when we did not.

Much like forgiveness and gratitude, right action just naturally follows from enough practice of compassionate, accepting awareness (on a foundation of faith, of course.) You can watch and try to control all of your actions and risk the occasional volcanic eruption, or you can spend your time using the seven tools to get to know yourself deep in your heart and just trust your actions to come from there. You know which strategy I would recommend.

Chapter Ten

Change

Now that we've gone through all of the seven tools in great detail, it is time to see how they work. We have established that what you believe determines not only what you create in your life, but also what you create as your life. Your ability to heal hinges on the fact that you get to choose what you believe. But, since most of your beliefs function in your unconscious mind, behind the scenes of your everyday awareness, in order to heal your life, you need some way to find those beliefs that are creating the things that you don't want, bring them into the light of your conscious mind, align them with higher truth, and then put the new beliefs back into your unconscious mind. I'm going to show you how to use the seven tools of healing to do precisely that.

But first, let's briefly review why so many of the techniques that you've most likely already tried to help yourself change and heal didn't work very well. Most of the self-help programs available today have two major flaws. The first flaw is that they only do half of the process needed to change beliefs. They explain to you what the latest psychological research has found about what people believe who already have what you want, and suggest that, to get what you want, you adopt the same beliefs. You can do this with affirmations, visualizations, autosuggestion, little inner pep talks, tapping, or whatever technique that particular self-help program is promoting.

But creating new beliefs and putting them into your unconscious mind just adds them on top of the beliefs that are already there. If you want to program your mind for success, whatever that means to you, you need to not only know how to put new beliefs into your mind, but also how to remove the old ones that are blocking you or no longer serving you. Without this step, the old limiting beliefs can rise up and wrest control of your creative flow from the new beliefs any time you turn your back on them for just a second. Practicing the seven tools of healing allows you to both clear out limiting beliefs and replace them with beliefs more in alignment with your soul's highest interest.

Most of the beliefs in your unconscious mind, especially the deep, primordial ones that seem to have the greatest hold over your creativity, got there during the first seven years of your life. You might not even know that they are there. To find them, just follow the clues in your life back to their roots using Rule Number One and the Three 'A's. Practicing the seven tools naturally leads to lasting inner change as directed by your inner wisdom.

The second major flaw shared by most self-help programs comes about because our society, in general, has a poor understanding of the laws of Consciousness, and so they violate one or more of them. Your creative Consciousness flows to wherever you are paying attention. If you focus on healing some problem you are having, that focus risks inadvertently creating more of what you are wanting to change, or, at least, of energizing it so that it is more difficult to change. Also, any time you start to work on yourself from the starting place that there is something wrong with you that needs to change, you risk creating your future out of fear. Practicing the seven tools of healing circumvents these flaws.

Healing implies change. I have spent my professional life searching for the answers to the questions "What is healing?" and "How can I best help you with yours?" So, naturally, I've thought about the process of change. Here are some of my thoughts.

Some people's healing is like a lightning bolt from Zeus, and these people's stories fill many books about healing. But in my experience, most people's healing is a long, slow, often tumultuous slog through the swamps of their wounds, repressed feelings, learned behaviors, neuroassociative conditioning, and false and limiting beliefs … in addition to all that needs to be done with lifestyle changes, diets, medicines, neutraceuticals, or other ways to best support their body. My patients and I go wandering through the cavernous halls of the dark night of their souls and all we have is the narrow flashlight of their conscious mind to illuminate one piece of the puzzle at a time. But, over time, and for those who stick with it, the pieces start to fall into place and a larger, spiritual view of their life starts to take shape. Most of my patients have to learn how to be open to letting the healing in. That, by itself, is a whole learning process. Carol had to try everything she knew about diet and supplements first before she turned her efforts inward.

Healing itself is a mystery. So, often, if you go at it directly, you miss the mark. But if you go after something deeper, such as love and understanding, as Evy McDonald, RN did, you often find your healing. Since healing implies change, it also implies moving from where you are now in your life—not healed—to where you want to be in your life— healed. Something somewhere has to change. The question then becomes, "What has to change and how do you get yourself to change it?" I've looked at that question for years and it turns out the seven tools approach has something to say about it.

> *Our dilemma is that we hate change and love it at the same time;*
> *what we really want is for things to remain the same but get better.*
> —Sydney J. Harris

Wouldn't it be nice if life worked that way? Change is the only constant, yet we seem to be hardwired to resist it. This seems counter to evolution, to the notion that living organisms adapt to their environment: we should be well adapted to change by now. Like we asked when we explored our need for safety, is our resistance to change another cruel cosmic joke or is something deeper going on? You are forced to change as you grow through your different developmental stages in life, as life changes around you, as people come into and leave your life, as your body ages. But have you noticed that, through all of these changes, there is some aspect inside of you that is constant? Your sense of who you are has been there as long as you can remember. When I look inside, I feel the same now, at sixty two, as I did at eighteen. That internal constancy of the sense of "I" is a spiritual truth. You can trust that constancy while you look for a healthy way to adapt to, flow with, and direct (when appropriate) the river of change around you. Resisting the flow is exhausting.

Remember the surgeon who said, "Whenever there are several different ways to try and get the same job done, that generally means that none of them works very well." Look at how many different ways we have in our society to help ourselves change: medical treatments, diets, psychological approaches, yoga, meditation, and spiritual practices. There must be hundreds of different diets out there. And more keep getting proposed all the time; yet their five-year success rates stay about the same. There must be almost as many different approaches to psychotherapy. Again, more keep getting developed all the time, as we continue to seek better answers to the perennial questions. The same can be said about all the different kinds of body work, meditation, addiction recovery programs, and such.

Of course, we need variety because no one size fits all; but, beyond that, in the bigger picture, all of these endeavors, including medicine, psychology, twelve step programs, religions, personal spiritual paths, yoga, education, indeed, the entire self-help industry, are all methodologies that we've devised to help us change … and, if we were really honest with ourselves, we'd have to admit that none of them works very well. Each has its ardent supporters and success stories, of course, or it would have never gained enough traction to make it to the world stage; but, taken as a group, the processes that we use to change ourselves don't tend to work very well. This observation has led David Hawkins[46] to conclude that most people don't raise their personal level of consciousness more than five points on his scale over their lifetime, no matter how much education they get.

Yet, perhaps as a result of our deeply held conviction that we can heal, that we can change, these ways to change make up some of the largest institutions in our society, and most of them are growing rapidly and continuing to develop new techniques. This huge self-help industry, in all its guises, is powered by our incessant dissatisfaction with where and who we are, coupled with the (mostly unspoken) knowledge that we can heal. You know in your heart that all of the seeking and trying are worth it. No matter how talented or developed you are, you somehow sense that more is possible, that you don't have to stay the same, that you don't have to keep suffering. This desire, that I call your holy restlessness, is based in truth and it keeps driving you forward, it keeps you searching and innovating. And you need to change (at least something) if you're going to heal. I wonder if we can figure out why self-help and personal growth techniques don't work very well and what to do about that.

To be honest, we have to start with the observation that some people who say they want to heal are not actually doing what they know in their hearts they need to do in order to heal. Many have gotten great advice from their practitioners then choose to not follow it. Many do not take the time to eat well or to face their discomfort. On the other side of the equation, many practitioners think that, if you are not responding to their program for you, you are lying to them about how well you are following it. The bottom line is that you are the only person who knows if you are sticking to your diet, doing your PT, or are honestly listening to your body. And you are the one most affected by your choices. Your innate resistance to change can sometimes also make you resistant to your own healing. The process of change can be a pretty high hurdle for so many of us. The practice of the seven tools is a way over that hurdle. You can apply the seven tools to your resistance to change, to why you might be sabotaging your well-being, and you can resolve that resistance. So, for the rest of this discussion, I am going to assume that you have resolved your inner resistance and are doing your best to follow what you know is best for you and will focus on the kind of advice you are getting from the different therapies that are available for you to try.

We humans are literally driven to change, if not by our burning desire to learn and grow and improve, then by our chronic health problems, relationship problems, business problems, and such. Tony Robbins[20] has said that the secret to inner happiness is "continuous and never-ending improvement." Yet some observers of human nature have concluded that people don't change. How could this be? Why is changing so difficult? Are we all blocked in some way? If you can answer these questions for yourself, then perhaps instead of looking for the next best supplement to take or technique to try, you can stop and look at what is going on behind the scenes of this massive failure of the self-help industry and, hopefully, find ways to improve your chances of changing. Here is what I found when I went through this exercise.

You probably have heard the saying that doing the same thing over and over again while expecting different results is insanity. Since most of us do this, I want to give us the benefit of the doubt and say that we may or may not be crazy, but such behavior does reflect a general lack of understanding of how thoughts and feelings lead to actions which lead to results. Incomplete understanding is not necessarily insanity: all of us have incomplete understanding of the laws of nature and Consciousness. That ignorance is often the aspect of ourselves we are trying to change when we seek out education and healing. And that is wise, not crazy.

I think that definition of insanity is trying to point out that there is a very strong correlation between what you do and the results you get. That correlation is so strong that, not only do you keep getting the same result if you keep doing the same thing, but you can turn it around and also assume that if you are getting the same result, you are somehow doing the same thing. (Simple math: if A=B then B=A.) So I looked at this huge panoply of all the ways that we've devised to help ourselves change and turned the question around. This is what I came up with: "If you are doing what, on the surface, appears to be different things, but you end up getting the same results anyway (i.e. not changing very well), could that mean that these techniques, which look so different from each other on the surface, are actually, in some critical and fundamental way, doing the same thing?" In other words, if you're trying to change and you're doing a bunch of things that look really different, like dieting, acupuncture, counseling, and yoga, but you get the same results, maybe the things are not really that different after all, on some important, causal level.

Next I asked myself, "What do these really different-looking techniques all have in common?" What I saw astounded me: they all start from the assumption that there is something wrong with you that needs to change. You are too fat or too weak or too stiff or too poor or too stuck in your head … the list is endless. And then they generally proceed by getting you to exert effort against that thing. The only ways they differ, really, are in what they see as the problem and in what kind of exertion they advise.

How could this similarity be what is blocking the whole self-help industry? It defies logic. Of course, the whole reason you want to change that aspect of yourself is because you don't like it. If you liked it, why would you want to change it? Seems like that would be insanity. And how can you change an aspect of yourself if you don't focus your attention on it? So, of course you would start there.

The reason starting there keeps you stuck has to do with how Consciousness works. Consciousness is very subtle. Small changes in intention or focus can have dramatic effects in your life. There are several steps in the reasoning process that led me to the answer to how to change, so please bear with me as we go through them. If how to change were a simple problem, we would have figured it out a long time ago and wouldn't be in many of the messes we are in now. I think this block has been missed and, as a society, we continue to beat our heads against it, because conventional medicine seems Hell-bent on trying to explain all of human experience solely from physical scientific principles before being forced to finally admit that there is such a thing as Consciousness. This, even though quantum physics has been postulating a non-physical Consciousness for decades.

I'd like to illustrate these esoteric ideas with an example. Let's start with the observation that you want to change. There are probably several qualities or attributes or physical characteristics about yourself and your life that you would choose to work on. That is what this whole book has been about. Wanting to change, wanting to be healthier, more successful, happier … that is not the problem. Your holy restlessness is an important part of who you are. How we generally go about trying to change is the problem and paradoxically creates the block to change. Here's how it works. Once you see something about yourself that you want to change, it is only natural that you would have some sort of judgment or feeling about that thing. That is where the problem arises.

Judgment differs from discernment. There is a value statement attached to judgment. If you judge part of yourself to be bad or less than or inadequate in any way, you have quite literally Forgotten that Everything is All Right (FEAR.) Then any action that you take from that perspective will be fear based, by definition. Do you see how subtle that is? Any time you judge a part of yourself, anything you do to change from that moment on is fear-based. So, at first, when I started looking at these questions, I saw that most of our methods to change inadvertently (or, in some cases, blatantly) keep you creating out of fear.

If it is true, and I believe that there is some truth to the notion, that you create your life moment by moment as you live it, then the present moment you are living is the result of past creativity bearing fruit now. If your present moment is created out of past fear-based creativity and you continue to create out of fear, then expecting your future to be any different than what you have now is crazy. So the vast majority of methodologies that our culture has developed to help you change unwittingly keep you creating your future out of fear. That is the bottom line; that is how most of our ways to change keep you doing the same thing over and over.

Also, most of them keep you focused too superficially: on the doing rather than on the motivation behind the doing and the limiting beliefs behind that. That is how the wide panoply of ways to change are the same. If you are creating out of fear, what are the chances that you'll like what gets created? If you are working too superficially, what are the chances you will ever get to the root?

But then I saw that fear-based creativity is not the only kind of creativity that can keep you stuck. Acting out of anger, grief, greed, or even happiness can keep you stuck. Whenever your creativity is based in an emotion—mad, sad, glad, and fear—it will be limited. What is the way out of this very subtle trap? How can you gain conscious control of your conscious creativity and free it from the blocks of emotion-based efforting? How can you use your access to Consciousness to create a life that is pleasing to your soul?

You already know how well you like it when you create your future out of fear. But if, on the other hand, you were creating your future out of love, what are the chances that you would like what is getting created? Your challenge, then, is to figure out how to get your creativity to flow from love rather than from fear or anger or greed or hedonism or any of the myriad other feeling states. The practice of the seven tools does just that.

For example, when I was in my medical training, I decided that doctors should not be judgmental of their patients. And so I set this as a standard for myself. I was going to listen to people and be really accepting of them and whatever they were dealing with in their lives. I worked and worked on this and I thought I was pretty good at it; yet, in my early years of practice, there were at least two times when someone yelled in my face out of anger and frustration at feeling judged. Both times I was completely surprised by this and had no clue what they were referring to.

When we moved to Seattle, I started riding the bus to work, which gave me built-in time each day to read. I read Stephen Levine, Bernie Siegel, Gary Zukov, *Astronomy* magazine, and many other great writers. One day on the way home, the bus was going up University Ave and I was thinking about the issue of being judgmental and how many years it had been since that fateful morning when, while sitting in a Quaker meeting while still a resident, I decided that I wasn't going to be judgmental anymore. People on University Ave sport every color of hair in the rainbow, sometimes all on the same head; and every sense of fashion from the saggers to the chic. Every time the bus stopped, I'd look up from my reading and this old fogey voice in my head would say, "Look at that person's hair!" or "Look at that person's clothes!" and I would say, "Stop it! Stop it!" and force myself to go back to my magazine. The next bus stop, the same thing all over. This went on all the way up the Ave.

Finally, I saw what I was doing. All the practicing I'd done over the years to accept people and repress my first instinct to judge, had not extinguished my basic judgmentalness one little iota. And I saw it was because I'd started with the judgment that judging people was bad and then I was judging myself for being judgmental. I was stuck on a hamster wheel.

I wondered how to get off of that hamster wheel. This was before I had started studying craniosacral therapy and was still practicing conventional family practice. Nothing in my medical training stepped forward to offer a solution, so I decided to try some of Stephen Levine's advice. In one of his books[100], he had talked about acceptance, so I said to myself, "I wonder if I can just accept that I'm one judgmental SOB?" And, to my great surprise, as soon as I had the thought, I had a sensation as though a huge knot made of two-inch thick rope was untying itself in my solar plexus. This was in the late '80s and I didn't know about the compassion tool at that time; but, quite often, just awareness and acceptance are enough to get change to happen. Since then, I don't know if I'm a judgmental SOB or not, and, even though my wife assures me that I still am, it doesn't seem to be much of an issue in my life ... and so far (knock on wood) no one since then has come into my office and yelled in my face about it.

The first step toward change is awareness. The second step is acceptance.
—Nathaniel Branden

At this point, I would add that the third step is compassion. Just be kind to yourself about whatever you are aware of and accepting at the moment. Your creative flow follows your focus. When you focus on compassion for yourself that you have some aspect of yourself that you want changed—rather than focusing on trying to change that aspect directly—your creativity starts to flow from compassion and more compassion gets created. If you focus on the aspect directly, your creativity starts to flow to it, creating more of what you are trying to eliminate.

The compassion then works the change; you don't have to force it with your ego mind. You may need to take that last statement on faith when you first start being with yourself this way. By focusing on compassion for yourself no matter what your truth, you are creating out of love and the chances increase that you will create for yourself a future that supports your health and happiness. So, if you asked me, "How do I stop creating my future out of fear or other emotion and get my creativity to flow from love?" I would answer, "Practice compassionate, accepting awareness of yourself just as you are right now." Take that part of yourself you want to change, admit the truth of it, and wrap it up in your heart. That is it. A loving heart can hold all hurts. That one simple practice repeated over and over again will change your life.

As you can see, individually, each of the seven tools is a familiar concept, entire books have been written about each one, different authors stressing one or another. What is unique here is how your inner love coaches you to combine these skills into a fully integrated package that empowers you to take whatever your life is handing you and use it to further the process of your personal growth and change. You already are your true authentic self, underneath it all. The challenge is to find that self and bring it out into the world. That is precisely what you will accomplish when you apply the seven tools of healing to whatever is happening to and within you. This life, with all of its traumas and triumphs, is one big invitation to find and be your true authentic self. "Courage, then, to take it." You've suffered enough already. It's high time you found the answers to your suffering. Practice the seven tools. They really are just a way of being with yourself, a way to squeeze the most learning out of each moment, a way to use whatever is in your life to ultimately find your health, happiness, and wholeness.

You can own all the tools in the world, but to get masterful results when you use them requires practice. I strongly encourage you either to find a group of people in your area who are meeting to help each other brainstorm and troubleshoot their practice of the seven tools or start your own group.

Masterful application of the seven tools to the stuff of your life will help you to skillfully find yourself, avoiding many of the traps and pitfalls along the way, avoiding getting stalled out for decades or missing the boat completely. Connect with your heart, trust your heart, it will lead the way.

The seven tools sound simple...and conceptually they are. But I've been observing my patients practicing their application to their lives and I've noticed some pitfalls. Some are learned, some are human nature, and some are a big part of the culture in which we live. I'd like to discuss the major most common pitfalls in the hopes that you may avoid them or recognize when you are caught in one and quickly extract yourself.

Chapter Eleven

Pitfalls

Being Oblivious

I put this pitfall first, perhaps, for personal reasons. Developing real-time personal awareness has been one of my biggest challenges. Remember, I was so oblivious to my words and actions that I did not even know I was behaving in ways that would make some of my patients feel judged. But that is how repression works: when you repress an aspect of yourself, you may succeed in hiding it from yourself, but everybody else can still see it. I started my own healing journey as sensitive as a cinder block, so I am living proof that these skills improve with practice. If I can do it, you can, too. I know you can.

Awareness is the second tool for good reason. And I spent so much time on it because of that. Remaining oblivious to your truth will keep you stuck no matter what else you do to heal yourself. You may be able to patch up your life for awhile or cobble some support together for a bit, but your real lasting freedom will come from facing your truth, from working with your truth in a healthy way. And your truth is anything and everything happening to you this moment, both inside and out.

Please take awareness seriously. Pay attention to the information coming to you from your life. Connect with your inner wisdom to help you know how to be with that information. Trust your gut sense.

Take the time to get really healthy with your feelings: they are the key to accessing what is going on in your unconscious mind. Hear their messages, get their clues. You have them with you wherever you go, so you can practice at any time. Hands off your feelings. Work with them at face value. If you are on a treasure hunt and every time you come across a clue, instead of working directly with what it says, you change it to say something else that you may like better, you greatly decrease your odds of ever finding the treasure. Failing to work with the naked, honest truth of their feelings and then follow them back to the root belief in their world view is probably the most common pitfall I help my patients overcome.

So often, when a person sees the limiting belief that they've been holding, they immediately jump in and try to change it. On the surface, this makes sense. But, believe it or not, it doesn't work. Any effort you put into trying to make a deeply held belief change just turns around and makes that belief more entrenched, stronger, harder to change. The way around this pitfall is to practice compassion for yourself having that belief and for all that that belief has done to you down through the years. Say to yourself, "I wonder how kind I can be to myself for having this belief." Whenever you say, "I wonder … (fill in the blank)" to yourself, you naturally arouse your curiosity. And "curiosity" and "cure" come from the same root word (cūra-Latin for care.)

That reminds me. Our society has many forces built into it that work to keep you sick. Some are overt, such as pesticides, GMOs, drug companies advertising on TV, Fox News, and the repression of women. But some are covert, like teaching that you need a priest or guru to connect with God or sayings like "curiosity killed the cat." This saying has catchy alliteration but is obviously designed to snub a person's (usually a small child pestering their parent) natural bent toward curiosity. Don't give your power over to these things. Go ahead. Be as curious about yourself and about your life and about how the world works as you want to be. If you happen to pass a couple of dead cats along the way, they much more likely died of stupification (if they listened to that saying) than curiosity.

Living in Fantasy

This pitfall is related to being oblivious. How rich is your fantasy life? Probably the far end of the fantasy spectrum are people who dissociate. Many people with dissociative disorders spend much more time in their fantasies than in real life. They can stay that way for their entire lives and not make progress toward self-knowing. Generally what helps them is to learn how they dissociate, when they do it, what triggers it, and how to make whether or not they dissociate their conscious choice. They then also benefit by learning how to spend more time in their bodies and how to be present in the moment.

But what if you don't have a full-blown dissociative disorder? What if you just like to daydream a lot? There is a difference between living in your fantasy as a way to escape from or avoid the present moment and having a vivid imagination. The former is a pitfall and will block your healing; the latter, as we will see, is an important skill for your healing.

Watch how fantasy works in your life. If you are using it like an addiction, that is, to avoid however you are feeling right now and to create some other feelings instead, it will stall your healing progress. If you are using it to imagine greater possibilities for yourself or to imagine how it feels to already have what you want to create for yourself, or to explore—in virtual space—possibilities you might not have thought of otherwise, fantasy might actually help with your healing. But notice how often I used the word "imagine."

Lack of Imagination

Your mind and body connect at the level of imagination. As we talked about earlier, your body is like a radio. A radio is a kind of information transformer. It takes information in the form of low frequency electromagnetic radiation and transforms it into information in the form of air vibrations. But your body is not just like a radio receiver, it is also like a radio transmitter: your body receives information from the universe and it can also transmit information back out into the universe. It is through the use of your imagination that you make use of your body's information transmitting abilities. Whenever you want to create something new in your life, imagine how it feels in your body to already have that something. This is one of the surest ways to let the universe know what you want. Mike Dooley[51] and other teachers of manifesting talk at length about this phenomenon.

Chances are you had a great imagination when you were a child. Chances also are that you got a message loud and clear that you had to give up that imagination to be a grown up. Most of the people I work with have allowed their imaginations to atrophy. They have given over their sense of wonder and enchantment to reason, logic, and skepticism. To be able to reason in your life is very important—no argument there. But, at the same time, a lack of imagination cuts you off to important parts of yourself... like your creativity, for instance. I wonder if there is a way to arrive at a healthy balance of both?

The mind and body are just two sides of the same coin, and information is constantly flowing back and forth between them, yet it seems that to gain conscious awareness and control over that flow of information requires imagination. Perhaps that is why imagery works so well. For example, if you are not already able to feel your energy—how it flows, where it is blocked, its frequency and intensity—to first start to open up to your energy often requires imagination. Similarly, when you first start opening up to your deeper intuitive knowing, you need your imagination. Imagination helps you have faith, the first and foundational tool for healing.

When I first started studying craniosacral therapy, I started feeling things that my conventional medical training said were not possible. I could lay my hand lightly on a person's thigh and feel down into their femur, or I could feel what emotions my patients were experiencing even if they were silent. This little voice in my head would say, "You can't feel that; it is impossible." By my third year of training, my progress had plateaued. Then, one day, I noticed that it was my scientific skepticism and medical training that was getting in the way of going deeper with the work. So I said to my rational, scientific, medical mind, "You go over to the sidelines and sit on the bench. You are welcome to watch but keep your trap shut. I'll invite you back when I'm ready for you." After that, what I was able to feel and sense in my patients took a big leap forward. Then, once I could get deep into a person's system and feel what was going on, I could invite my scientific medical side to come in and render its opinion: "Okay, that thing that feels like a ball of wadded up energy in their solar plexus is their pancreas which has been irritated by the alcohol they had last night". Craniosacral therapy is a perfect example of a discipline that benefits from a balance of the left and right brains: of the rational, logical, scientific, and of the intuitive.

Rational, logical, linear thinking is often ascribed to the left brain.

Intuitive, creative, global thinking is often ascribed to the right brain. Life works better when you have full access to both. You were given two halves a brain for a reason. One need not ever diss the other; develop the strengths of both. You don't have to give up your imagination to be a responsible adult. Perhaps the way you were parented made you close that part of yourself down; perhaps your education did that to you. If you are shut down to your imagination, you may very well find that connecting to your inner love, hearing it accurately, and being able to act on its advice is very difficult. But you can wake your imagination back up.

Keep reminding yourself to trust the little nudges and glimmers you get from inside. If you are around children, get down on the floor and play with them. If you are so inclined, take an art class, a pottery class, a writing class; cook without a recipe. Do creative things. Trust yourself; get into the flow. Learn Reiki; take a class to open to your psychic abilities; study with a shaman. Stretch yourself, get curious, challenge yourself to find out what all these weird fringy things are about. Learn to meditate. Look within and trust what you see and hear. Trust those things that you seem to know without knowing how you know. These practices and activities will wake up and grow your imagination. Then you can use your new-found power of imagination to explore and get to know yourself a whole lot better. And, when you are ready, you can invite your rational analytical side to render an opinion.

Wanting What You Want

I am always impressed by how powerfully we want what we want. Our egos will go to such great lengths to help us. At least, they think they are helping us. The pitfall is when wanting what you want blinds you to the truth of your moment. If you want to get a particular job done, for example, you may repress how you really feel in order to get it done. If you really don't want (another form of wanting something) to deal with the ramifications of divorce, you may deny how your spouse really is and choose to not look at any evidence that makes you see them in a bad light.

Keep an eye on your wants. If you see that they are interfering with your access to your truth, be kind to yourself about that. Ask yourself, "Is that what I really want, in my heart of hearts, if I was being really honest with myself?" How you treat yourself and others is more important than having stuff.

Addictions

Addictions are a perfect example of what can happen when what you want causes you to evade your truth. Whenever you really want to feel one set of feelings and really do not want to feel another set of feelings, whatever you do to accomplish that is an addiction. It might be TV, video games, work, sex, drugs, or alcohol. Whenever you give yourself over to your addictions, you are stalling your personal growth. The flip-side is also true: the addict is a spiritual seeker…they just might not know it yet. If you are challenged by addictions, that is life's way of saying that you cannot ignore your spiritual growth; that, for you, finding yourself and being yourself is paramount. So don't give up on yourself. If you are in despair, follow that feeling to its roots and be exquisitely kind to yourself.

Some addictions are obvious, like those listed above, but many are not. Since addiction is feeling management, nearly everyone I meet is addicted in some way or another. Most people do something to manage their feelings rather than experience them moment to moment in their raw, natural state. Wanting what you want with respect to how you feel often interferes with what it takes to have a healthy relationship with your feelings. Letting their feelings be messengers and getting the messages from them is one of the most difficult skills for my patients to master. We often have decades of practice managing our feelings and have developed a whole toolbox of tricks that need to be unlearned before we can just let our feelings be so that we can hear them in their unadulterated state.

I can't emphasize this enough: your feelings are the keys to your world view. Your world view determines your life. If you want to change your life, you've got to change your world view. If you want to be free, you've got to face your truth head on without blinking. Only your true feelings will show you your true world view. If you want to heal, you've got to stop diddling with your feelings and accept their truth.

Since addiction is feeling management, the cure for addictions is to learn to be present in the moment with your feelings no matter what they are, to get their message, and to act accordingly. Substance addictions are a big problem in our culture. Have you ever noticed that nearly all addicting substances are also mood-altering? This is not a coincidence. These substances can come into your body and literally drop a curtain between certain feelings and your awareness. If you are using a mood-altering substance such as alcohol, tobacco, opiates, anti-anxiety medications, sleep medications, and/or antidepressants, first focus on whatever you need to do to get chemical-free. You may need a recovery program, a twelve step program, alternative treatments, digging deeper and finding the root causes of your physical pain and treating those, etc. Functional medicine is often more effective and supportive than is conventional medicine for this work. I strongly encourage you to get chemical-free on your healing path earlier rather than later. Use Rule Number One and the Three 'A's to work with any feelings that are exposed as the chemicals taper down.

But there are also many ways to be addicted without using any substances. The work-a-holic, the rage-a-holic, the sex-a-holic, the superficial-a-holic, the worry-a-holic, the help-a-holic, the list goes on. Nearly any behavior can be used addictively. Whatever you do to stuff or avoid your feelings or to create one feeling in an attempt to replace another feeling is an addiction. Wrap a red ribbon around your finger and catch yourself any time you feel the need to manage your feelings. Instead, be the observer. Say to yourself something like, "Ah, there's that feeling again. My usual MO is to _____ (stuff it, rationalize it, blame somebody else, fill in the blank with what you know about yourself) but, this time, I wonder if I can just sit with it a moment longer? I wonder if I can follow it back to its roots?"

See how you relate to your feelings and ask them how they would like you to relate to them. Observe how you have learned how to manage your feelings. At the very least, practice asking the feeling to take you to its roots before you make it go away. Over time, you will see that the feeling, per se, is not the problem.

If you are avoiding your feelings, you cannot have a deep and intimate relationship with yourself. If you cannot do that with yourself, you cannot do that with others and others cannot deeply relate to you. The lights are on but nobody's home. You are lonely in a group of friends. You feel like no one understands you, like no one really knows you. And you are right, because all social interactions start with you knowing yourself. Practice the seven tools faithfully. The third tool, acceptance of what is, will help you free yourself from denial, repression, transference, excuses, rationalizing, and all those other tricks you've learned to bury your truth.

You may also have adopted group or cultural fantasies rather than determine your own truth for yourself. The extreme end of that spectrum would be joining a cult or a gang, but identifying with any group—whether that group is a religious sect, a political party, a professional association, or even a nation—can be done addictively. It doesn't have to be, though; it depends upon what aspects of Consciousness you are accessing and the health of the relationship you have with your feelings.

If you want to heal your life, first heal your relationship with your own feelings. Get their message. Let them take you deeply into your world view and align it with higher truth. Review the section on Rule Number One and the Three 'A's. If you are reading this, chances are whatever you've experienced so far in your life, you've survived it. Revisiting it to see what conclusions you drew when you went through it the first time is not going to kill you. In other words, you need not fear your feelings. You have the wisdom and resources to get through your life and come out healthy.

Loss of Trust

Your healing path will also be blocked if you lose trust in yourself. If a woman keeps getting into abusive relationships, she may lose trust in her ability to choose a good partner. If the entrepreneur keeps losing money, she may lose trust in her ability to start and run good businesses. Parents facing difficulties with their teens may lose trust in their parenting abilities. If this has ever happened to you, almost always this loss of trust happened because you drew the wrong conclusions from your experiences. The conclusions you drew may be perfectly reasonable and rational, but by "wrong" I mean the conclusion is too limiting, it closes you off from love in your life, it paints you into a corner, it is not true from a higher or spiritual perspective.

Over and over I witness my patients having trouble because they are unwilling to cooperate with their higher self. Your higher self often asks you to risk, to do something you've never done before, to act without knowing all the details. This can be very unnerving. But I bet you have examples from your life or you've heard your friends telling their stories of being in a place of uncertainty or a situation in which things seemed to be going all wrong and you've just given yourself over to total acceptance and things worked out well in the end. This message to trust is a common theme in many fairy tales. The hero (you) leaves the comfortable village where you grew up (your ego mind) and enters the trackless forest from whence no one ever returns (your unconscious and societal fear of the unknown) and meets a funny old man (your higher self) who gives you a strange present that you can't make heads or tails of at the time. Later in the story, the gift comes in handy and saves your life. Other characters in the story refused the gift and spurned the old man and went on to die later (an unfulfilled life). If you didn't have lots of fairy tales read to you when you were young, I hope you have your own kids or grandkids you can read them to and then you both can benefit.

Often my patients don't believe their inner voice because it feels too dreamlike and we're taught that dreams are not real. Yet dreams are probably the most common method your unconscious uses to communicates with your conscious. So the conscious mind often associates any communication from the unconscious with dreams, even if that communication happens when you are awake. So practice trusting that inner voice, no matter how quiet or dreamy it seems at first. (Besides, who's to say that dreams aren't real? See the section on dreams in the Awareness chapter.)

People who have lost trust in themselves often feel like that astronaut who is out spacewalking and the lifeline to their ship gets cut: no matter how you flail your arms and legs, you're not getting any closer to where you want to go. If you relate to this and you've lost trust in yourself in some way, once that trust is lost, how is it regained? Review the section on Faith. Trust is a choice that can be revisited and re-evaluated in each moment. In other words, with enough awareness in the moment, you can choose trust. To rebuild trust you often have to stop giving your power to your fears. Review the section on fear.

To not trust yourself and your ability to hear and heed your own inner guidance is a very painful way to exist. When you are in the middle of such a phase in your life, it is hard to see anything else. When I've gone through such periods myself, it's like "hang on and just do the best you can do." And then, when I get through such periods and look back, I see them as times of intense learning, generally of something really new or of a really deep and particularly opaque block that I didn't know I had. Whatever you are going through, try to have the presence of mind to keep practicing the seven tools. That will perhaps help you get through the rough times a little more quickly and gracefully and learn all that such experiences hold for you to learn. You are actually not like that astronaut; you can find your way back to yourself, even if you feel like your lifeline has been completely cut.

Ineffective Use of Therapies

Another huge pit that many of my patients fall into is the improper use of many of the treatment modalities that are available. Most treatment modalities have something of value to offer. The problem is often not with the modality, but with the consciousness with which it is applied. Just about anything can be used addictively. Take positive thinking, for example. On the surface, thinking positively sounds like a good idea: trying to keep a positive outlook on life, looking for the best in people, and such, can have a very beneficial influence on your healing. But, looking deeper, if forcing yourself to think positively is in direct denial of your personal truth in that moment, you will be blocked. For example, to keep telling yourself that you are having a wonderful, glorious day, when in reality everything is going to hell, will only make sure you get there faster. Rather than force your thoughts to be positive, watch the thoughts you judge to be negative, follow them back to their roots—to that aspect of your world view that created them—and use compassion to align that aspect of your world view with higher truth. Do this, and the negative thoughts will stop coming and your outlook will just naturally gravitate toward being more positive.

Watch yourself carefully for any tendency you have to use treatments to avoid, warp, or sugarcoat your truth. With full willingness to be aware of and accept your truth, just about any therapy that you are likely to hear about could conceivably help you … assuming it is appropriate for your condition.

Conventional medicine and many forms of alternative medicine are constantly fighting among themselves about which therapy is better. They use words like "scientific validity" or "evidence-based." But there is a major problem with how medical science is being conducted right now, with drug companies and vitamin manufacturers funding most of it and deciding what does and does not get published. Top that off with advertising budgets the size of Argentina's GNP and nobody knows what is true and what isn't any more. But as far as I, as a clinician, and you, as a patient, are concerned, our challenge is to find the right therapy for you at the right time and use it with the right level of consciousness. With clear vision and a clear mind and in steady consultation with your inner wisdom, you will be able to reap the benefits of whatever kinds of therapies you are drawn to use, conventional and/or alternative, and not get trapped or detoured by them.

So let's say that you have just become aware of a health issue that you are having. For example, your blood pressure is creeping up or your blood sugar is too high or you've just started reacting to a bunch of different foods. If you look at all the healing traditions around the world, you will come up with dozens of ways to treat just about any malady you can think of. Which one is best for you? Which ones ought you to avoid? Because your health issues are clues that there is an imbalance somewhere in your system and because deeper healing implies increasing your understanding of yourself, I look for therapies with two characteristics. First, I look for therapies that try to get to the root of the imbalance, not just treat the symptom of the imbalance. And, second, I look for therapies that help you use the imbalance to deepen your understanding of yourself: how did it get there, what does it need in order to go back into balance, what you can do to prevent it from happening again, is it asking you to change any limiting or spiritually incongruent beliefs? If I can find a single therapeutic approach that does both, all the better.

When deciding which therapy to try, you probably consider what you are hoping to get out of it. Perhaps you might like your symptoms to go away. Obviously, some symptomatic treatments are important; for example, that you keep breathing until your asthma resolves. So a bronchodilator is a good thing to have … just don't stop there. The same can be said about medication for your blood pressure or your blood sugar or your seizures. Control the symptoms but don't stop looking for the root cause. A common pitfall I see with symptomatic therapies is that often, once a person's symptoms are gone, their motivation to go deeper and ask the hard questions is also gone. But then they are left with taking the medication over and over, year after year. If you want to get off of your symptom-controlling medications, get to and treat the root causes of your problems. Practice the seven tools.

Let's say that you want both: to control your symptoms and to go deeper with your understanding and healing. Conventional an alternative medicine are good places to look for good symptomatic treatments. So let's explore the several steps on the path to a deeper understanding of yourself and getting yourself to live your own truth…and their possible traps.

Faith that you can find and be yourself is the first step. Any modality or practitioner that tries to disempower you or make you dependent upon it or them should immediately raise some red flags. I recommend you very carefully evaluate such therapies and practitioners before committing to them. Many different kinds of therapies, from drugs to diets, can fall into this category. Trust your gut sense about this. If the therapist can describe a clear plan of action and a timeframe that leads to the results you really want, that would be reassuring. Nobody can know for sure how you will respond to their treatments, but if they at least have thought about it, that is a good sign.

The next step is to become aware of your truth. Your feelings, both physical and emotional, are simultaneously part of and clues to your truth. Many forms of psychological therapy teach you fancy and powerful strategies to control your feelings, as if your feelings were the problem. Watch carefully. If you are working to change feelings rather than get their message, this is a red flag. You can beat your head against your feelings all day long and, unless you make some fundamental changes to your life or belief system, they will just keep coming back. Most psychological therapists really do want you to explore your feelings and get their meaning and deepen your understanding of whatever situation you are in. Please make sure you are working with your therapist in such a way.

I think you are at more risk of forcing changes on your system without deepening your understanding when you work with energy healers than with psychologists. Many see energy blocks as the problem and use tools to remove those blocks. But an energetic block is a symptom just as much as a headache is a symptom. It is a clue to an imbalance. Rather than dynamite the blockage, explore it, get its side of the story, follow it to the imbalance and work to correct that. If you are receiving energy work, make sure you talk with your therapist and let them know that you want to explore blockages and get to their roots, not just clear them. Clearing blocks might give you temporary relief from some pretty uncomfortable feelings but, in the long run, they are very likely to return.

Find a therapist and form of therapy that helps you explore the deeper life of your symptoms, physiological imbalances, feelings, their origin, and the conclusions behind them, and you will make much more progress in your search for health and yourself.

Once a feeling, in its full spectrum as physical, emotional, and energetic (every feeling that you have can be viewed independently and even simultaneously from each of these three perspectives), is listened to and the underlying aspect of your world view uncovered, the next step is to admit fully to yourself the truth of all of it: the experience that you went through, the conclusions that you drew, and how those conclusions have been affecting you ever since. Most good therapists would help you with this acceptance piece. If they skip it, do it for yourself. If they deny your truth, minimize it, or try to get you to rationalize it away, first try to educate them in the error of their ways and, if that doesn't work, find a new therapist.

The next common block occurs once the belief or conclusion or physiological imbalance is uncovered. Our human nature tells us that when we see a problem, fix it. Once we find a limiting belief, we want to change it. If we see a blatantly false belief, we want to jump right in and correct it. If your blood pressure or blood sugar is high, we want to give you drugs to bring them down. Believe it or not, our tendency to use our ego-based cognitive mind to jump in and fix these imbalances and false beliefs is a block. It will keep you stuck. This took me a long time to understand, as the basis of my medical training and even my psychological training is to work on the level of fixing. In the short run, it was often helpful to my patients, but, in the long run, they stayed stuck, just creating more symptoms to take the place of the ones that we'd fixed. So often when a treatment takes away a symptom, we are so grateful. And we give a lot of credit to the treatment. But later, when another symptom arises in our life, we don't often realize that it is the same hydra just raising a different head. We can spend decades chopping off hydra heads and never really touch the heart of the beast.

Steven M. Hall, M.D.

(I think this block goes unrecognized because in order to see it, you must work deeply with the same people for years, watch their course carefully, and be focused on helping them get to the root. Today's medicine, with so many cookie-cutter doctors plugged into slots in corporate-owned clinics, and today's society, with people moving around so much and changing doctors when their insurance changes, just doesn't lend itself to that level of long-term observation.)

Once you uncover an imbalance anywhere in the system of who you are (see Appendix A), first notice your desire to fix it, acknowledge that desire, and have compassion for yourself that you have that imbalance and desire to fix it; then sit with the imbalance and ask it what it wants from you. Learn about it. How did it get there? What can it teach you about yourself? How does it want you to be with it? How can you help it? Let the answers to these questions rise from your gut knowing. In my experience, this is where the imbalance will most likely ask for compassion, both for itself and for you having the imbalance. If you can just allow yourself to rest in that place of compassionate observation of the imbalance and all that it is doing to you and all that it is asking of you, most likely a good and effective answer to how to correct the imbalance, once and for all, will come to you.

What did I just say? Can you repeat it back to me? "If I can just allow myself to rest in that place of compassionate observation of the imbalance and all that it is doing to me and all that it is asking of me, most likely a good and effective answer about how to correct the imbalance, once and for all, will come to me." This is the ladder out of just about any pitfall on your path to healing. Tattoo it to the inside of your eyelids.

At first, you may have to have faith that being the compassionate observer of your life will actually work any real change, but, once you've experienced it a few times, you'll be a believer. It may ask for a specific treatment, such as a medication or lifestyle change and, in my experience, treatments arrived at through this process work really well and don't generate bothersome side effects or complications. Any lifestyle modifications that may be asked for just make sense. They are not a struggle nor do they engender feelings of deprivation in you. You are working with your system, freeing it to just be, rather than ignoring it or forcing it to be any preconceived ego-based way.

But the most important consequence of letting your doing rise from that place of compassionate, accepting awareness is how it affects your creativity. You basically have two choices for the source of your creative flow. You can create out of emotions or you can create out of love. Any therapy or treatment that starts with the assertion that there is something wrong with you that needs to change risks keeping you stuck in your ego- or emotionally based creativity. When you or anyone you are working with needs to jump in and fix you in any way, that action is coming from a Forgetting that Everything is All Right (FEAR) perspective. By definition. And this is the problem that I see with most conventional and alternative therapies: they start with the assumption that there is something wrong with you that needs to change. This is as opposed to the view that whenever you are ill, that is an invitation to learn, to be curious, to wonder.

The fix it mentality keeps your creativity flowing from fear. If your present moment, that you so desire to change, was created by past fear-based actions and you continue fear-based actions now, no matter how you change them up by trying different therapies, your future is going to be substantially the same as your past has been. On the other hand, actions that arise from the deep knowing that comes from compassionate, accepting observation are based in compassion, in love. If you are creating your future out of present love-based actions, what are the chances that you might like what gets created?

By avoiding this last block, the need to fix, you can shift your creativity from a foundation of fear or any other emotion, to a foundation of love. And, as you may remember, one healing imperative is to consciously source your creativity from love.

Honest, sincere, consistent practice of the seven tools of healing will help you avoid these pitfalls or at least help you identify when you have fallen into one and help you to get out of it.

Chapter Twelve

Summary

The seven tools of healing are a skill set I've observed my patients acquire as they heal whatever life has given them. Their need to heal drives their search for answers, and, as they practice and improve their competency in these skills, the depth and effectiveness of their healing improves. The same can happen for you. Practice these skills. Apply them to whatever you face. Get the information that is hidden in your experiences; learn to live what your heart says; be true to your authentic self. You can do this.

Your inner wisdom detects when your body, energy, mind, and beliefs are out of balance, and it will rebalance them if it can. If it can't, it will create a symptom to get your attention so you can help in some way. Listen to these symptoms, interpret them correctly, and take the right action that will actually correct the imbalance. The root of the imbalance can be in your biochemistry, energy, mind, belief systems, relationships, or environment. An imbalance in one area can cause symptoms in another or in all areas at once. But such complexity will sort itself out and the right path through the maze will make itself known, if you keep watching, listening, and working with your truth in an accepting, open-hearted way. If you are injured physically and/or emotionally, apply the seven tools to whatever is going on in your life: how much you are able to function now, how your relationships are, all the feelings that you are having, and you will reach resolution more quickly.

Learn about your body. What does it need to function properly? No published list of shoulds knows your moment-to-moment biochemical needs, so learn to listen to what your body wants to eat, what supplements it might want, how to exercise, when to sleep, and such. Watch your physical feelings and follow them back to their roots.

Learn to listen to your mind. Watch your thoughts, see how they affect your body. Learn to choose supportive thoughts without repressing or denying any aspect of yourself. One way to do that is to choose to stay in touch with your heart. Since you can choose what to focus your attention upon, why not choose your heart?

Learn to watch your energy. There is much information available to you in how your energy flows, how it is blocked, its frequency and intensity and such. Again, get its message and listen for the right action it is asking for.

Learn to watch your beliefs. Beliefs are so powerful. They both shape the way you see the world and set the boundaries on what you're able to create. Limiting beliefs and beliefs that go against higher truths will create symptoms in your life.

Whatever you observe with all your watching, see the real truth of it. Admit that truth and choose kindness for yourself that this is your truth. The truth, fully accepted and lovingly observed, will set you free. The truthfully informed, open-hearted perspective will allow you to choose how best to act in any given situation.

All that really exists is this very moment. We are here to learn to love better. All there is to love is this present moment. Ask yourself, "I wonder how much more I can love this present moment?"

Faith. Awareness. Acceptance. Compassion. Forgiveness. Gratitude. Right action. Your soul knows who you are; it knows what you came into this life to experience. Practice the seven tools until you are a master at them. Use the seven tools to work your soul's purpose.

Though we seem to be sleeping,

there is an inner wakefulness

that directs the dream,

and that will eventually startle us back

to the truth of who we are.

~Rumi

Appendix A

The Vedic Model of a Human Being

The goal of science is to understand nature. Each scientific discipline focuses on its particular aspect of nature. Biologists focus on living systems, astronomers on the stars, ichthyologists on gross and disgusting religious practices (not really, just making a joke about the sound of the word. I have nothing against people who study fish or who put bumper stickers of fish on their cars).

We don't understand all the complications and interrelationships of nature, so scientists start their study by designing simplified models of their particular subject. These models are always based upon foundational assumptions about nature. From the models, they make predictions about how nature would respond to a particular perturbation. They then design an experiment to actually carry out the desired perturbation, trying to control as many possibly confounding variables as they can, and watch to see how nature responds.

For example, if you were studying an ant hill, you would notice that ants scour the countryside in search of food and carry it back to the hill. So you might predict that if you sprinkled a few bread crumbs around, the ants would find them and carry them back to their hill. You might even make some predictions about how long that might take or, if you want to get really fancy, develop a mathematical expression relating the distance of the crumb from the hill and how long it takes the ants to find it and fetch it back. You then spread some breadcrumbs and watch to see what the ants do. If your predictions are correct, then you start to believe that perhaps your model of an anthill actually captures some truth about nature. Scientists continue to think up more and more ways to test their models, until they are sure that the model is either true or needs revising. Most scientists are excited by experimental results that do not fit predictions, because that means that a deeper understanding of nature is needed.

The process of science is arguably the best method humans have yet devised to arrive at a true understanding of a question about nature (one could also argue that contemplation by an adept is also an excellent methodology for understanding truth). When done correctly, the process of science is self-correcting, inevitably honing in on the truth. The biggest problem with science is that it is performed by humans. Even scientists are susceptible to ulterior motives and prejudicial beliefs. Sometimes their theories become their life's work and they cannot stand to think that they have been wrong for so long. Other times, as in the case of conventional medical science, the process has been hijacked and subverted by drug companies in the name of greater drug sales and profits[101]. A similar hijacking has happened in the food and agriculture sciences by high-tech agribusinesses[102]. These forces benefit by views of nature that support their business plans and do all they can to keep science from growing beyond that. But I believe that, in the end, truth wins out and science continues to progress.

In medicine, the aspect of nature that scientists study is you ... and your experiences of health and disease. One of the problems we're having in medicine is that, on one hand, we have very good data to support the thesis that every aspect of your life exerts some sort of influence upon your health (therefore, the ideal medicine would be able to take into account every aspect of your life, including your beliefs, your energy, and your soul) and, on the other hand, narrow scientists have unilaterally claimed the right to decide reality ... and they only acknowledge as real that which can be measured with their instruments (therefore, they want to limit the scope of their study of you to those aspects that show up on blood tests, biopsies, and various scans and such).

To the conventional medical scientist, you are a skin-bag of chemical reactions. Their belief is that if we could but know what those chemical reactions are, then we could pour in other chemicals and cure all of human disease and suffering. No doubt curing all of human disease and suffering is a noble goal. The problem is that this view of you is based upon a late-nineteenth-century Newtonian insight that life is chemistry. The drug companies have fixated on this notion ... because it so niftily serves their needs ... while, in the meantime, the rest of science has moved on to more accurate and reliable theories, theories that require the existence of Consciousness.

This purely physical view of you is not as innocuous as it sounds; it has profound consequences. To the conventional medical scientist, your mind is a byproduct of the neuronal activity in your brain, the same neuronal activity that somehow mysteriously creates the illusion of consciousness. This antiquated view is powering the search for "designer drugs," the attempt to explain everything human in terms of genes, and the brain initiative. (Studying the brain is great for deepening our understanding of the brain, but studying the brain in an attempt to understand how it is that we are conscious makes about as much sense to me as dissecting the heart in an attempt to understand how we love. See Appendix C for a more quantum theory of consciousness, mind, and body.)

Because of this prevailing world view, practitioners routinely tell depressed patients that their depression is just due to a chemical imbalance in their brains so they should just take the drugs and save their breath: counselling is of no value. This is just one example of many practices that are based upon the conventional medical view and that greatly prolong human suffering.

A scientific model is just some person's idea (more usually, a consensus of a group of scientists), and it is based on a set of simplifying assumptions. In any scientific discipline you care to look at, the prevailing models will have some observations of nature that do not fit or cannot be explained by the model. This is because the model is not yet a complete description of nature. That we already know. So, as a scientist, my loyalties lie more with the data than with the models. Models are meant to be refined and updated, not defended to the death. (In the early years of physics' painful growth toward quantum mechanics, a prominent physicist once lamented that physics changes one funeral at a time. I fear the same is going to happen as medicine changes.) In medicine, the data that our scientific models need to explain are your experiences, all of your experiences, all of human experience for that matter.

Even as early as the second year of medical school, I was starting to hear of people's health experiences that could not be explained by the conventional medical model I was taught. As I got further into my training, I became more and more distressed by how often physicians would ignore aspects of a patient's history that they could not explain, discard experiences that their patients were trying to tell them about that did not fit the conventional medical world view, and some would even get hostile toward the patient and blame them. From where I sit now, after 30+ years of practice, I know these physicians who were supervising my training were just doing what they were trained to do. I do not think they even realized that what they were doing, in reality, was practicing scientism, the religion of science. When the dogma supplants the data, when adherence to the medical model is more important than acknowledging the patient's experience: that is practicing the religion of science, believing that the prevailing model is the gospel truth. That is not science.

I knew from my undergraduate training that the most unscientific thing a scientist can do is discard data just because it doesn't fit the prevailing model. Such data is called "outlying data" and is vital to the progress of science, as it is the data that any new, supplanting model must also take into account, along with all the data already adequately explained by the previous model. So I started collecting patients' experiences that were outlying. That's not difficult, as so many are. Some examples of medical outlying data include the placebo effect, and the proven clinical effectiveness of acupuncture, homeopathy, therapeutic touch, visualizations, Reiki, and clinical hypnosis.

According to the science historian Thomas Kuhn[14], outlying data continues to accumulate until the weight of it unbalances the prevailing theory and the theory topples over. At that point, the foundational assumptions get reformulated to incorporate the changes in world view. Some examples from history include the changes in the phlogiston theory of combustion when oxygen was discovered and the change from Newtonian mechanics to quantum mechanics in physics. Kuhn delineated a series of symptoms that a scientific discipline exhibits as it nears such a "paradigm shift" (a term he coined). Currently, conventional medicine is exhibiting all of those symptoms. I think the conventional medical model would have toppled long ago if it weren't so vehemently propped up by drug companies and their large and loyal sales force: conventional physicians.

One of the symptoms Kuhn described is the proliferation of competing theories, all attempting to better explain the outlying data and get traction on the world stage. Eventually, one of the competing theories starts to rise to the surface and becomes the new prevailing model. Until a critical amount of outlying data accumulates again. And so science marches on. Just as climate change deniers will eventually have to give way to the weight of the data, someday even the drug companies will weaken their grip. There will come a time when they will see that they can embrace a more humanistic view of medicine and still make plenty of profit. There will always be plenty of naturally occurring illness and human suffering to go around. They will come to realize that they don't have to suppress real healing and manipulate the market to keep people sick just to sell drugs (am I still naïve?).

As I witnessed more and more the limitations of the conventional medical model, I started to think about and search for a better model. The model I operate from now, the integral medical model, has several components that I describe in other publications, but the aspect of the model I want to explain to you here is a proposed model of a human being. Since the human being is the part of nature studied by the sciences that underlie medicine, I think it is important to have as complete a working model of one as possible.

I searched many of the world's healing traditions and the model I found that best explains the process of healing, as I observe people's inner wisdom walking them through it, is the model that underlies the Vedic traditions of yoga and Ayurvedic medicine. This model goes back, as far as I can tell, about 6000 years. It has been used by yogis and sages for eons and has withstood the test of time and scrutiny by some of the most enlightened beings ever to live on the planet. That said, it is still just a model, a grossly simplified description of a human being. I have just found it very useful for understanding relationships among mind, body, energy, beliefs, experiences (including treatment modalities), consciousness, Consciousness, and creativity … many of the ingredients important to health and disease.

This model has helped me make sense out of all kinds of my patients' experiences that don't fit neatly into the current conventional medical model. This model helps explain mind-body interactions, body energy, how the mind works, how Consciousness relates to our body and mind, how diseases can affect the body and mind simultaneously, how beliefs work, how creativity works, and several other phenomena.

The ancient Vedic sages saw the human as made up of six aspects, or irreducible perspectives. To make the model more complete for medical purposes, I also add the concept that a person is immersed in, and influenced by, a social milieu made up of his or her family, friends, culture, and the like as well as in an environmental milieu made up of food, air, water, weather, land, pollutants, and such.

One model of a human being:

1. You have a body. This is the part of you that conventional medicine pays the most attention to. It is your "skin-bag of biochemical reactions." It needs food, water, air, sleep, exercise, and the like. The body's biochemical and physiological processes can fall out of balance in myriad ways and conventional medical therapies are aimed at coercing those processes back to normal.

2. You have energy. This is the part of you that energy workers, such as practitioners of Reiki and Therapeutic Touch, pay most attention to. This is what enlivens you; it is prana, chi, the vital life force, or whatever you want to call it. It has many attributes in common with electricity, such as direction of flow, frequency, amount of flow, or current, and pressure or strength of flow, like voltage; but it is clearly not electricity. Your body does generate electricity and uses it for many physiological processes. Electrical energy is physical and included in the body. This vital life energy is different. It needs to flow freely. Energy anatomy and physiology are just as complex as body anatomy and physiology. The energy can go out of balance in about as many ways as can the body.

3. You have a mind. The mind comprehends and processes data and assigns meaning. This is the part of you that bridges between the physical world and Consciousness. The mind takes the data

from your senses and makes conscious sense out of it. It needs information and images to process. Mental processes are also very intricate and complex and can go out of balance in many different ways. In this model, your brain is part of your body and your mind is its own unique perspective on you.

4. Your mind has content. This is the part of you that psychology pays the most attention to. These are your thoughts, beliefs, personality traits and such. Researchers estimate that two to five percent of your mental activity is conscious, so ninety five to ninety eight percent of your mental activity takes place in your unconscious.

5. You have an inner observer. This is the part of you that many forms of meditation focus on. It can watch your mind think, your body feel, and your energy flow. It can watch all other aspects of you. It is often called the "seat of the soul."

6. You are a social being. You are greatly influenced by your family, culture, language, and relationships. Research is showing that community exerts a stronger influence upon your health than does diet, exercise, and even smoking.

7. You live in a physical environment. You are greatly influenced by nutrition, environmental factors like the weather, electromagnetic fields, pollutants, and countless others.

8. You are a spiritual being. You have an aspect of you that is outside the laws of time and space, that is immortal, that is wise and loving. This aspect of you will not be hurt or tarnished by anything that happens within the laws of physics. This is your own individual "piece" of pure, undifferentiated Consciousness.

The ancient sages saw these aspects arranged like sheaths within sheaths, sort of like the wooden nesting dolls. These sheaths are called "koshas" in Sanskrit. Alternatively, they are also portrayed as concentric circles, like a target. For the five outer-most aspects, the first five listed above, the Sanskrit name included the suffix "maya", which gets variously translated as "impermanent" or "illusory." The sages knew your body is not an illusion but it is impermanent in time and space. There was a time when you didn't have a body and there will be a time when you don't have a body again. But, of all the possible translations for "maya," the one I like the best is "not as it appears to be." Thinking about the first five aspects that way reminds me that there are deeper truths or realities than just those appearing on the surface. I often call the first five sheaths "the mayas", for future reference.

Figure 1 Russian Nesting Dolls

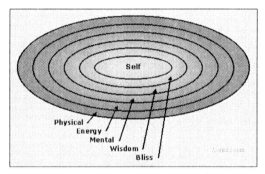

Figure 2 The Five Koshas Surrounding Self

I have thought long and hard about how these aspects relate to each other. In Appendix C, I present one possible quantum explanation for these things, which also helps explain what we see clinically. But before getting too geeky, I want to describe a few clinical observations.

First, have you noticed that you have a fairly constant sense of self inside that has been there as long as you have been self-aware? It is ageless and unique to you. It is your own personalized piece of pure Consciousness. Also, mind, body, and energy seem to be correlates of each other; in other words, they do not seem to function as separate aspects that are somehow "connected" but rather as different, simultaneous perspectives of something deeper.

Spinoza[15], when he was working on the problem of mind/body duality, concluded something very similar. He said that who we really are as humans is a mystery. He said that mystery is composed of "divine substance." If you look at that divine substance for physical characteristics, such as your height, weight, blood chemistries, and CT scans (he didn't mention CT scans, I just threw that in), you can find those things. If you look at that divine substance for mental characteristics, such as what you love, what inspires you, what motivates you, you can find those things. One might also add that if you look at that divine substance for energetic properties, such as the color and intensity of your aura, how your energy is flowing, what is happening in your chakras, you can find those things. The ancient Vedic sages saw that we have five such ways to look at that divine substance which is your true self, your spiritual self.

Pure Consciousness, the heart of who you are, did not have "maya" in the Sanskrit name, Atman. This implies that Atman is outside the laws of physics, outside time and space. Atman is the unchanging, the timeless, the pure potential, the source of your creativity. The inner observer is also your inner wisdom, inner guidance, or inner love that you use the seven tools to open your mind to. As discussed in the body of the *Seven Tools of Healing*, beliefs play a pivotal role in your access to Consciousness and the access Consciousness has to your life. For these reasons, rather than as simple nestings, I see these aspects acting more as in Figure 3

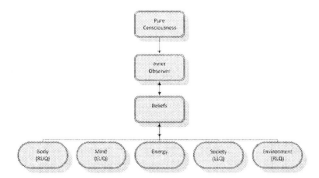

Figure 3 Proposed interrelationships of the different aspects of who we are.

To get a fairly realistic understanding of how these aspects interrelate will require, for most, a shift in how you think about the world. For example, if you were going to build a robot, you'd start with a machine that would be the robot's body. You would then add a battery pack or some other form of energy. Then you would add a computer to run the machine and program the computer with the software and data it needs to do its job. So the outer four aspects of a human make sense. Even a simple robot would have them. And this is pretty much as far as most conventional and even alternative medical models go.

But the ancient sages saw that we have two more aspects deeper than these four. The fifth aspect is labeled "bliss" in figure 2 because this part of us can directly experience spiritual bliss. It is still a maya, still within the laws of physics, but it has many of the same properties as does Consciousness. Clinically, I see this fifth aspect function as your inner observer. But it is not just any cold, aloof, scientific observer: it is spirit; it is wise, loving and understanding. Walt Whitman and some of his other Romantic poet buddies talked about this watcher, but, other than that, it is mostly unacknowledged in Western thought. But this fifth aspect is an important part of most Eastern philosophies and has been fairly well introduced into the West over the last seventy years or so. The Sanskrit name for this fifth aspect is Anandamayakosha. Ananda means spiritual bliss then maya means not as it appears to be, or impermanent in time and space, and kosha is a sheath over the true self. But it goes by many other names around the world, such as our true self, our higher self, Buddha nature or Christ Consciousness.

And, lastly, deeper than your higher self, you have your own piece of pure undifferentiated Consciousness that is outside time and space, which we can call God within, your immortal soul, pure undifferentiated Consciousness, Atman, etc.

When we make a robot, we can clearly see that it is made of the four separate aspects of body, energy, computer, and software. These aspects do have interrelationships and interdependencies but are clearly separate parts. As human beings, our aspects also have interrelationships and interdependencies, but thinking about them as parts added together to make a whole leads to paradoxes (such as the mind-body duality) and does not explain our observations and experiences very satisfactorily.

Instead of thinking about your body, mind, energy, etc. as separate parts of yourself that have been assembled like pieces of a robot, I invite you to try thinking about them as different perspectives, different ways of looking at yourself. I have found this view more helpful. Remember the story of the blind men feeling an elephant? Thinking about the basic six aspects of a human as just different ways of looking at an essentially mysterious "divine substance" makes it easy to understand how a change in thinking can be associated with a change in physiology, or how taking a pill can change moods, or how acupuncture can change physiology and the like.

Your body doesn't change in isolation. Your mind doesn't change in isolation. Your energy doesn't change in isolation. A change in one will cause instantaneous correlated changes in the others. You could also include society and the environment in this argument. That is why, in Figure 3, I put these five factors all on the same line; they are not hierarchical with each other. This is explained more in Appendix C.

The potential for the pure Consciousness, your true self, is unlimited and is beyond mind and, thus, beyond comprehension. This is your source of creativity. The fifth aspect, the part that can experience the spiritual, sits like a transparent glass sleeve around the pure light of Consciousness, silently observing out through the other layers. The first layer that limits and determines what creativity you are able to manifest in your life is the fourth aspect, your beliefs. Divine substance doesn't change, but as we're able to "let out," so to speak, different frequencies or different aspects of our divine self, all the other aspects change simultaneously, since they are just ways of looking at divine substance. As explained in Appendix C, the quantum mechanical way of looking at these things makes these interdependencies and interrelationships make even more sense.

For simplicity's sake, I use the mobile metaphor to help to understand how the first three perspectives function as correlates of each other. Imagine a mobile hanging down from the ceiling. One bar holds your body and from it hangs all of your organ systems. From another your mind and from it all your thoughts and feelings, from another your energy. You get the point. What happens if one aspect gets out of balance with the others? What happens if you walk up and bump one part of the mobile?

Who you are as your divine, "child of God" self is mostly hidden in your daily life. As you heal, this side of you starts leaking out more. As these changes unfold, you will automatically and simultaneously see changes in your body, mind, thoughts, energy, interactions with others, interactions with your environment, and so on.

This model helps us get a better look at questions like, "Is my depression due to a biochemical imbalance in my brain?" (This is the current tack taken by the pharmaceutical industry's advertising campaign.) The answer given by this model is, "Yes, there is a biochemical representation of your depression in your brain, and also in your kidneys, and liver and skin and … There would also be a representation of your depression in your energy, in your mind and in your beliefs. This leaves open the question about what is causing your depression. Treatments could be pharmacological, cognitive, and/or energetic." And, indeed, all of these kinds of treatments have been used for depression and each has its own probability of success.

What does this model say about causation? This model would suggest that Consciousness is causal. By Consciousness, I am referring to the last listed perspective labeled as "Self" in Figure 2, or the mysterious "divine substance." Everything in the physical universe, including your five mayas, is just an expression of some aspect of pure, infinite Consciousness. Many Native American cultures understand this. They see spirit in the Earth, the air, the wind, the water, everywhere they look. Animals each express a particular aspect of Consciousness as does each disease.

What does this model say would be the cause of disease? A disease can develop due to an imbalance in any of the factors in Figure 3 below pure Consciousness. I don't have any proof, of course, but I like the belief that spirit doesn't get sick; there are no mistakes on the spiritual level; everybody's soul is competent to live their life. But imbalances can occur within any other factor in this model. Triggers could be environmental pollutants, toxic relationships, poor nutrition, physical injuries, excess stress, fear or hatred, limiting beliefs—there is a very long list. And an imbalance in one factor will show up in your life as changes in all the other factors. So finding the primary imbalance, the lynch pin, the Rosetta Stone, for example, can be daunting and is one adventure that makes the practice of medicine so intriguing.

But any disease that you may find yourself contending with must also be reconciled with the Law of Consciousness that states that you are not a victim. From one perspective, as a child of God, you are a free being. Yet so many diseases, disasters and other events in your life seem to just show up uninvited. How do you reconcile that? More importantly, how can you be in a situation over which you have no control and exercise your personal power at the same time? This is a question you have to answer for yourself, but people's inner wisdom reminds them over and over to put themselves in the role of the student (see Appendix B). Disease, like any other experience, is a chance to learn more about yourself and bring your choices and actions more into alignment with who you really are. The bodily responses to your diseases can be seen as your body's way of getting your attention. The mental angst associated with disease can be thought of as your mind's way of getting your attention. All of it is calling for some kind of change. One purpose of this book is to prepare you to be able to respond in a healthy and timely way to the messages, in the form of your life, coming to you from your Consciousness.

Note the ramifications of this model: the disease pattern in your body, in your mind, in your energy, in your relationships, etc., is some aspect of Consciousness expressing itself in your life. Since what you believe determines what aspects of Consciousness get expressed in your life, it is theoretically possible to find and change the beliefs that are allowing the disease-causing aspects of Consciousness into your life, thus stopping the process of the disease being created and allowing you to heal. The practice of the seven tools of healing is the best way that I have found to help my patients find and change these beliefs. Please practice them for yourself. I have yet to witness someone truly heal and remain a victim at the same time.

Next, I would like to take a deeper look into each element of this model, of each unique perspective into who you are, with an eye on how they can help you get to know yourself better and help you regain and remain healthy.

The Physical Body

Many wisdom traditions think of the body as a house for the soul during this life. Judeo-Christian traditions refer to the body as a "temple." What is meant by that? Many in our culture interpret this saying to mean that they better take good care of their body. Taking care of your body is always a good idea, but to this I say, "Yes, some people go to the temple to mow the lawn or clean the bathrooms, but that is not why most people go to the temple." What are people doing while they are in the temple? They worship or connect with something that feels greater than themselves. Calling the body a temple implies that you can have the same connection with spirit … that you can commune with God … by living in your body with the necessary frame of mind.

I see the body as the physical mouthpiece or spokesperson for the inner wisdom, the teacher. As mentioned earlier, any communication from Consciousness can be simultaneously perceived from all of the different perspectives we have available: physical, energetic, mental—but the body, as the outer most of your perspectives, is the easiest to believe is real and is often the easiest for most of us to pay attention to.

Your inner wisdom knows when something in your life is in balance, out of balance, and, most importantly, how to get it back into balance. When something is out of balance, it generates symptoms, hoping to get your attention so you take action to get the imbalance back into balance. Those symptoms show up in the body. The body can speak to you about:

- imbalances in your biochemistry, such as when you are thirsty or hungry
- imbalances in your physiology, such as when you need to relieve yourself or get up and stretch
- imbalances in your thoughts and beliefs, such as when you are anxious or depressed
- imbalances in your energy
- social and environmental imbalances will also show up as physical symptoms

Imbalances anywhere in your life will be felt by your body as a physical symptom. But, as you can see from this model, not every physical symptom has a physical cause. Not every physical symptom is asking for a drug or supplement or physical treatment.

The aspect of you that generates the symptom knows the answer that will satisfy it. Remember the example of thirst and how you learned that thirst meant go get some water.

You would benefit greatly from being able to continue the kind of listening and knowing that helps you interpret your symptoms correctly.

Learning how to listen to your body, how to interpret the information correctly and then take the proper steps to respond appropriately to what it is asking of you are the most important skills to help you regain and/or keep your health and to be a good student of life.

Because of the mobile effect—imbalances anywhere in your life will have some kind of effect on your body—the body can be used to "sense in", so to speak, to the congruency or incongruency of many different possible scenarios. One way to look at the body is to see it as an attention-getting device. The feelings that come through your body are messengers bringing you information about what is really going on inside. For this reason, you can learn to use bodily sensations as a meter for what fits and what doesn't fit with who you are. That is why the body meter exercise works.

With practice, you can get quite skilled at using the feelings in the body to stay in balance and in the flow each moment.

Energy

The subject of your energy was covered in detail in Chapter 2. Just remember that this is vital life energy and is different from the four kinds of energy described by physics (and is used for simplicity's sake in the robot analogy). It is sometimes referred to as your vital body, to differentiate it from your physical body. I have met people who can see this body, also referred to as your aura or your etheric body. I have also had patients for whom listening to their energy was easier for them than listening to their body. Since the information presented by each of their bodies is the same, they were still able to get to the roots of their imbalances.

Many treatments are specifically directed toward this energy. Food contributes to your energetic body as well as to your biochemical body. So do herbs. Homeopathy and flower essences are also primarily energetic treatments. Acupuncture, Reiki, therapeutic touch, and craniosacral therapy, to name a few, are therapies that work directly on energy and how it flows.

Energy can also be directed by Consciousness. When asked how they can do so many amazing things with their bodies, yogis often respond, "I can direct the flow of prana in my body." Have faith that your energy is real (if you're not already convinced) and practice listening to it. The more lines of communication you have open between our conscious mind and Consciousness, the easier you can heal.

The Mind

In this model, the mind is thought of as our ability to apprehend and process data: to make conscious sense of our information. We get information from our five physical senses and from our intuitions and inspirations. The mind functions like a bridge between pure Consciousness and the physical world. The mind is also, along with the body and energy, yet another window into the divine mystery that is you.

There is currently a big confusion between the mind and the brain. Articles in even the most rigorous scientific journals use the two words synonymously. There is also a big argument going on about whether or not the mind is just a by-product of neurons acting inside the brain or is it somehow something outside the body, existing separately from the body. This argument is often referred to as "the mind-brain problem" and has been going on for centuries.

The brain is a physical organ; it has physical properties such as mass and chemical composition. The brain is included in the physical perspective in the model I'm describing. Most people working in the neurosciences speak as if they believe that activity in the brain is the root cause of how you think, feel, and act; that something in the way your neurons are interacting determines those things. They believe that what we construe as Consciousness is a by-product of the neuronal activity in the brain. They must not have talked to Max Plank.

Consciousness, with a small "c", is arguably produced by the specific orchestration of neuronal activity in the brain, but this consciousness is not the source of your creativity, your volition, or your intuition. They look at what parts of the brain are more active in people who are depressed or anxious or who play the piano or participate in athletic activities, and they say that this brain activity is causing the depression or anxiety, that the brain activity is causing the piano playing or athletic activity. In the model I am presenting here, the mind is not physical, it has no mass that we know of; it has no chemical composition. The mind is not limited to the brain.

The mind is another way of viewing "divine substance." See Appendix C for a quantum mechanical theory of mind.

Sure, the function of the brain is important to the physical expression of the mind, but the same can be said about the lungs, heart, intestines, kidneys, or any part of the body. Certainly if you had a stroke or developed Alzheimer's, these things can affect how your mind expresses itself in the physical world. But that expression of your mind would also be affected if your lungs stopped putting oxygen into your blood or if your heart stopped beating or if you stopped absorbing your nutrients. Our current intense scientific examination of the brain and how it functions is helping us understand the brain. But it is shedding very little light on the characteristics of the mind or of Consciousness itself.

You might ask why the confusion between the brain and the mind is so important. The answer is that it shapes research priorities and therapies. In the model I'm proposing here, the job of the mind is to take in information from the senses, from your imagination and intuition, and make conscious sense out of it. The brain follows orders from your mind and distributes the necessary information to the body by way of the nerves and neurohormones. What the neuroscientists are seeing on functional MRI, PET scans, and EEGs are whatever your brain has to do inside of itself in order to comply with what is being asked of it. Your brain does not originate the asking. You, your volitional self, your Conscious self, initiates the asking. Your brain functions like an intricate switchboard to funnel the information where it needs to go. The neuronal axons are even structured like the wires in the old manual switchboards.

Years ago, I attended a basic science conference at Swedish Hospital in Seattle entitled "The Mind-Brain Conference." I thought to myself, "maybe they're getting it; I'd like to go hear what they have to say." The conference started with the story of Phineas Gage.

The Strange Case of Phineas P. Gage

In the summer of 1848, Phineas P. Gage was managing a group of men laying railroad tracks across a rocky stretch of Vermont countryside. Tall and athletic, the twenty-five-year-old Gage was a model employee, "efficient and capable," according to his boss, as well as temperate, shrewd, smart, and "persistent in executing his plans of action." One of Gage's tasks was to set explosive charges in rocks. His men would typically drill a hole in a rock, place gunpowder and a fuse in the hole, cover the powder with sand, and then tamp the sand with a three-foot long, thirteen-pound iron bar, so the explosion would be directed downward into the rock.

Gage was expert at this task, which he had performed many times. One day, after the fuse had been placed, but before sand had been poured in the hole, someone called to Gage. Distracted, he dropped the bar into the hole, igniting the fuse and the powder. The resulting explosion launched the bar like a rocket upward into Gage's face. The bar penetrated his left cheek, went through the top of his skull and landed a hundred or so feet away, covered with blood and portions of Gage's brain. Still conscious, Gage was taken to a nearby doctor. Miraculously, he survived. Even without antibiotics he fought off infection and eventually the hole in his skull healed. In less than two months, Gage's doctors pronounced him "cured."

While Gage's wounds had healed and he could walk, talk, and use his hands like any normal man, he was hardly his old self. In fact, he was a new person, one so different that his employers refused to take him back. Friends noted that "Gage was no longer Gage." This new Gage could not manage his emotions. He was fitful, irreverent, and profane. He was impatient and acted on his desires without restraint. At times, he was stubborn and yet, at other times, he could not make up his mind. He couldn't plan for the future.

He went from job to job, sometimes getting fired, sometimes quitting capriciously. He traveled and joined the circus as a freak, posing with the iron bar from his accident. Finally, he ended up living with his mother and sister as their dependent. In 1861, at age 38, he died during a seizure. What had happened to this once capable, temperate man, who seemed from the outside to have healed from his horrific wounds?

Researchers found the answer in the early 1990s, after creating computer simulations of Gage's skull. They learned that the accident had damaged a specific part of Gage's brain, the prefrontal cortex. They concluded that this damage impaired his ability to plan and make decisions."[103]

People have been using the story of Phineas Gage to support the idea that brain structure and function are primary in how the mind works, in our personalities and such, for over a hundred years. The rest of the mind-brain conference was dedicated to describing experiment after experiment in which monkeys were trained to do specific memory tasks. Very specific parts of their brains were then destroyed and observations were made about how that brain damage affected the monkeys' ability to perform their memory tasks. In this way, very specific information was being learned about what the different parts of the brain did.

As I was sitting there that afternoon, I imagined that if some aliens came to Earth, they would see that the dominant life forms on many parts of the planet are these pleomorphic organisms rolling around on ribbons of asphalt or concrete. If they took a bunch of cars and systematically broke parts of the cars, they could, theoretically, find out how a car works, right down to the individual transistors in the radio. But, I reasoned, that line of research would never be able to answer the question "Why is that car on that road going that direction at that time?" And from a human perspective, that is a more interesting question than how the car works.

Also, if you were driving down the road and someone blew a tamping rod through your steering column and you started swerving all over the road, other drivers might think that you were a very crazy and unpredictable driver. How many would think that perhaps you are still a good driver but that the machinery is no longer responding to your orders? In this metaphor, the car would be your body, including your brain, and you, the driver in the car, would be your volitional mind. How much use is a car without a driver? On the other hand, could you even call yourself a driver if you didn't have a car? The body needs Consciousness; otherwise it is no more than a skin-bag of biochemical reactions. Consciousness needs a body; otherwise it has no way of being in the material world. How much use is your body without your mind or your mind without your body? They are so intertwined and we have no way of measuring mental activity separate or independent from brain activity, so the mind-brain confusion is understandable. This confusion is also dangerous and interferes with healing.

Conventional medicine believes that issues such as anxiety, depression, mood swings, anger outbursts, post-traumatic stress triggering, disassociation, ADD, addictions and such are all due to chemical imbalances in your brain. This leads to the logical conclusion that the best way to treat all of these conditions is to pour in other chemicals in an attempt to get your brain chemistry back into balance. You might as well just save your breath and not do any counselling. You are just a victim of these things, so there are no lessons to be learned or meaningful changes that you can initiate on your own. This view of psychiatry is being promoted by some of the wealthiest and most powerful corporations on the planet. They are expert at watching out for their own interests; meanwhile, people's suffering is prolonged with suppressive, rather than curative, therapies.

There are chemical representations in the brain for all of your thoughts and feelings. That is true. And the brain adapts, some people refer to this as "wearing grooves in your brain." So, of course, if you think a lot of depressing thoughts, your brain is going to get better at doing depression. But that doesn't mean that the brain cannot be trained to get better at something else as well. The important therapeutic question is, "which is more causal, the thought or the chemical representation of the thought in the brain?" If you believe that the chemical representation in the brain is more causal, you believe in the primacy of the brain; drugs, surgery, ECT, and the like are therefore therapies that make sense. If you believe, instead, that the thought is more causal and the chemistry and all of the brain's information transfer happens second (thoughts and feelings also have chemical implications all throughout the body, not just in the brain. See Candice Pert and the *Molecules of Emotion*[19]), then you believe in the primacy of Consciousness. Then the existence of creativity and therapies like psychoanalysis, dialectical behavior therapy, insight work, mindfulness, Focusing, and meditation make sense. The quantum mechanical theory proposed in Appendix C offers an explanation for the simultaneous appearance of thoughts in the mind and chemical representations of those thoughts in the body. One does not precede the other. Both are the simultaneous consequences of quantum principles so, according to that model, neither are causal.

The brain and the skin come from the same embryonic layer of tissue called the ectoderm. We know the skin adapts and changes in response to what you ask of it. If you went outside and worked hard in the yard for a month, your hands would callous. They'd toughen up. Are you working in the yard because your hands are toughening up? Of course, as your hands adapt, what you are able to do in the yard before your hands get sore increases. That is the whole reason our bodies can adapt. The brain is no different. It will adapt to what you ask of it. But are you asking of it because it is adapting? Who's doing the asking? This interrelatedness of mind and body has been perplexing for centuries. The quantum mechanical model in Appendix C may be one possible resolution. But, either way you look at it, bringing Consciousness into the healing equation, bringing free will and creativity into the healing equation, offers you much more hope for finding and treating root causes and getting back to a healthy life than if the equation only contained drug and surgery options. You are not a victim of your brain. You do not have to believe everything you think.

Society, and our healing, would be much better served if researchers stopped arguing about mind vs. brain and researched both perspectives equally. I think there are many very powerful and beneficial mind-based therapies that are not being utilized optimally because they get excluded from the conventional scientific conversation. And people are staying sick longer and suffering more because of it. Seeing the body, mind, and energy as different and irreducible perspectives on who we are provides a model that could be the basis of such research. (I get that scientists only want to study things that can be measured, but, personally, I don't understand why scientists resist the concept of Consciousness so rigorously. Doing science is such a creative process; it cannot even be done without the scientist connecting with Consciousness.)

Getting back to how all of this relates to you, to review, you have only one mind, but we divide it into two parts to talk about how it works. You have what we call the "conscious" mind (an unfortunate use of the same word for two different concepts. The consciousness of your awake mind grounded in a mutually agreed-upon physical reality is a part of the greater undifferentiated Consciousness, of course, but is so much less) and then we have all the rest of your mind, the "unconscious." We really don't need to get into whether or not something outside the conscious mind is sub-conscious or supra-conscious. I have not found that distinction clinically necessary.

How are the resources of the mind divided between the two? I'm not sure how anyone arrived at an answer to that question because the unconscious is so vast and, by definition, we don't know a whole lot about it, but the generally agreed-upon answer is about five percent conscious and about ninety five percent unconscious. That may be on a good day. Here's where the mind-brain confusion actually gets humorous. The old estimate used to be that ten percent of the mind is conscious. Many people interpreted that to mean that we only use ten percent of our brain. There is a column entitled "Ask the Experts" in the back of *Scientific American* magazine. A child wrote in asking if it were true that we only use ten percent of our brain. The "expert" answered that, as near as they could tell with EEG's, MRI's, and PET scans, all the brain is working pretty much all the time. He missed a golden opportunity to explain the confusion and also point out that just because something is not conscious, doesn't mean it's not going on or that it is unimportant. Sigh.

To use a computer analogy, the conscious mind can be thought of as your computer screen. It is what is in front of you and contains the information that you're working on now. Behind the screen, several different programs may be running. Your computer has an operating system that coordinates much of what the computer is doing and it may have other programs like security software screening for viruses and such. This is a fairly useful analogy since most people know what happens if they try to open too many programs on their computer at once. This is like sensory overload, which I get every time I go into a shopping mall. Also, if you know how your computer works, you can open all kinds of files that are normally hidden from the casual computer user.

The same can be said about the mind. Anything in the unconscious is potentially available to the conscious mind, if you just know how your mind's filing system works. Dan Millman tells a funny story about this point in *The Way of the Peaceful Warrior*[79]. He was a college student at the time, a world-class gymnast, and he was getting spiritual tutoring from an old man he calls Socrates. One afternoon, Socrates challenged Dan to a feat of physical ability. Dan looked at the old man incredulously, did a one-handed handstand pushup on the corner of the counter, hopped down and said, "Okay, beat that." Socrates looked at him, walked into the bathroom, came out with a glass of water, drank it, set the glass down and said, "There, I win." Dan said, "What!?" Socrates calmly replied that he sensed into his left kidney and it told him that, if he didn't drink some water soon, it would start giving him problems. Dan conceded.

Your body is constantly feeding information to the mind. Most of that information is dealt with without much ado. With the guidance from your unconscious mind, your body runs itself pretty well most of the time without bothering your conscious mind with the details of maintaining skin temperature, balancing electrolytes, digesting your food, running your immune system, and repairing all the little wears and tears, among myriad other tasks. But, with practice, you can learn to watch and even influence these processes in your body.

With practice, you can increase your conscious awareness of the body, leading to the seemingly amazing things yogi's can do with their bodies. The opposite is also true. The conscious mind can control what it pays attention to. When you walk into a friend's house, often there is a smell that you notice. After a few minutes, you don't notice it anymore. That is not because your nose has filtered out all of the chemicals in the air that are causing that smell; it is because your mind has determined that there is nothing harmful or threatening and the conscious mind doesn't have to take up precious attention with that. But if you caught a whiff of smoke or natural gas, your conscious mind would be alerted immediately. The same goes for background noises, familiar objects in your vision, shoes touching your feet, the list goes on.

The unconscious mind has its own data monitoring and data processing functions; it is not just a bank of filing cabinets full of static files waiting for you to take one out, open it on your desk and work on it. The unconscious is making its own decisions, drawing its own conclusions, holding its own beliefs, and it has the power to communicate directly with your body. The unconscious mind controls the majority of your creative capacity, and understands, and probably helps to derive, the symbolism in mythology, dreams, paintings, cinematography, and body language. It's a busy place.

Hypnosis is one way to increase the communication between the conscious and unconscious. Many pain clinics are now utilizing hypnotherapists to help people learn how to tune out chronic pain that cannot be alleviated by other therapies. Biofeedback and neurofeedback are examples of other techniques to consciously access body processes that are normally handled by the unconscious. This model, by putting the mind, with its ability to bridge the physical and the Conscious, in control of the body and energy, explains most of what we call mind-body interactions, "mind over matter", and that sort of folk wisdom.

To apply these concepts to your healing, all you need to know about the mind are two things: a) anything in your mind can be accessed consciously if you learn how and b) the mind's capabilities improve with practice. The mind responds to exercise in much the same way as does the body. Many successful people are in the habit of taking time each day to practice thinking. The practice of awareness, the second of the seven tools of healing, is an excellent mental exercise. Learning how the mind works and how to access information and processes that take place in the unconscious is very useful for healing. Practicing the seven tools of healing help you do this.

The Contents of the Mind

In this model, the contents of the mind are beliefs, conclusions, results of conditioning, language, and such. In the machine metaphor, this perspective of ourselves could be thought of as the software loaded into the computer, as well as the data that the software works on. The contents of the mind, to a very great extent,

- determine your individual personality
- determine how you interpret your experiences
- provide the basis for the choices you make
- make the world look the way it does to you
- determine what you can create
- set the boundaries on the Consciousness you are able to manifest in your life

Since ninety five percent of mental activity goes on behind the scenes (seens) of your conscious mind, most of the beliefs you hold are also in the unconscious part of your mind. You may not know they are there. All you may see of them are the results of their influence showing up in the form of feelings and actions and how the world looks to you. There is a constant flow of information between your conscious and unconscious mind all day long. And the more you learn about how your mind works, how the filing system works, the easier it is to access the unconscious information when you need it.

Your structure of interpretation is included in the contents of the mind, and, since a major thrust of the practice of the seven tools of healing is to align this structure with higher truth, the contents of your mind is very important in your healing process.

Inner Observer

You might have noticed that each perspective gets progressively deeper inside, which makes it harder to grasp for most people. The body is pretty obvious: we can see it and touch it, weigh it and measure it. Hard narrow science can deal with it. The mind and its contents are a little slipperier. They're obvious if we stop and think about them. The sciences that explore them are often referred to as the "soft" sciences. The other perspectives are not even recognized by science at this time, though there is absolutely no reason the scientific process could not be used to study them, too. The study of energy, inner wisdom and Consciousness has been practiced in the East and in the fringe elements of our culture, just not by the mainstream as yet. Perhaps someday.

The fifth perspective is no exception. It is perhaps more difficult to grasp than is the concept of energy. Putting this aspect into some sort of historical context may help in understanding it.

In the ancient Vedic texts, each of the perspectives we've been discussing in this model of a human being has a Sanskrit name. The ancient sages used the metaphor of sheaths, one slid over the other, to describe the relationship of these perspectives. The body was the outer most sheath; then the energy, the mind, and intellect come next; then this fifth aspect.

The Sanskrit name for the fifth perspective is "anandamayakosha." Kosha means sheath, maya means impermanent, and ananda can be translated as "bliss" or "spiritual bliss." In other words, this fifth aspect is that temporally manifest ability we have to experience spiritual bliss. When people rest in the perspective of this fifth aspect, they often feel very calm and peaceful, unperturbed by anything that happens on this Earthly plane.

Sometimes anandamayakosha gets translated as "outer soul" but I'm not sure what that means. For a time, I thought of anandamayakosha as a kind of antenna that connected our minds to what Jung called "the collective unconscious" or to spiritual knowing. It was the conduit for our intuition or inspiration. Now, functionally, I think of it as our inner observer.

You may have noticed that you have the ability to watch your body, as in the body meter exercise. And you can watch your mind thinking thoughts and processing feelings. With practice, you can also watch your energy. Who's doing the watching? Who are you ... independent of all of the wounding, abandonment, limiting conclusions you've drawn, or any of the other experiences you've had in your life? The answer to these questions is what I think of as the fifth perspective: the inner watcher.

But your inner observer is not just any impassive observer: it is the most direct translation of Consciousness, spirit, or God into the physical world. It is a wise, understanding, kind, and compassionate observer. So far, in my own exploration, I've had difficulty telling a difference between the feeling of spiritual bliss and the feeling of pure compassion. The sixth aspect, our soul, or what the Vedic sages called Atman, is the source of compassion. It is our "piece" (for lack of a better word) of undifferentiated Consciousness. Our inner observer is the foot-in-the-door, so to speak, to let that compassion into the manifest world. Compassion is what I call it when love is acting in the world.

As my patients heal, they are more and more able to identify themselves as this kind wise observer. Their "I," their conscious sense of self, shifts from their ego and becomes this kind, wise observer of their life: whatever is happening in their bodies, however their energy is blocked or flowing, how their mind works, what they believe and how those beliefs are impacting themselves, how their relationships work, how their diet and other aspects of their environment impact them, and they are able to hold the whole picture of their present moment in a kind, open-hearted way. The more they heal, the more they are the compassionate observer of themselves. In a circular feedback sort of way, the more they observe themselves compassionately, the more they heal.

I suspect that the almost total absence of this aspect from Western thought is one reason why so many in our culture find healing so challenging; and, perhaps, also why so many of our human constructs, such as corporations, can let profit be the highest ethic, no matter how people or the planet get treated in the process.

Soul

The sixth perspective in the model of a human being could be thought of as the same thing Spinoza was calling "divine substance." It is the perspective that includes all perspectives. Some call it "unity consciousness." In the Vedic texts, it is called Atman. It is the ageless, timeless, pure Consciousness, the true Self over which the five maya sheaths are slid. Many world traditions teach that this perspective can be experienced but not known. There are no good words to describe it.

Many cultures hold strong opinions about these topics and many heated (as in bullets and bombs) discussions have been held in their honor. In this book, we don't need to go there. Each person is allowed their own conception of these matters.

All that we need for this model of a human being is to agree that there is some sort of knowing that can inform the body/energy/mind/contents of mind/observer with some sense of inner consistency; that there is some sort of standard against which we can compare our currently held beliefs and conclusions for truth and accuracy. Whether you conceive of this knowing as coming from God, a channeled ascended master, a power animal, your own higher Consciousness, or whatever, is up to you.

I've found this model of a human being to be very helpful in deepening my understanding of myself, my patients, and the processes of disease and health. It has helped me understand the forces affecting us and the range of choices, often in the form of therapies, available to us in response to these forces. I hope it helps you put some pieces of your experience together in helpful ways as well.

Appendix B

Metaphors

The metaphors used by a particular discipline can be very telling. For example, conventional medicine uses two dominant metaphors: the machine metaphor and the war metaphor. Conventional medicine is constantly comparing aspects of your body to aspects of machines. Your brain is a computer, your heart is a pump, your joints are hinges, your lungs are bellows, your arteries are pipes, nerves are wires, and so on and so on. Treatments are fixing and repairing the machine.

The war metaphor sees disease as the enemy to be vanquished, drugs and other treatments are the weapons, and your body is the battleground. Look at the language that conventional medicine often uses: "we have new drugs in our armamentarium in our war against cancer," "you are a victim of your heart attack." Microbes are the invaders; tumors are the enemy. Treatment focuses on killing, eradicating, annihilating, and conquering.

But a sad irony is playing out in conventional medicine: doctors think they are the generals calling the shots, making the decisions, being in control, when really they are just the foot soldiers dutifully following orders. The CEOs of the big medical corporations, like the drug and insurance companies, are the real generals. The soldiers just do as they are told or they are dishonorably discharged.

Just because these metaphors have nothing to do with healing doesn't mean that they are not powerful. They have led to the development of many powerful techniques that you can put to good use at the appropriate time and for the right reasons. Just use them with a healing consciousness: you are far more than a machine and healing is not about war. No one ever wins a war. More importantly, the unifying consciousness needed to heal is very different than the "us vs. them" consciousness used to wage wars.

Healing very often asks you to transcend the war consciousness. So often when a person first comes to see me, they are at war with themselves. They hate their headache and are fighting with it. They hate their weight and are fighting with it. Usually, the first thing I do with them is get them to stop the war they are having with various aspects of themselves. Every aspect of you is on the same team. Teams work much better when all members work together rather than fight with each other. Other healing traditions often do the same thing. For example, in Alcoholics Anonymous, the first of The Twelve Steps is intended to stop the war.

Ironically, while the war metaphor is not helpful for healing, the warrior metaphor is. The true warrior is a survivor. The true warrior is a master of their mind and body, of their creativity. The same skills are important in healing. The warrior, in the martial arts sense, is good at healing themselves as long as they keep their consciousness in honest communication with their heart.

Naturopathic medicine often uses the garden metaphor. Your body is the garden. Disease happens when the garden is taken over by weeds. Therapies help to cultivate the characteristics you want while weeding out those you do not want. The more organic the gardening, the better. You can't force plants to grow—that is up to nature—but you can provide fertilizer, water, favorable soil, and other supportive conditions to optimize those aspects of nature that you want.

Again, this metaphor has merit. Gardening generally causes less destruction than war. Many of the therapies used by naturopaths are safer than those used by conventional medicine and, in the right circumstance, equally or more effective. For example, in 2013, an estimated 440,000 deaths occurred in US hospitals as a result of potentially preventable errors[104]. This number does not include those injured or killed by drug side-effects, lack of effective treatments due to the high costs of conventional care, and such. The number of people estimated to be harmed but not killed by conventional medicine may be ten times the number killed.

Standard naturopathic strategies, such as removing toxins and allergens;

hormone balancing; optimizing nutrition, physical conditioning, sleep quality, the functioning of the immune system, and such just make good sense. Conventional medicine is aware of these ideas and is developing functional medicine, a way to incorporate the best of conventional and natural medicine in a coherent framework. But most conventional and natural treatments are still used in an allopathic way: merely to treat symptoms, to get your body to be and work the way you want it, heedless of why it's working the way it is right now.

But things don't just happen to you in a vacuum. Sure, your lifestyle choices—how you eat, exercise, relate, and stress out—have big impacts on your health, there are motivations behind your lifestyle choices and beliefs behind those, but even these are not the only influences on your health. Years ago, a thirty three year old man came to me after his rheumatologist diagnosed him with a mixed connective tissue disorder. This is the diagnosis given to people when they are all stiff, sore, and inflamed but they do not have rheumatoid arthritis, Lupus, or any of the other well-defined auto-immune syndromes. He didn't want to take the toxic medications the rheumatologist offered.

After a brief explanation of how I like to work with people and what I would have to offer him, he agreed to try a session of integrative bodywork, in which we are able to converse with his body to see what it is trying to accomplish by generating his symptom complex. After a few minutes of working on him, I asked him what he was experiencing. He was having memories of being a three-year-old, standing in his older brother's bedroom. His parents, aunts, and uncles were all standing around his brother's bed as his brother breathed his last breath, dying from childhood leukemia. His brother had had a long, hard "battle" with it, suffering enormously from the side effects of chemotherapy. One of his aunts made the observation out loud that at least he wasn't suffering any more. You can just imagine the level of emotions in that room.

In that instant, the man realized that what he, as a three-year-old, heard his aunt say was that if he wanted to live, he had to suffer. He saw that his mixed connective tissue disorder was just trying to make good and sure that he was going to live. We were able to explore the belief that the three-year-old formed, driven all the deeper into his psyche by the emotional intensity of the moment, to see if it was really true. His adult self could easily see that his aunt meant nothing of the sort, that what she said was intended to be compassionate. His intellect knew that he didn't need to suffer to stay alive or to even feel alive. He was able to see how that belief had been affecting him down through the years, and he was able to let it go. After the session, his mixed connective tissue disorder resolved.

Functional medicine has many good approaches to getting inflammation to go away: fish oil, Evening Primrose oil, anti-inflammatory herbs, Low-dose Naltrexone, improving intestinal permeability, removing allergens, and the like. I often wonder what would have happened with that man if we'd done all those things to make the inflammation go away but he'd continued to live with the unconsciously-held belief that he needed to suffer. As I said, a healthy lifestyle is important, but healing is often more than just exercising, eating right, and not stressing out. You also want to align your beliefs with higher truth. And even safe, natural ways to control symptoms may inadvertently prolong suffering by delaying getting to the real roots.

The Education Metaphor

I have found that a fourth metaphor, the education metaphor, more accurately captures what is happening when a person contacts their inner wisdom for healing assistance. It helps me stay focused on getting to real roots of problems. If you decide to adopt it as well, I believe it will help you work with the Consciousness of your experiences while freeing you to use whatever conventional and alternative treatment modalities make the most sense.

I have proposed that healing is the process of you getting to know who you really are and then being that. This is an educational process. (That is why this planet is often referred to as "the school of hard knocks.") We have also established that every experience you have exerts some sort of influence upon your health. Putting this all together, the education metaphor sees all of your life, including your health issues, as a series of opportunities to learn.

Education is not preparation for life; education is life itself.
—John Dewey

Education's purpose is to replace an empty mind with an open one.
—Malcolm Forbes

The education metaphor has several parts. There is a student, a teacher, a classroom, a curriculum, and learning objectives. *The student is your conscious sense of self*; everything that comes to mind when you say "I." Psychology calls this aspect your ego. When Freud wrote about these ideas, he wrote in German and used the word "Ich" for this aspect. "Ich" literally translates into "I" in English. Freud disliked the materialism of the United States, so, when he directed the translation of his works into English (which he spoke fluently), he purposefully changed "I," with all of its intimacy, warmth, and familiarity to "ego," a word that is remote and intellectual. Your ego is the part of you who thinks it knows who you are. Your ego is that part of you that learns and grows and changes.

The teacher is your inner wisdom, your higher self, your Buddha nature, your soul, your spirit, Christ consciousness, Atman. Whereas your ego thinks it knows who you are, your inner wisdom really does know who you are. It is the wisdom that is monitoring all of the receptors in your body and notifies your ego, through symptoms, when it detects an imbalance that needs attention. It knows why you are here and what you need to experience and do in order to feel like you have lived a fulfilling and meaningful life. It functions as the choreographer of your life, feeding you your experiences. It is your personal window into pure, undifferentiated Consciousness. We all have a teacher. It is the source of your intuition and your guidance.

The classroom is all of physical creation.

The curriculum is all of your experiences. I want to make a very important point here. Sometimes we call whatever we are experiencing our teacher. I used to do that. I called my back pain my teacher. Then someone pointed out that, when you are seeking Truth in life, you like to have a teacher; you don't want your teacher to go away. Do I really want to keep my back pain around? No, I want to heal it. So I started looking at it as curriculum, it is representing any number of lessons. But my teacher is my own inner wisdom, and I don't want that to go away.

And the learning objective is to answer the question: Who am I?

The education metaphor is a very powerful way to view your experiences. For example:

- How does the teacher feel towards the student? Your inner teacher loves you; it understands you perfectly and holds you in the deepest respect.

- Does the teacher have the student's best interests at heart? Yes. Your inner teacher really wants you to be happy, fulfilled, enlightened.

- Will the teacher ever give up on the student? I don't think so. I used to think people can give up on themselves at times. But, in the grander scheme of things, who is to say that even happens or matters? You can learn from any experience, even self-abandonment, when the time is right.

- Who plans the curriculum-the student or the teacher? I think that when you get advanced enough in your self-exploration you can do some independent study projects, but, for the most part, you (meaning your ego) don't consciously ask for much of what happens to you moment by moment.

- Does the teacher ever ask the student to do things they don't want to do? Guess that's a stupid question. The real issue, though, is what do you do when that happens? Do you conclude that the teacher is an idiot and doesn't know what they are doing and go in search of a different class? (Good luck with that one.) Do you lose trust in the teacher? Or do you knuckle down and do whatever it takes to get the assignment done? You choose what kind of student of life you are.

- If the student really wants to learn, how ought the student attend to the teacher and the teachings? Do you sit near the front, listening intently, taking notes, or are you in the back shooting spitwads? Do you move forward eagerly in your life or do you get dragged along kicking and screaming? Even though you don't always feel like you choose the lessons, you can choose what kind of student of life you want to be. That makes all the difference in the world.

The education metaphor is particularly helpful when you face experiences that you didn't ask for and don't want, such as injury, illness or abuse. If you can trust the teacher and hold on to the idea that perhaps buried somewhere in these experiences is some important bit of learning, then you can face your experiences with courage and keep your eyes open for ways you can deepen your understanding of yourself as the experiences unfold. The learning often comes as you are working to heal from the experience.

We deem those happy who from the experience of life have learnt to bear its ills without being overcome by them.
—Carl Jung

Take a moment to reflect upon a few important things you've learned as you've gone through life so far. What inside of you allowed you to learn that lesson at that time? How is that lesson influencing your life now? Have your conclusions closed you down or opened you up to more possibilities, to more degrees of freedom, in your choices? Have your conclusions opened you up to love or closed you down?

Life's education progresses as an endless questioning of conclusions. Even when you have learned from your very own personal experiences, you may need to be open to reconsidering your conclusions. Remember what I learned from my creaky knees.

When you heal, you often have to work with two truths. One of the truths is generally not true and the other is deep within, only accessible by connecting with your deep inner wisdom. The first truth is your own personal truth (the conclusions that you have drawn from your own experiences, the conclusions you have absorbed, as by osmosis, from your families and society). Your own personal truth is that you are holding that belief, so, for you, in that moment, that belief is true. The second truth is the higher spiritual perspective. So, even though that belief is in you controlling your physiology and directing your creativity, the belief itself may not be true from a spiritual perspective.

In other words, your own moment by moment personal truth is composed of the beliefs that you are holding, no matter what those beliefs are. There is also a higher—I think of it as Spiritual, as the gold-standard—truth that you can compare your beliefs to. (Not everything in ethics, morality, or human comportment is relative, as some contemporary philosophers are arguing. For example, using any reasonable metric, kindness is innately preferable to cruelty.)

One of my favorite sayings is "question conclusions." Mark Twain tells the story of his cat who, one cold morning, sat on a hot stove burner. For the rest of that cat's life, he never sat on another stove burner. Most of us, hearing the story, think to ourselves, "smart cat." But the point of the story was that the cat concluded that the stove burner was the problem when really the temperature of it was the problem. Because of that confusion, for the rest of that cat's life, he limited his seating options. How often are you like that cat? You draw conclusions from your experiences, and maybe in that moment those conclusions make perfect sense, but maybe those aren't the conclusions your teacher intended for you to draw, and, as a result, you live a life more limited than it needs to be.

Conclusions that promote your healing open you up to more love in your life. Limiting conclusions are just that: limiting. If you ever draw a conclusion from some experience you have gone through and later feel like you have painted yourself into a corner, feel free to revisit and question that conclusion. Just maybe there is an entirely different way to look at that experience now that you have gotten more perspective on it.

For example, let's say that you are from a very abusive family. Your parents are alcoholic narcissists and your siblings are just plain mean. Every time you see or talk to one of them they attack you, put you down, slander you, or in some other way abuse you. (I have several patients in this situation.) So let's say that you decide to cut off contact with your family. On the surface, that may seem like a limiting conclusion. But healing is challenging in the best of circumstances; it is even more challenging when you are putting yourself in the direct line of fire. Upon further examination, you can see that, for now, cutting off contact is an act of self love and respect. It is giving yourself a breather. Then, later, when you have healed some of the pain from childhood and no longer need so much from your family (that you're never going to get from them anyway), you can re-establish contact with them and continue to address whatever learning those relationships hold for you. You can also heal a relationship without ever talking to that person. Choose whatever option seems most loving for you.

See life as an educational process and hold the goal of getting as much learning out of each experience as you can. You get to choose your perspective and goals. The education perspective is an important part of an internal construct that allows for the process of change, personal growth, and healing. You are going through those experiences anyway, so you might as well get something positive from them. Remember, "We each have our own personal challenges we're working with, but we're all really trying to do the same thing. We're all just trying to learn how to love better."

I think that sums up the healing path. As you learn how to love yourself, others, and the planet better, you heal. As you heal, you are better able to love yourself, others and the planet.

Appendix C

The Quantum Mechanical Perspective on Human Consciousness

For years, I just knew that the neuroscientist's classical explanation of mind and consciousness as epiphenomena derived, somehow, by the activity of neurons in the brain just didn't make sense with respect to how we as people really work. There was too much outlying data.

Take spontaneous creativity. If activity in the brain is the source or primary causation of all of human experience, where does spontaneous creativity come from? The brain just processes data that comes into it; spontaneous creativity is more than stimulus-response.

And intuition? Have you ever just known something but not known how you know? Or volition? How do you ever start something new? Something that is just not a continuation of what you have already been doing? And meaning. Meaning seems to be critically important to us, yet the physical sciences, which see all of reality resulting from the interactions of particles with each other and energy fields, cannot weigh in on meaning. Even computers, with their powerful information-processing abilities can only process symbols, not meaning[105]. There are more examples, of course, of human experiences that do not lend themselves to the idea that the brain, with its electrical activity, is the highest authority in your life.

So I made up my own theory about how Consciousness is actually primary. I theorized that Consciousness, the Consciousness that is behind the creation of the entire universe, gets filtered through your beliefs. Your beliefs determine what aspects of infinite Consciousness get through the apparent barrier between what lies outside the laws of physics—the timeless—and what lies within the laws of physics—manifest creation—to be able to manifest as your life. Your beliefs determine your thoughts and then the thoughts somehow get translated into activity in your brain. The brain then transmits that information from Consciousness to the rest of your body. In my theory, the brain was a big, fancy switchboard.

Consciousness is overarching, determining the thoughts in your mind; your mind then controls your body through the brain. Our society calls this relationship "mind over matter." I took the interrelationships one step further up the ladder and thought of this top-down flow of causation as "Consciousness over matter": a more precise description of where the control really comes from, though I mourned the loss of the alliteration.

The functioning of the brain is, of course, critically important, my theory espoused. If it is damaged and unable to carry out its task of translating the thoughts into physical electrical activity and communicating that information to the body through its wide network of neural connections, hormone synthesis, and the like, of course there will be dysfunction in the person's life. But the same can be said if there is heart damage, or lung damage, or liver damage, etc., etc. In fact, one of my medical school professors once pronounced to the class that a good set of bowels contributes more to a happy life than a good set of brains. Now that we are learning so much about how the bacteria in your intestines influence the brain, I think he was right.

To explain the brain/mind connection in my theory, I often used the analogy of a car and a driver. If the car represents your physical body, the driver is the intelligence directing the body. If the car breaks down, the intelligence gets stranded, like in shut-in syndrome. If your car is a Ferrari, you can do more in your life than if it is an old VW Beetle. But a car without a driver isn't going anywhere (at least before Google) and a driver without a car, well … you can't really even call that person a driver, can you? So, I reasoned, they obviously need each other to be a functioning system, but the driver is the intelligence; it decides where and when the car goes where it goes. The car just follows commands to the best of its abilities. In this metaphor, the brain is part of the car.

Here is a clinical observation that I had to explain in my theory: when I work on someone and they have a thought, it feels to me like that thought gets represented in their whole physical and energy bodies instantaneously, not just in the brain. So I reasoned that the mind's interaction with the brain and the brain's subsequent communication with the body happened pretty quickly. (The new theory presented here explains my clinical observations even better.)

The theory I made up seems to match more accurately what I observe in my patients than does the neuroscientists' theory. And I liked how the addition of Consciousness to conventional medicine made it a more complete system of healing which, in turn, made integrating other healing systems from around the world much easier.

But, fundamentally, my theory was no better than that of the neuroscientists, because I still could not explain how the mind, in its non-local, non-material form, could effect changes in the localized, material biochemistry of the body. I puzzled about this for years. Then I came across Amit Goswami's wonderful book *The Quantum Doctor: A Quantum Physicist Explains the Healing Power of Integral Medicine*[34]. (He even used my word, "Integral"!) Some of the aspects of the quantum mechanical world view answered my questions. I am so excited!

For those of you who are not quantum physicists, I would like to give a little background. In the late 1600s and early 1700s, Isaac Newton not only developed calculus (in competition with Leibnitz) but also a system of mechanics that explained mathematically the movement of apples that fall from trees, cannon balls shot from cannons, the deflection of beams as they were weighted, and most other natural movements that scientists and engineers used to create the Industrial Revolution.

Newtonian mechanics says that energy and velocity change continuously, that initial position and velocity of a body can be known accurately and future position and velocity calculated using physical laws. All interactions between bodies are local, coming from the vicinity with the help of signals traveling through space taking certain amounts of time, like gravity and magnetic fields. Newtonian mechanics leads to a very deterministic view of the universe, the proverbial clock that God wound up and let go to run on its own.

Newton's equations were so successful that, by the 1890s, the dean of physics at Harvard was advising students not to go into physics, since there would be nothing for them to do with their careers. The only observation not explained was that pesky phenomenon called "black box radiation." Well, trying to explain that bit of outlying data led to the development of the idea of quanta.

Quanta are small packets of discrete energy. Energy increases not smoothly, like going up a ramp, but in steps, like going up a staircase. This idea was counterintuitive to our worldly observations but made sense because the quanta are very, very small. But this observation about energy broke open the floodgates and, by the 1920s, physics was going through a Kuhnsian[14] paradigm shift from Newtonian mechanics to quantum mechanics.

In quantum mechanics, objects are described as waves of possibility that can be in two or more places at once. But in which place the object will be found, based upon a specific kind of measurement, cannot be predetermined by any physical laws or mathematical equations. Also, there are non-local interactions that allow for signal-less instantaneous communication between particles (called quantum entanglement). And movements don't have to be smooth and continuous, allowing for "quantum leaps" to occur. Entering the quantum mechanical world is akin to going down Alice's rabbit hole.

Interestingly, you don't need quantum mechanics to describe the motion of a basketball through the air, but you do to describe the movement of a single photon. When you apply the equations of quantum mechanics to macroscopic, everyday-sized bodies, they reduce to the equivalent of Newtonian equations, though with very different assumptions behind them. So why is quantum mechanics such a big deal for medicine? Humans, after all, are more the size of basketballs than photons.

Well, as early as the 1930s, physicists were starting to marvel at the congruencies between the quantum mechanical world view and the world view put forth by Eastern meditative traditions. Fritjof Capra even wrote a whole book on it: *The Tao of Physics*[106]. Some materialists wonder if this remarkable convergence of world views is because certain critical functions in the brain are quantum events. For example, we know that the dark-adapted human eye can detect a single photon and that the quietest noise that most people can hear moves the tympanic membrane a distance on the order of the diameter of a hydrogen atom. And, because the synaptic clefts between neurons are so small, that the interaction of neurotransmitters with their receptors within neuronal synapses could also be a quantum event would not be hard to believe.

Another interesting quantum phenomenon is that the flow of time might not be linear. There is some evidence that the brain is sensing the environment about two seconds into the future. This may explain the rapidity of the stress response and how, often, a noise in the environment, like a door slamming while you are asleep, gets seamlessly incorporated into your dream by events in the dream leading up to the door slamming. How did your unconscious mind, that is generating the dream images, know ahead of time that the door was going to slam? These are fun things to think about. But since the brain is not primary, there is a better explanation for the congruencies between the quantum world and the human psyche. We will get to that.

Back to the background. In Newtonian physics, objects are things whose movements are completely determined by physical laws and initial conditions, such as starting position and velocity. In quantum physics, objects are seen as waves of possibility and initial conditions cannot be precisely known. (For example, the Heisenberg uncertainty principle sets a boundary upon how precisely you can know simultaneously both the position and velocity of a particle.) Also, the wave equation that is used to represent the subatomic particle has many possible solutions. Which possibility actually manifests as an event in the manifest universe depends upon how that possibility wave is observed or measured. As Goswami puts it: "It is observation by an observer that *precipitates* (italics his) a definite event out of the various possibilities." This precipitation of possibilities into an actual measured event is called "collapse" of the possibility wave function. It is as though the act of measuring causes all the potentialities to collapse into the one experienced event. One possibility gets chosen and expressed as a physical event and the other possibilities disappear. Goswami maintains that it requires a non-material consciousness to collapse a possibility wave into an actuality; it takes a consciousness to do the choosing. The act of measuring both a) causes the probability wave to collapse and b) determines which of the probabilities gets expressed as a material, physical event.

This is important. I want to be very clear here. The way we understand the behavior of matter/energy/information at the quantum level, consciousness has to exist. Without consciousness, there would be no material reality. This is in stark contrast to Newtonian materialism.

For reasons that Goswami explains very well but are too long to go into here, in order to avoid dualism, the consciousness called for by quantum mechanics must be seen as the "ground of being." In other words, all of the possibilities contained within the possibility wave are possibilities of consciousness, not separate from consciousness. The material possibilities are possibilities of consciousness from which consciousness may choose: nothing in material creation is outside of or separate from this consciousness.

(Wow! That last statement is about as woo-woo as it gets; but it is being made by (I'm sure most of the time) sober mathematicians and physicists who are interpreting hard, empirical observations of the material world; led to these conclusions by rigorous adherence to the scientific process. To stay current with scientific thinking, conventional medicine needs to start taking the influence of Consciousness on human health and disease into account.)

This consciousness required by quantum mechanics is very similar in properties to Atman in the Vedic model of a human being, or to Brahman in the Vedic cosmology or to God Transcendent in Christian mysticism or Wakan Tanka in the Lakota tradition. So I will now denote it with a capital "C" as in the rest of the book. It is the infinite potential out of which the strings appear and into which the strings disappear in string theory. This concept appears all over the world and down through human history, and it is starting to show up again in the physical sciences. Any honest pursuit of the truth discovers the concept of this Consciousness, so there must be some validity to it.

I hope that is enough background. Here is the quantum theory of Consciousness, matter, energy and information as I understand it.

- Each sentient being in the universe has the ability to take a measurement of the possibility wave, contained within infinite Consciousness, which represents themselves in each moment of their existence.

- All the different aspects and dimensions of that sentient being's existence and experience collapse out simultaneously from the possibility wave.
- The very act of being aware, being a sentient being, does the measuring.
- All of the aspects of a human being (the five Mayas) are contained within the possibility wave of that person and all precipitate or collapse into temporal, physical experience simultaneously.

The possibility wave of a photon is relatively simple, it contains the possibility of being a wave or a particle, having a certain amount of energy or frequency, and such. As you may imagine, the possibility wave for you, which is collapsing moment by moment as your experience of your life, is much more complex. So which aspects of infinite Consciousness are commonly contained within the human possibility wave?

Goswami answers this question in Chapters 3 and 4 of *The Quantum Physician*. These are the properties as he describes them:

- "The physical body which is the hardware and where representations are made of the subtler bodies."
- The Vital Body which he sees as similar to Steiner's etheric body and I think of as the original matrix of osteopathic medicine. It holds the blueprints for the forms and programs of morphogenesis or the generation of biological forms, what Sheldrake[107] refers to as "morphogenetic fields." This is the second Kosha, your vital life energy.
- "The mental, which gives meaning to the vital and the physical and of which the brain makes representations." It is a non-local, non-physical aspect. The mind assigns and processes meaning in a way a computer, limited to manipulating symbols, will never be able to.

- "The supramental intellect, which provides context for mental meaning and vital functions and associated feelings, and the laws of physical movement."
- "The bliss body, which is the unlimited ground of being. In this ground of being with unlimited possibilities, the other four compartments exert progressive limitations."

These five aspects that collapse simultaneously out of a human possibility wave you might recognize as the five mayas in the Vedic model of a human being (see Appendix A.) The sixth aspect of the Vedic model is Consciousness, the ground of all being out of which the possibility waves collapse.

In his writings that I have read so far, Goswami seems to combine Atman with the bliss body, also called Anandamayakosha. But this still works well, because Anandamayakosha is essentially the essence of pure Consciousness, just within the laws of time and space, after the possibility wave has already collapsed. Before the wave collapses, all aspects of the possibility wave, all potential mayas, are Consciousness, Atman, outside of time and space. The process of measuring the possibility wave with your awareness as a sentient being, collapses the possibility wave into time and space, which is what makes them mayas. And it is the products of that collapse that you experience as this present moment, with all the properties that you can become aware of that were discussed in chapter four on Awareness.

This theory explains the apparent "interaction" of mind, body, and energy. Clinically, we observe that a therapy that induces a change in one instantaneously induces correlated changes in the other two. For example, if you take a medication that changes your biochemistry, there will also be corresponding changes in your energy and mental aspects. If you receive Reiki and change your energy, corresponding changes will instantaneously show up in your physical body and mind. If you go through therapy and change your mind, corresponding changes will show up in your physical body and energy. These observations have been reported for decades. This theory explains how that can be. The physical body, vital life energy, and mental activity are three of the five aspects of the potential wave that simultaneously precipitate into measurable reality as your potential wave collapses into your present moment. They are seen as simultaneous products or representations of "divine substance," the divine you. This theory resolves the problems of dualism in Descartes' and Leibniz's ideas about mind-body interactions and affirms Spinoza's and Steiner's intuitions.

It also gives us a way to integrate many different kinds of medicine. Most approaches focus on one of the mayas and tend to minimize the others. Conventional medicine focuses on the physical body, primarily. Psychology focuses on the mind and intellect primarily. Acupuncture, homeopathy, and Ayurvedic medicine focus primarily on the vital energy. Integral medicine sees any sort of focus on any maya by any system of medicine as supportive and important in the right circumstances, but, since the mayas are created out of Consciousness, to get to the curative, to get to the root or cause and create real change, one must focus on the determinants of creativity. And those determinants are whatever sets up the measurement of your possibility wave.

So that is an interesting question. If measurement of the possibility wave triggers the collapse of the wave into an event in time and space and simultaneously decides what aspects of the possibility wave get expressed physically in, or as, that event, what sets up the experiment, so to speak, that gets measured as you? In the physics lab, it is easy to see that it is the physicist, with her own intelligence and Consciousness, who determines the set-up of the experiment and what kind of measurement gets made. But how does this process work in real life? In your real life?

When I look at this question, I see that the answer is complicated, because several factors may be involved. One influence, and one that you potentially have some personal control over, is your system of beliefs. What you believe in this moment exerts influence over what you are able to create in the next moment. This allows for a smooth transition from one moment to the next and also explains why, when you have one of those "aha!" moments and a belief suddenly changes, your creative flow also changes. Have you ever noticed that about those "aha!" moments? And gaining conscious control over your beliefs, so that you can gain conscious control over your creative flow, is what the practice of the seven tools is all about.

This theory also explains why beliefs are so important and powerful, not only composing the lenses through which you peer out into the world, but also functioning as the gatekeepers of your creativity. But there are other influences, besides your beliefs, that also contribute to setting up the experiment that measures your possibility wave: your genetics, the environment around you (and within you in the form of your nutrition, microbiome, and such), the culture in which you live, how others treat you, and so forth.

So, if there are toxins in your environment creating cancer in your body, if someone drives by and shoots you, if the economy collapses, all these things also get experienced as your present moment. I do not think that you control all of these things but, and this might seem paradoxical to you, at the same time, you are not a victim of these things. How could that be? It goes back to beliefs. No matter what factors go into creating your present moment and no matter what your present moment contains, exactly how you experience your present moment and how you choose to respond to it is also impacted by your beliefs; and those you can potentially control by practicing the seven tools of healing. Looking at all of these influences that help to shape how your possibility wave collapses helps explain why bad things can happen to good people and vice versa and why it appears that we can create our own reality but only up to a certain point.

Multiple factors determining how your possibility wave collapses also explains why sometimes just changing your beliefs is enough to get you better but many other times it is not. You must question deeply and persistently into your experiences and follow them back to their roots to see all of the determinants of your creativity. Once you do that, you are in a position to do whatever is in your power to modify those determinants, if need be. You may also need to ask for help from family, friends, and practitioners.

Based upon this theory of quantum Consciousness, in the ideal medical system, practitioners would be trained to:

1. do whatever is needed to support your five mayas with physical, psychological, and/or energetic treatments while they then
2. help you question into your experiences
3. uncover the determinants of your creativity
4. help you connect with your inner wisdom that knows how to shape those determinants so that you become able to create health and happiness.

This would be the ideal primary care, a true Integral medicine.

References and Notes

1   Wilber, Ken. *The Integral Vision: A Very Short Introduction to the Revolutionary Integral Approach to Life, God, the Universe, and Everything.* Boston: Shambhala Publications, Inc., 2007.

2   McQuaid, Michelle. "Can You Create Lasting Change? Four Ways to Make Your Habits Stick." Accessed 11/30/2017 *www.psychologytoday.com/blog/functioning-flourishing/201507/can-you-create-lasting-change* ;
Dole, Janice, Gale M. Sinatra. "Reconceptualizing Change in the Cognitive Construction of Knowledge." *Educational Psychologist* 33(2/3) 1998:109-128.

3   Seligman, Martin. *Authentic Happiness: Using the New Positive Psychology to Realize Your Potential for Lasting Fulfillment.* New York: Atria Paperback, 2013.

4   Vivekananda, Swami. *Vedanta: Voice of Freedom.* Ed. Swami Chetanananda. St. Louis: Vedanta Society of St. Louis, 1990.

5   Basically, every book written by Ken Wilber is recommended, just to name a few:
A Brief History of Everything. Boston: Shambala Press, 1996. This is a great introduction into his ideas about the Integral World View.
The Marriage of Sense and Soul: Integrating Science and Spirituality. NY, NY: Random House, 1998. Here Ken applies the Integral World View to a proposed solution to the conflicts between science and the world's spiritual traditions.
Integral Psychology: Consciousness, Spirit, Psychology, Theory. Boston: Shambala Press, 2000.
Integral Spirituality: A Startling New Role for Religion in the Modern and Postmodern World. Boston: Integral Books, 2007.
Integral Life Practice: A 21ˢᵗ-Century Blueprint for Physical Health, Emotional Balance, Mental Clarity, and Spiritual Awakening. With Terry Patten, Adam Leonard & Marco Morelli. Boston: Integral Books, 2008.

6   O'Donohue, John. *To Bless the Space Between Us: A Book of Blessings.* New York: Doubleday, 2008.

7   Webster, Miriam. *Webster's Unabridged Dictionary.* New York: Random House, 2005.

8   Tzu, Lao. *Tao Teh Ching.* Trans. John C. H. Wu. Boston: Shamballa Press, 1990.

9   "Serenity Prayer." *Wikipedia*. 4 April 2016. <https://en.wikipedia.org/wiki/Serenity_Prayer>.

10 Brimble, A. "Bereavement Among Elderly People: Grief Reactions, Post-bereavement Hallucinations and Quality of Life." *Acta Psychiatrica Scandinavica*: vol 87, issue 1: pp 72-80, Jan 1993.

11 Brown, Brené. "Brené Brown Quotes." *Brainy Quotes*. <http://www.brainyquote.com/quotes/authors/b/brene_brown.html>.

12 Egginton, William. *In Defense of Religious Moderation*. New York: Columbia University Press, 2011.

13 Wilber, Ken. *The Marriage of Sense and Soul*. New York: Broadway Books, 2000.

14 Kuhn, Thomas. *The Structure of Scientific Revolution*. Chicago: Chicago University Press, 1996.

15 Curley, Edwin M., ed. *The Collected Works of Spinoza, Vol 1*. Princeton, NJ: Princeton University Press, 1985.

16 Kasser, Jeffrey L. "Philosophy of Science, vol I-III." *The Great Courses*. Chantilly, VA: The Teaching Company, 2006.

17 Kiyosaki, Robert. *Rich Dad, Poor Dad*. Scottsdale: Plata Publications, 2011.

18 Lipton, Bruce. *The Biology of Belief: Unleashing the Power of Consciousness, Matter, and Miracles*. Carlsbad: Hay House, 2008.

19 Pert, Candace. *Molecules of Emotion: Why You Feel the Way You Feel."* New York: Scribner, 1997.

20 Robbins, Tony. < https://www.tonyrobbins.com/>

21 Siegel, Bernie. *Love, Medicine and Miracles: Lessons Learned about Self-Healing from a Surgeon's Experience with Exceptional Patients*. New York: Harper & Row, 1986.

22 Boroditsky, Lera. "How Does Our Language Shape the Way We Think?" Conversations, *Edge*. 06/11/09, 04/16/2016 < https://www.edge.org/conversation/how-does-our-language-shape-the-way-we-think>.
    Plebe, A., Vivian, M. "When Language Shapes Perception." *Reviste Italiano di Filosofica del Linguaggio*, 2015.
    Athanasopoulos, P., et. al. "The Worfian Mind: Electrophysiological Evidence that Language Shapes Perception." *Communicative and Integrative Biology* 2:4, 332-334; July/August, 2009.

23 Rorty, R. "Postmodern Bourgeois Liberalism." *The Journal of Philosophy* Vol. 80 #10 Part 1. Oct 1983: pp583-589.

24 McLeod, S. A. "Maslow's Hierarchy of Needs." *Simple Psychology* updated 2017. 1/27/18. < https://www.simplypsychology.org/maslow.html>.

25 Tay, L., Diener, E. "Needs and Subjective Well-being Around the World." *J. of Personality and Social Psychology*, vol 101 (2), 2011 pp.354.

26 Watts, Alan. *The Way of Zen*. New York: Random House, 1957.

See also: Steiner, R. *Spiritual Science*. Blauvelt, NY: Steinerbooks, (a division of Barber Communications, Inc.), 1989.

27 Murray, W. H. *The Scottish Himalaya Expedition*. London: J. M. Dent & Co., 1951.

28 Henley, W. E. "Invictus." *Poetryfoundation.org*. 1/27/2018. <<u>https://www.poetryfoundation.org/poems/51642/invictus</u>>.

29 Bargh, J. A. "How Unconscious Thoughts and Perceptions Affect Every Waking Moment." *Scientific American,* vol. 310 Issue 1, July 2014.

30 EMDR Institute, Inc. < <u>http://www.emdr.com/</u>>.

31 Cognitive Behavioral Therapy. < <u>http://www.mayoclinic.org/tests-procedures/cognitive-</u> behavioral-therapy/home/ovc-20186868>.

32 White, E. B. *The Once and Future King*. United States: Perfection Learning, 1987.

33 Chopra, Deepak. *Creating Health: Beyond Prevention, Toward Perfection."* Boston: Houghton Mifflin Company, 1987.

34 Guo, Bisong, Andres Powell. *Listen to Your Body: the Wisdom of the Dao."* Honolulu: University of Hawai'i Press, 2001.
    Heller, Joseph, William Henkin. *Bodywise*. Berkeley: Wingbow Press, 1991.
    Berry, Carmen Renee. *Is Your Body Trying to Tell You Something?* Berkeley: PageMill Press, 1997.

35 Goswami, Amit. *The Quantum Doctor: A Quantum Physicist Explains the Healing Power of Integral Medicine*. Charlottesville, VA: Hampton Roads Publishing Company, Inc., 2011.

36 Davidson, R. J., W. Irwin. "The Functional Neuroanatomy of Emotion and Affective Style." *Trends in Cognitive Science* vol 3 (1), Jan 1999.

37 Kabat-Zinn, J. *Full Catastrophe Living: How to Cope with Stress, Pain and Illness Using Mindfulness Meditation*. New York: Bantam Doubleday Dell Publishing Group, 1996.

38 Dienstmann, Giovani. "Types of Meditation-An Overview of 23 Meditation Techniques." Meditation. *Live and Dare: Master Your Mind and Master Your Life.* 1/27/2018. <<u>https://liveanddare.com/types-of-meditation</u>>.

39 Goldman, Daniel. *Emotional Intelligence: Why It can Matter More than IQ.* New York: Bantam Books, 2005.

40 Faber, Adele, Elaine Mazlish. *How to Talk so Kids will Listen & Listen so Kids will Talk*. New York: Scribner, 2012.

41 Gallese, Vittorio. "The 'Shared Manifold' Hypothesis: From Mirror Neurons to Empathy." *J. of Consciousness Studies*, 2001.

42 Hesse, H. *Siddhartha*. New York: Bantam Doubleday Dell Publishing Group, 1990

43 McKay, M., J. C. Wood, J. Brantley. *The Dialectical Behavior Therapy Skills Workbook: Practical DBT Exercises for Learning Mindfulness, Interpersonal*

Effectiveness, Emotional Regulation and Distress Tolerance. Oakland, CA: New Harbinger Publications, 2007.

44 Dalai Lama XIV. *Healing Anger: The Power of Patience from a Buddhist Perspective.* Ithaca, NY: Shamballa Press, 1997.

45 Kubler Ross, E. *On Death and Dying.* New York: Simon and Schuster, 1997.

46 Hawkins, D. R. *Power Vs. Force: The Hidden Determinants of Human Behavior.* Hay House, 1995.

47 Horowitz, M. J. *Stress Response Syndromes: PTSD, Grief and Adjustment Disorders Fifth Edition.* Northvale, NJ: Jason Aronson, Inc Press, 2013.

48 Sapolsky, R. M. *Why Zebras Don't Get Ulcers: The Acclaimed Guide to Stress, Stress-related Diseases, and Coping.* New York: St. Martin's Press, 2004.

49 Hall, Steven M. "Taming the Bear: Taking the Bite Out of Stress" *The Seven Tools of Healing.* 1/27/2018. <http://the7tools.com/classes/>.

50 Noë, A. *Out of Our Heads: Why You are Not Your Brain, and Other Lessons from the Biology of Consciousness.* New York: Hill and Wang (A division of Farrar, Straus and Giroux), 2009.
    Ornstein, R. *The Right Mind: Making Sense of the Hemispheres.* New York: Harcourt Brace and Company, 1997.
    Searle, J. R. *Mind: A Brief Introduction.* New York: Oxford Press, 2004.

51 Dooley, Mike. *Infinite Possibilities: The Art of Living Your Dreams.* New York: Atria Books, 2009
    Manifesting Change: It Couldn't be Easier. New York: Atria Paperbacks, 2010.
    Leveraging the Universe: Seven Steps to Engaging Live's Magic. New York: Atria Books, 2011.

52 Collins, S. F. *Our Children are Watching: 10 Skills for Leading the Next Generation to Success.* United States: Our Children Are Watching, Inc. 2014.

53 Googled "Guides to Meditation" and got this: <https://www.google.com/search?q=guides+to+meditation&oq=guides+to+&aqs=chrome.2.0j69i57j0l4.5814j0j7&sourceid=chrome&ie=UTF-8>.

54 Mafi, M., A. M. Kolin. *Rumi's Little Book of Life.* Charlottesville, VA: Hampton Roads Publishing Company, Inc., 2012.

55 Rocca, J. "Review of Galen and Galenism. Theory and Medical Practice from Antiquity to the European Renaissance." *Early Science and Medicine,* 9(4), 2004 362–364. Retrieved from http://www.jstor.org/stable/4130205.
    García-Ballester, L., J. Arrizabalaga, M. Cabré, L. Cifuentes, F. Salmon. *Galen and Galenism: Theory and Medical Practice from Antiquity to the European Renaissance.* UK: Taylor and Francis, Ltd, 2002.

56 Hahnemann, S. *Organon of Medicine: The First Integral English Translation of the Definitive Sixth Edition of the Original Work on Homoeopathic Medicine.* Los Angeles: J. P. Tarcher, Inc., 1982.

57 This is a fairly good review of D.D. Palmer, the founder of chiropractic: <https://en.wikipedia.org/wiki/Daniel_David_Palmer>.

58 This is a good description of Southerland's concept of "The Breath of Life" by one of the best Cranial practitioners alive today: < http://www.craniosacral-biodynamics.org/thebreath-of-life.html>.

59 Here is a good summary of Wilhelm Reich and Orgone: Cantwell, A. Jr. "Dr. Wilhelm Reich: Scientific Genius-or Medical Madman?" *New Dawn Magazine #84*, May-June 2004. Accessed at: <http://newdawnmagazine.com/Article/Dr_Wilhelm_Reich_Scientific_Genius.html> April, 2016.

60 There are several good summaries of the four fundamental forces in physics. See: https://en.wikipedia.org/wiki/Fundamental_interaction, or: http://sciencepark.etacude.com/particle/forces.php.

61 There are several sources of information about Vega machines, here is one: http://www.wholisticresearch.com/info/artshow.php3?artid=80.

62 Rife machines claim to work on radio frequencies, which are electromagnetic energy and not subtle energy, but have been disproved and discredited by conventional and integrative practitioners alike: http://www.drweil.com/drw/u/QAA401104/Ready-for-Rife.html.

63 Kirlian photography remains an interesting avenue for artistic expression: http://www.lightstalking.com/what-is-kirlian-photography-the-science-and-the-myth-revealed/.

64 Dossey, Larry. *Meaning and Medicine.* New York: Bantam Books, 1991.

65 Hill, Napoleon. *Think and Grow Rich.* New York: Jeremy P. Tarcher/Penguin, 2008.

66 Talbot, Michael. *The Holographic Universe.* New York: HarperCollins Publishers, Inc., 2011. See also, for an interesting idea: http://www.wakingtimes.com/2014/04/16/proof-human-body-projection-consciousness/

67 Here is a good starting reference on pranayama: http://www.yogapoint.com/info/pranayama.htm.

68 Here is some information about scientifically proven benefits of Tai Chi: https://nccih.nih.gov/health/taichi/introduction.htm. Search "Tai Chi" to find experienced instructors in your area.

69 Chi Gong, or, more accurately, Qigong, also has proven health benefits: http://nqa.org/about-nqa/what-is-qigong/.

70 Myss, Caroline. *Energy Anatomy: The Science of Personal Power, Spirituality, and Healing.* Lousiville, CO: Sounds True, 2002.
Myss, Caroline. *Anatomy of the Spirit: The Seven Stages of Power and Healing.* New York: Random House, 2009.

71 Holloway, Gillian. *The Complete Dream Book: Discover What Your Dreams Reveal about You and Your Life.* Naperville: Source Books, 2006.

Hall, James A. *Jungian Dream Interpretation: A Handbook of Theory and Practice.* Toronto, Canada: Inner City Books, 1983.

Pierce, Penney. *Dream Dictionary for Dummies.* Chichester, UK: John Wiley & Sons, 2008.

72   Schwarz, N., G. Bohner. "Feelings and Their Motivational Implications: Moods and the Action Sequence." In Gollwitzer, P., Bargh, J. A. (eds) *The Psychology of Action: Linking Cognition and Motivation to Behavior.* New York: Guilford, 1996. Pp 119-145.

73   Weston, D., P. Blagov, K. Harenski, C. Kilts, S. Hamann. "Neural Basis of Motivated Reasoning: An fMRI Study of Emotional Constraints on Partisan Political Judgment in the 2004 U.S. Presidential Election." *J. of Cognitive Neuroscience.* Vol 18 Issue 11 Nov 2006 pp 1947-1958.

74   There are several references to the psychological benefits of beautifying our living spaces:http://www.sciencedaily.com/releases/2013/03/130325160522.htm, http://www.sciencedaily.com/releases/2010/11/101101171240.htm, http://lhhl.illinois.edu/crime.htm, http://www.theatlanticcities.com/neighborhoods/2012/05/can-trees-actually-deter- crime/2107/.

75   Here are a couple of good books to get you started on Feng Shui:
Brown, Simon G. *The Feng Shui Bible.* London: Octopus Publishing Group, 2009.

Collins, Terah Kathryn. *Western Guide to Feng Shui: Room by Room.* Carlsbad, CA: Hay House, 1999.

76   Gendlin, Eugene T., PhD. *Focusing.* New York: Bantam Books, 1981.

77   Jones, Lisa. *Broken: A Love Story.* New York: Simon & Schuster, 2010.

78   Kant, Immanuel. *Groundwork of the Metaphysics of Morals.* Revised edition, Mary Gregor and Jens Timmermann, eds. New York: Cambridge University Press, 2012.

79   Milliman, Dan. *The Way of the Peaceful Warrior: A Book that Changes Lives.* Tiburon, CA: H. J. Kramer, 2000.

80   McDonald, Evy. "Another Perspective of ALS." *American Holistic Health Association, Journey to Wholeness-True Stories.* 4 Apr 2016 http://ahha.org/selfhelp-articles/another-perspective-of-als/.

81   Beck, Martha. *Finding Your Own North Star: How to Claim the Life You Were Meant to Live.* London: Little, Brown Book Group, 2003.
Steering by Starlight: the Science and Magic of Finding Your Destiny. Emmaus, PA: Rodale Press, 2009.
Findiing Your Way in a Wild New World: Reclaim Your True Nature to Create the Life You Want. New York: Simon & Schuster, 2013.

82   Chopra, Deepak. "The Properties of Your Higher Self" I suspect it is now out of print, I listened to it in the early '90s but could not find reference to it on his website.

83 Leff, Sonya. *You, Your Health, Your Community.* Butterworth-Heinemann, 1970.

84 Richard Miller, PhD. Private communication.

85 Gladwell, Malcolm. *Outliers: The Story of Success.* New York: Little, Brown and Company, 2008.

86 Myss, Carolyn. www.myss.com.

87 Gurumayi   Chidvilasananda.   http://www.siddhayoga.org/ gurumayi-chidvilasananda

88 http://www.siddhayoga.org

89 Ruiz, Don Miguel. *The Four Agreements: A Practical Guide to Personal Freedom.* San Rafel, CA: Amber-Allen Publishing, 1997.

90 Jung, C.G. *Synchronicity: An Acausal Connecting Principle.* Princeton: Princeton University Press, 2010.

91 Tolle, Eckhart. *The Power of Now: A Guide to Spiritual Enlightenment.* Novato, CA: New World Library, 1999.
    A New Earth: Awakening to Your Life's Purpose. New York: Plume, 2006.

92 Rankin, Lissa. *Mind Over Medicine: Scientific Proof that You can Heal Yourself.* Carlsbad: Hay House, 2013.

93 Dispenza, Joe. *Breaking the Habit of Being Yourself: How to Lose Your Mind and Create a New One.* Carlsbad: Hay House, 2012.

94 Here are some internet resources for Asperger's Syndrome: https://www. theatlantic.com/magazine/archive/2014/03/letting-go-of-aspergers/357563/. https://www.autismspeaks.org/what-autism/asperger-syndrome.

95 Cousins, Norman. *Anatomy of an Illness as Perceived by the Patient: Reflections on Healing and Regeneration.* New York: Norton, 1979.

96 Hay, Louise. *You Can Heal Your Life.* Carlsbad: Hay House, Inc., 1999.

97 Wahls, Terry, and Eve Adamson. *The Wahls Protocol: How I Beat Progressive MS using Paleo Principles and Functional Medicine.* New York: Penguin Putnam, 2014.

98 Katie, Byron. *Loving What Is: Four Questions that can Change Your Life.* New York: Random House, 2003.

99 Chaoud, G., Y. W. Aude, J. L. Mehta. "Dietary Recommendations in the Prevention and Treatment of Coronary Heart Disease: Do We have the Ideal Diet Yet?" *Am J. Cardiology* 2004;44: 1260-1267.
    https://www.huffingtonpost.com/entry/no-one-size-fits-all-diet- plan_us_564d605de4b00b7997f94272 Accessed 1/14/18.
    https://www.psychologytoday.com/blog/rhythms-recovery/201603/there-is-no- one-right-diet-everyone Accessed 1/14/18

100 Levine, Stephen. *Healing Into Life and Death.* Garden City: Anchor Press/ Doubleday, 1987.

101 Lo, B., M. J. Field (eds) "Conflict of Interest in Medical Research, Education, and Practice" *Institute of Medicine Committee on Conflict of Interest in Medical*

Research, Education, and Practice. Washington D.C.: National Academies Press, 2009.

And here are more articles on the conflict of interest in medicine: https://www. huffingtonpost.com/dr-mark-hyman/dangerous-spin-doctors-7- b_747325. html. Accessed 1/21/2018.

Marcia Angell worked for a time as the editor of the New England Journal of Medicine. http://bostonreview.net/archives/BR35.3/angell.php Accessed 1/21/18.

102 Here are several resources about the same kind of conflict of interest in agricultural research and policy: https://blog.ucsusa.org/gretchen-goldman/ how-is-the-usda-doing-on-scientific-integrity Accessed 1/21/18.

https://blog.ucsusa.org/genna-reed/monsantos-four-tactics-for-undermining-glyphosate-science-review Accesses 1/21/18

What do you think about their side of the story? https://monsanto.com/company/commitments/our-pledge/ Accessed 1/21/18

103 Quoted from *Descarte's Error* by Antonio Damasio, MD., who, by the way, is a big believer in the primacy of the brain.

104 Makary, Martin, Michael Daniel. "Medical Error—The Third Leading Cause of Death in the US." BMJ 2016, 353: i2139.

Also see: James, John T. "A New Evidence-based Estimate of Patient Harms Associated with Hospital Care." *J. of Patient Safety* Sept 2013, vol 9 issue 3 pp 122-128. And

Young, Matthew. "Medical Errors—The Third Leading Cause of Death in the US." *Harvard Law School.* posted Oct 14, 2016, accessed 1/24/2018, <http://blogs.harvard.edu/billofhealth/2016/10/14/medical-errors-the-third-leading-cause-of-death-in-the-us/>.

105 Harnad, S. "Computation is Just Interpretable Symbol Manipulation: Cognition Isn't." *Minds and Machines.* Special issue on "What is Computation?" 4:379-390. Penrose, Roger. *The Emperor's New Mind: Concerning Computers, Minds, and the Laws of Physics.* London: Oxford University Press, 1989.

106 Capra, Fritjof. *The Tao of Physics: An Exploration of the Parallels between Modern Physics and Eastern Mysticism.* New York: Bantam Books, 1977.

107 Sheldrake, Rupert. *A New Science of Life: The Hypothesis of Morphic Resonance.* Rochester, VT: Park Street Press, 1995.